D0902671

JORDIE BELLAIRE
COLORIST

FONOGRAFIKS
LETTERING & DESIGN

ELLE POWER
PRODUCTION ASSISTANT

IMAGE COMICS, INC.

Robert Kirkman
CHIEF OPERATING OFFICER
Erik Larsen
CHIEF FINANCIAL OFFICER
Todd McFarlane
PRESIDENT
Marc Silvestri
CHIEF EXECUTIVE OFFICER
Jim Valentino
VICE PRESIDENT
Eric Stephenson
PUBLISHER
Corey Murphy
DIRECTOR OF SALES
Jeff Boison
DIRECTOR OF PUBLISHING PLANNING
& BOOK TRADE SALES
Chris Ross
DIRECTOR OF DIGITAL SALES
Jeff Stang
DIRECTOR OF SPECIALTY SALES
Kat Salazar
DIRECTOR OF PR & MARKETING
Branwyn Bigglestone
CONTROLLER
Kali Dugan
SENIOR ACCOUNTING MANAGER
Sue Korpela
ACCOUNTING & HR MANAGER
Drew Gill
ART DIRECTOR
Heather Doornink
PRODUCTION DIRECTOR
Leigh Thomas
PRINT MANAGER
Tricia Ramos
TRAFFIC MANAGER
Briah Skelly
PUBLICIST
Aly Hoffman
CONVENTIONS & EVENTS COORDINATOR
Sasha Head
SALES & MARKETING PRODUCTION DESIGNER
David Brothers
BRANDING MANAGER
Melissa Gifford
CONTENT MANAGER
Drew Fitzgerald
PUBLICITY ASSISTANT
Vincent Kukua
PRODUCTION ARTIST
Erika Schnatz
PRODUCTION ARTIST
Ryan Brewer
PRODUCTION ARTIST
Shanna Matuszak
PRODUCTION ARTIST
Carey Hall
PRODUCTION ARTIST
Esther Kim
DIRECT MARKET SALES REPRESENTATIVE
Emilio Bautista
DIGITAL SALES REPRESENTATIVE
Leanna Caunter
ACCOUNTING ANALYST
Chloe Ramos-Peterson
LIBRARY MARKET SALES REPRESENTATIVE
Marla Eizik
ADMINISTRATIVE ASSISTANT

www.imagecomics.com

INJECTION, VOLUME THREE. First printing. November, 2017. Copyright © 2017 Warren Ellis & Declan Shalvey. All rights reserved. Published by Image Comics, Inc. Office of publication: 2701 NW Vaughn Street, Suite 780, Portland, OR 97210. Originally published in single magazine form as INJECTION #11–15, by Image Comics. INJECTION, its logos, and the likenesses of all character herein are trademarks of Warren Ellis & Declan Shalvey, unless otherwise noted. IMAGE and the Image Comics logos are registered trademarks of Image Comics, Inc. No part of this publication may be reproduced or transmitted, in any form or by any means (except for short excerpts for journalistic or review purposes), without the express written permission of Warren Ellis & Declan Shalvey or Image Comics, Inc. All names, characters, events, and locales in this publication are entirely fictional. Any resemblance to actual persons (living or dead), events, or places, without satiric intent, is coincidental. Printed in the USA. For information regarding the CPSIA on this printed material call: 203-595-3636 and provide reference # RICH–769878. For international rights, contact: foreignlicensing@imagecomics.com. ISBN 978-1-5343-0248-8. Big Bang Comics/Forbidden Planet variant ISBN 978-1-5343-0728-5

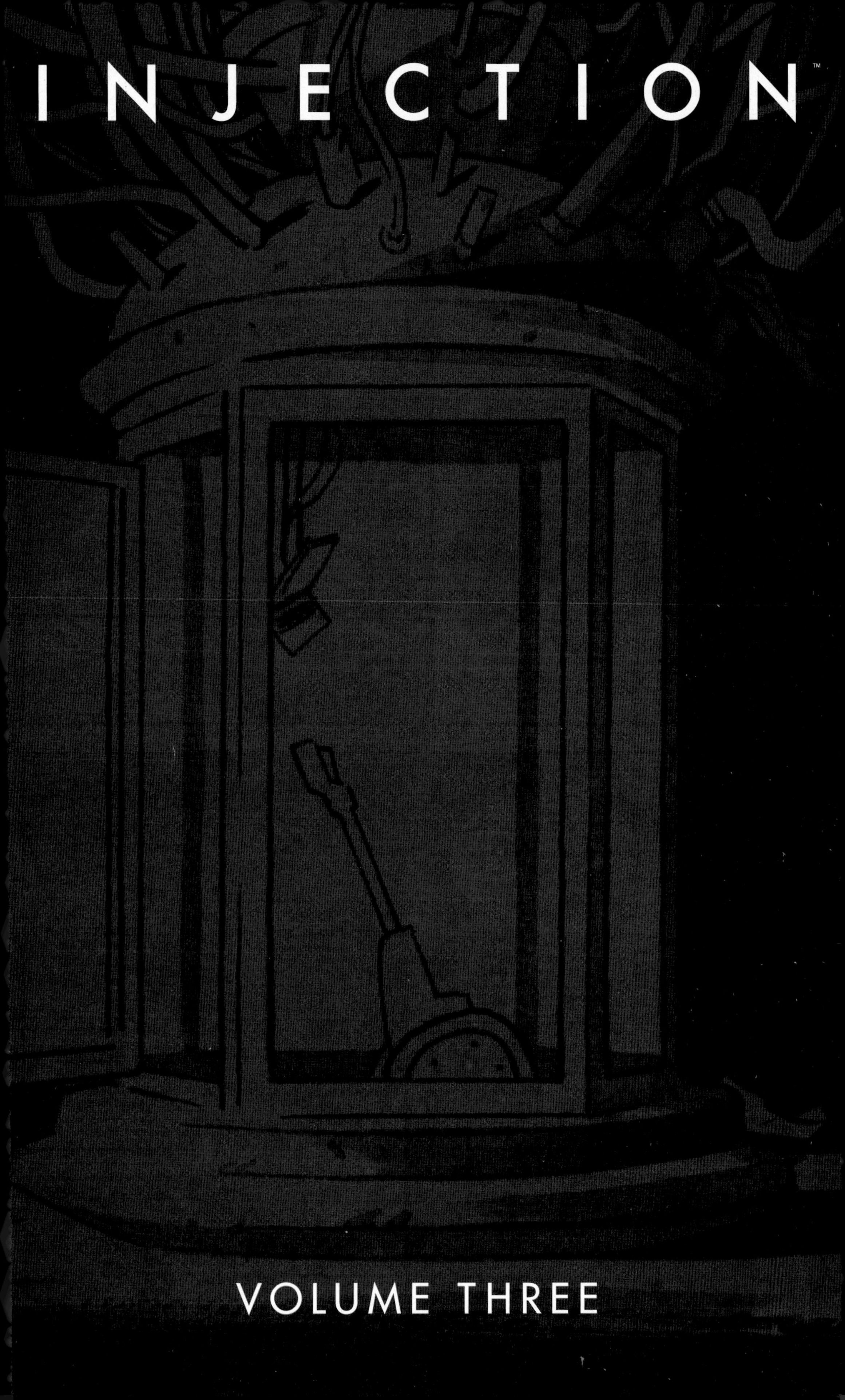
INJECTION™
VOLUME THREE

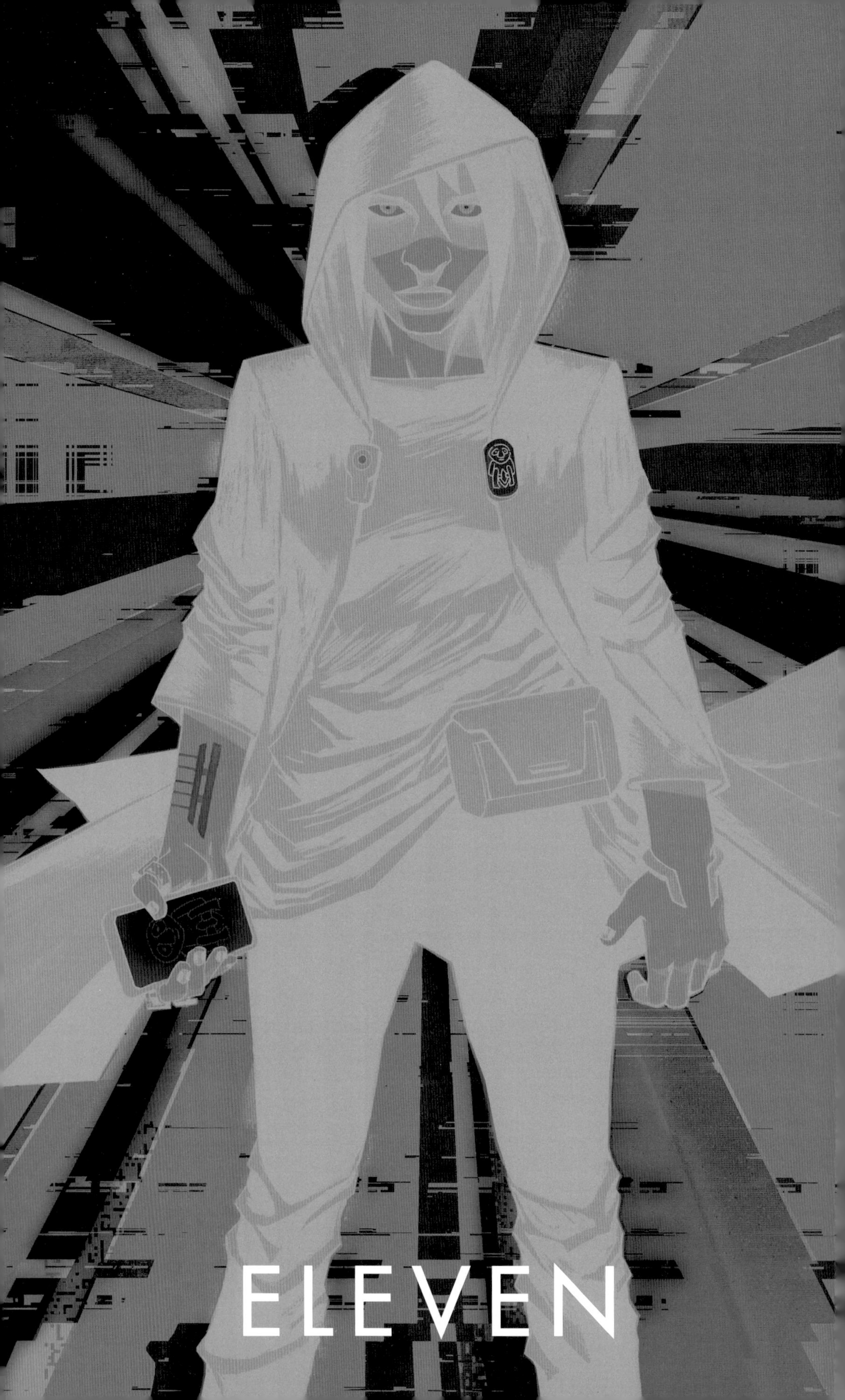

ELEVEN

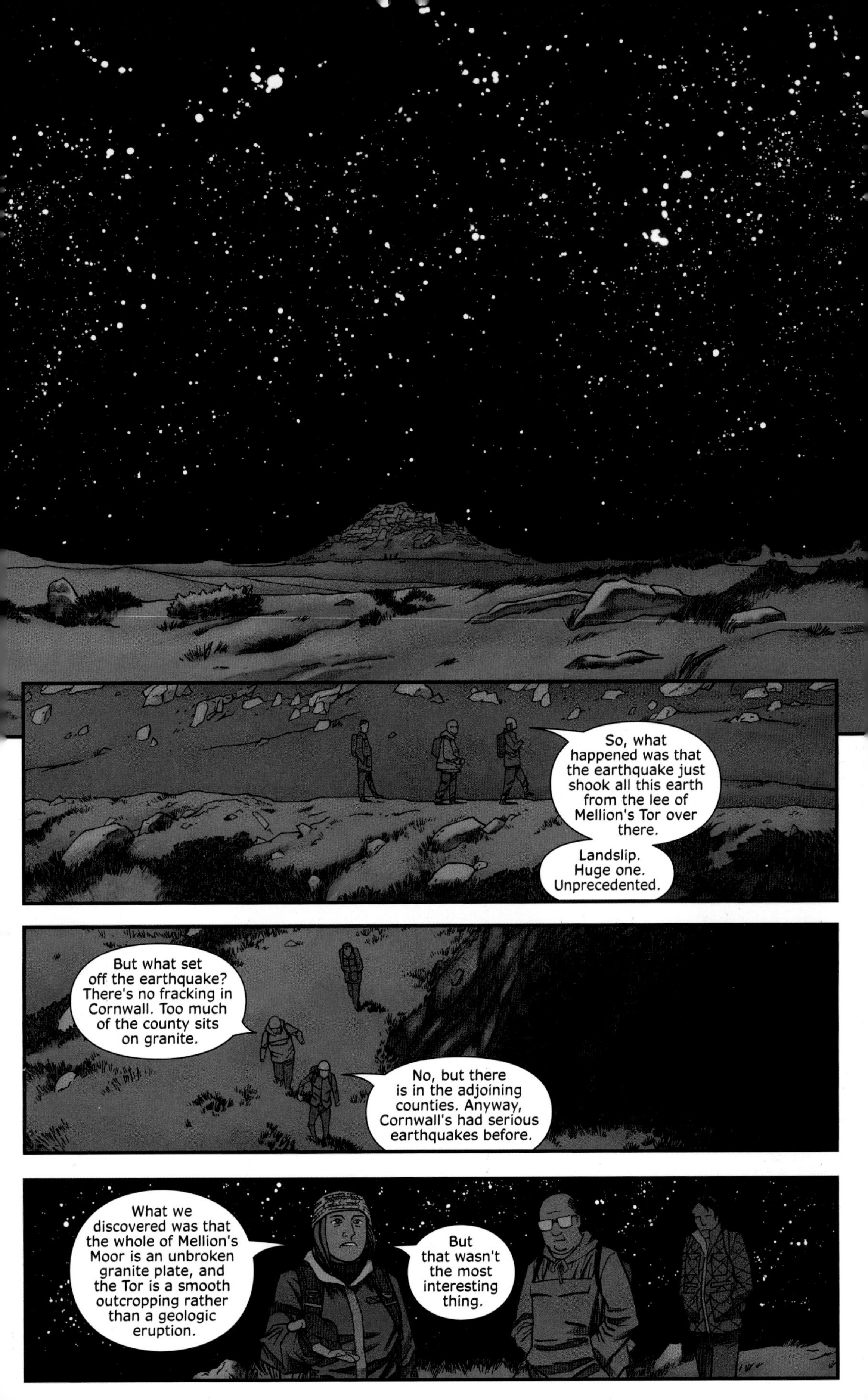

So, what happened was that the earthquake just shook all this earth from the lee of Mellion's Tor over there.
Landslip. Huge one. Unprecedented.
But what set off the earthquake? There's no fracking in Cornwall. Too much of the county sits on granite.
No, but there is in the adjoining counties. Anyway, Cornwall's had serious earthquakes before.
What we discovered was that the whole of Mellion's Moor is an unbroken granite plate, and the Tor is a smooth outcropping rather than a geologic eruption.
But that wasn't the most interesting thing.

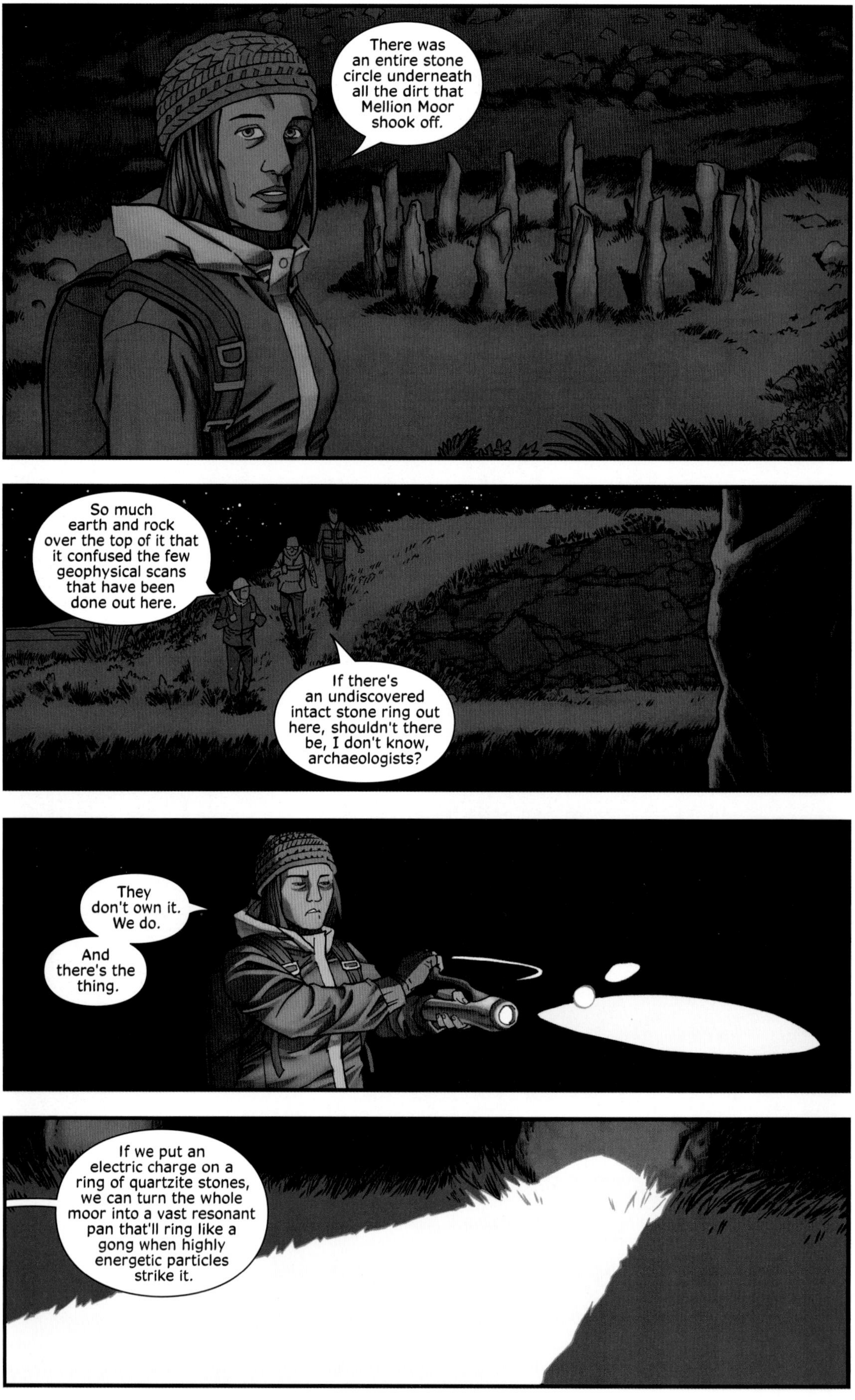
There was an entire stone circle underneath all the dirt that Mellion Moor shook off.
So much earth and rock over the top of it that it confused the few geophysical scans that have been done out here.
If there's an undiscovered intact stone ring out here, shouldn't there be, I don't know, archaeologists?
They don't own it. We do.
And there's the thing.
If we put an electric charge on a ring of quartzite stones, we can turn the whole moor into a vast resonant pan that'll ring like a gong when highly energetic particles strike it.

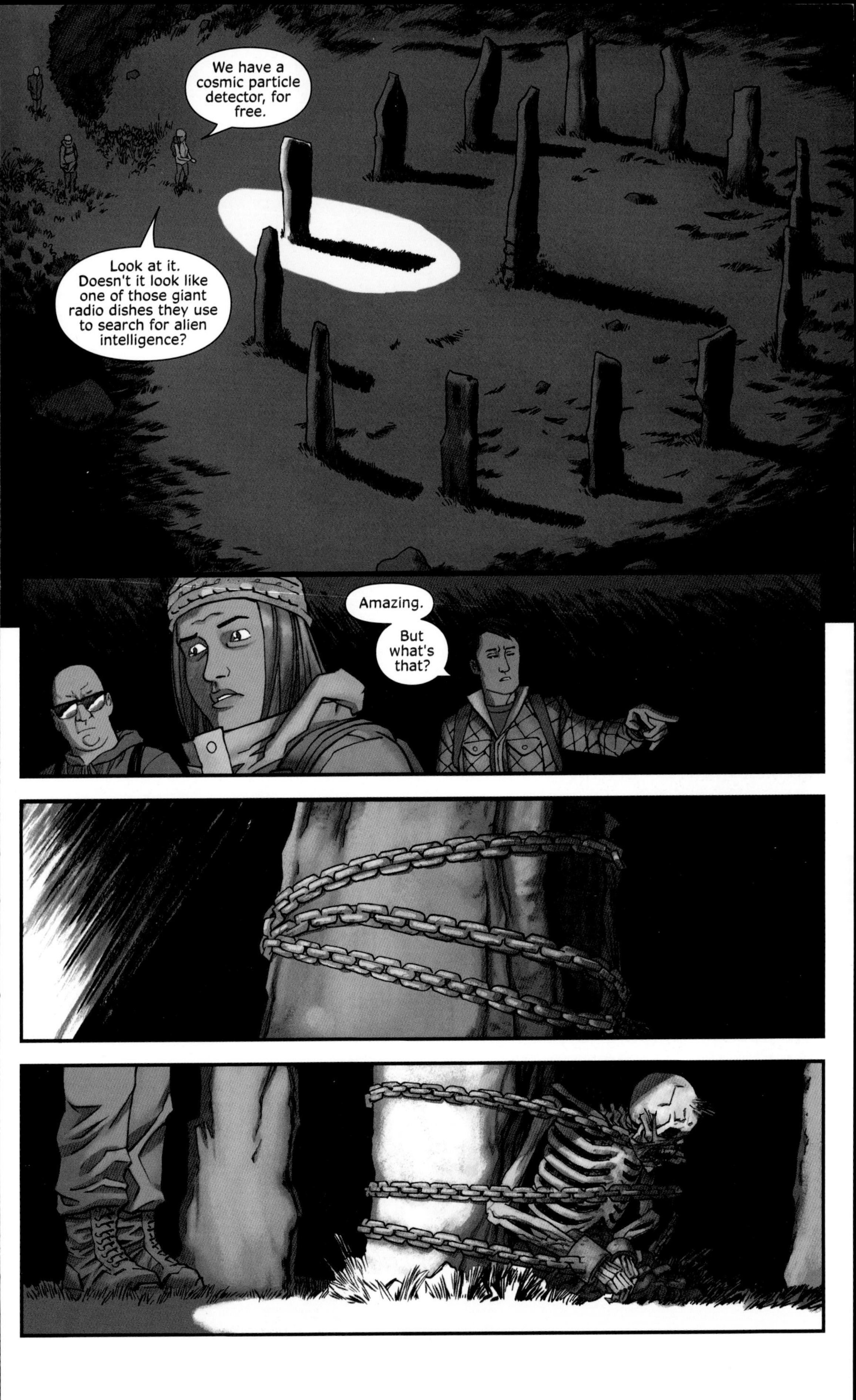
We have a cosmic particle detector, for free.
Look at it. Doesn't it look like one of those giant radio dishes they use to search for alien intelligence?
Amazing.
But what's that?

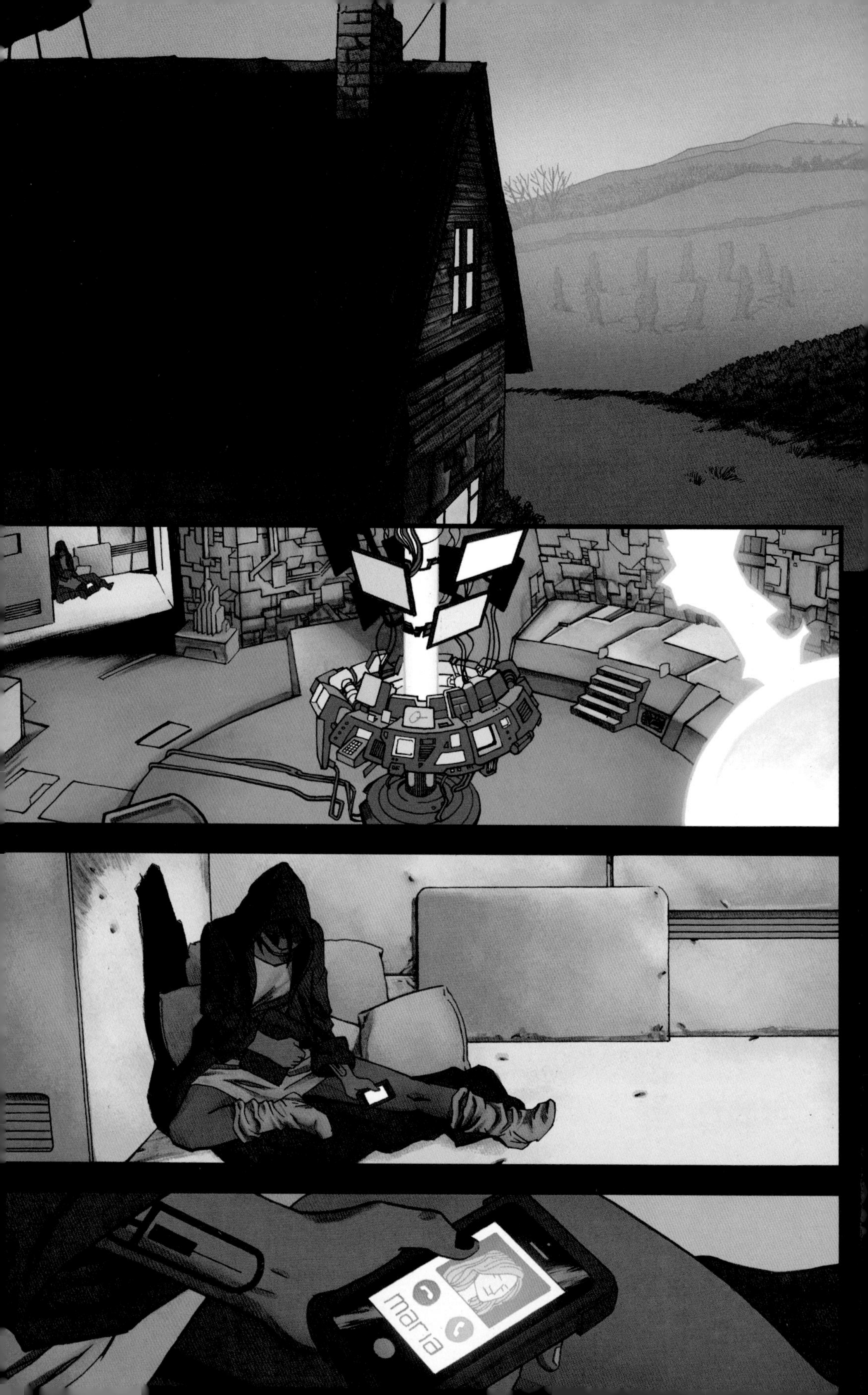
maria

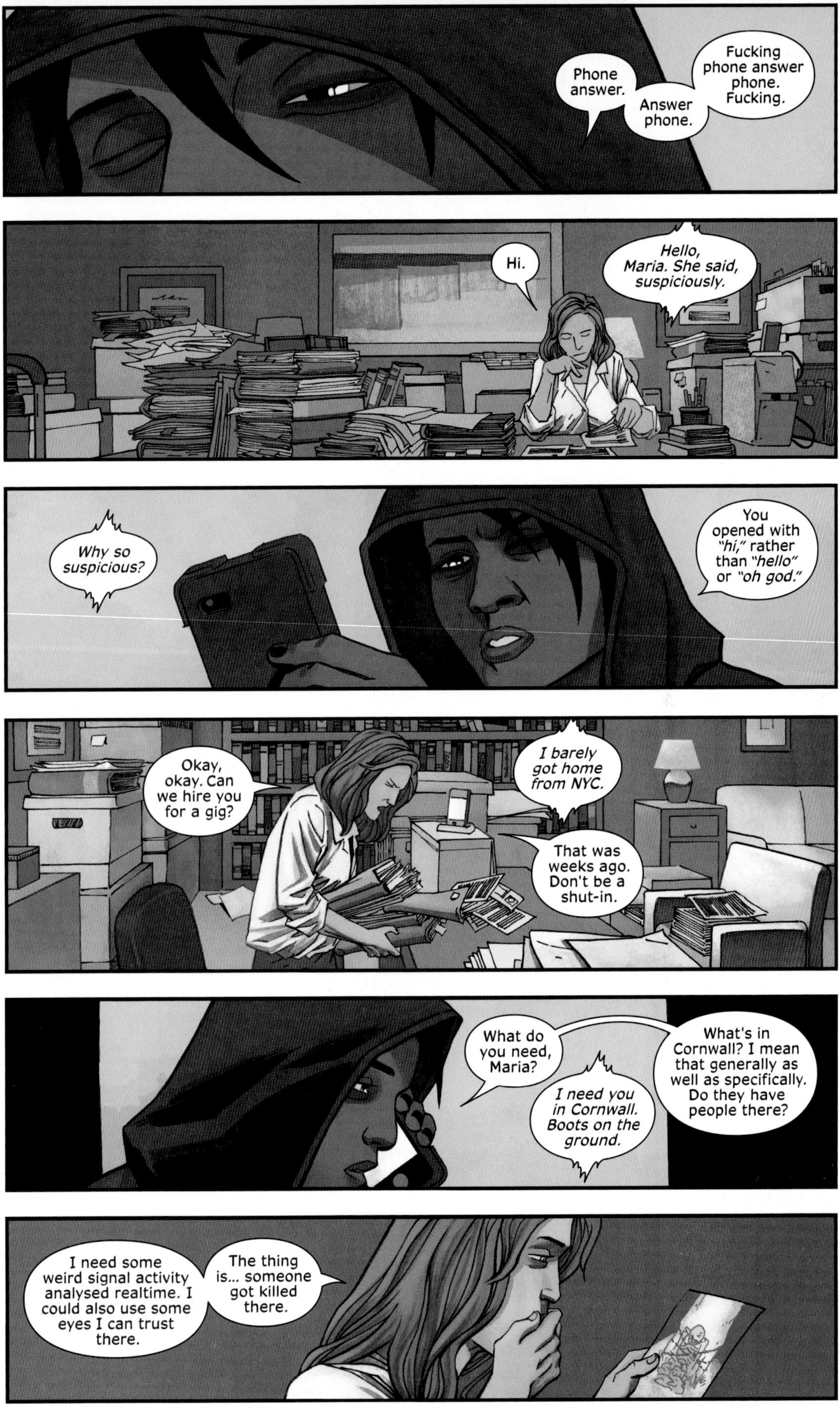
Phone answer.
Answer phone.
Fucking phone answer phone. Fucking.
Hi.
Hello, Maria. She said, suspiciously.
Why so suspicious?
You opened with "hi," rather than "hello" or "oh god."
Okay, okay. Can we hire you for a gig?
I barely got home from NYC.
That was weeks ago. Don't be a shut-in.
What do you need, Maria?
I need you in Cornwall. Boots on the ground.
What's in Cornwall? I mean that generally as well as specifically. Do they have people there?
I need some weird signal activity analysed realtime. I could also use some eyes I can trust there.
The thing is... someone got killed there.

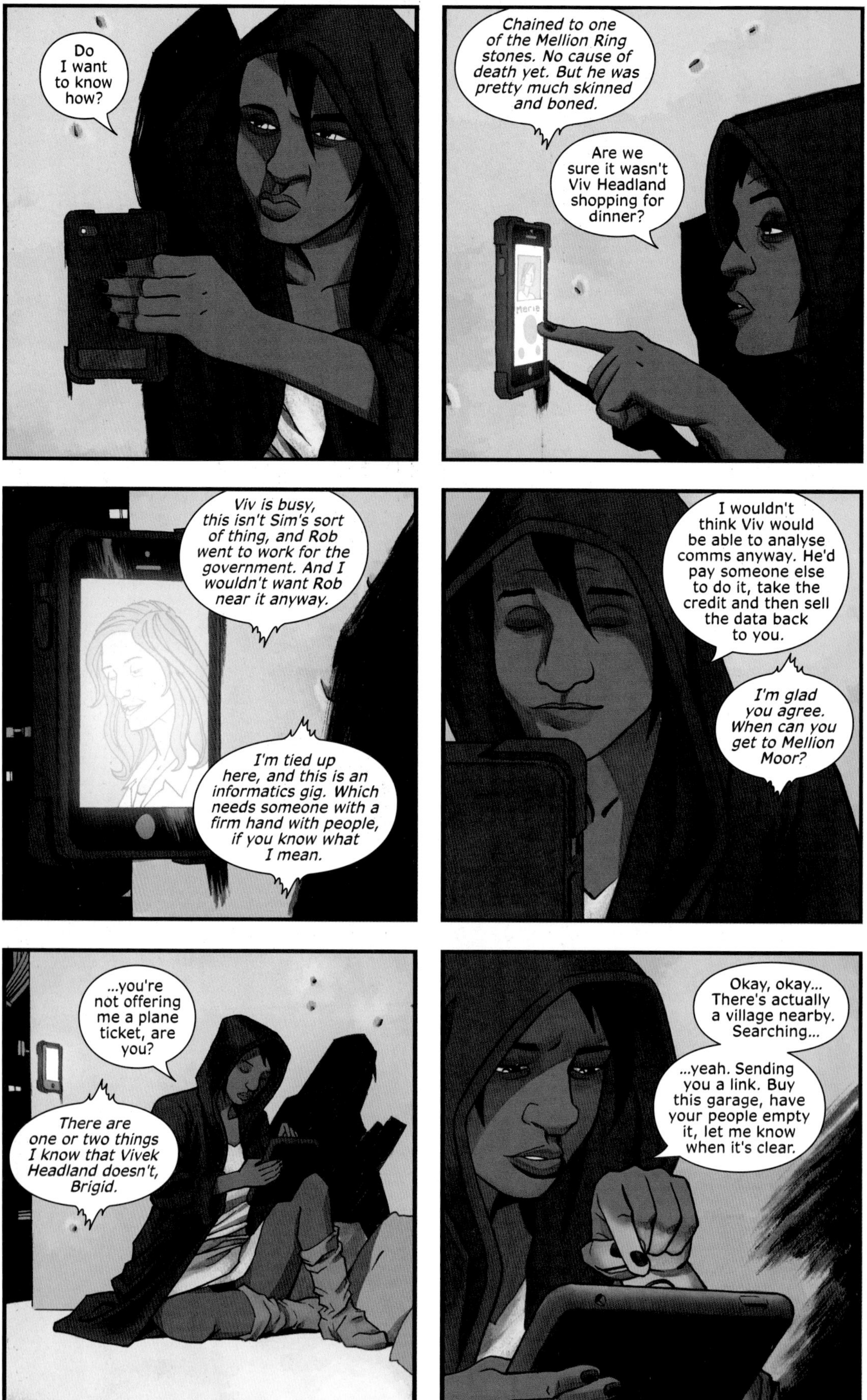
Do I want to know how?
Chained to one of the Mellion Ring stones. No cause of death yet. But he was pretty much skinned and boned.
Are we sure it wasn't Viv Headland shopping for dinner?
Merle
Viv is busy, this isn't Sim's sort of thing, and Rob went to work for the government. And I wouldn't want Rob near it anyway.
I'm tied up here, and this is an informatics gig. Which needs someone with a firm hand with people, if you know what I mean.
I wouldn't think Viv would be able to analyse comms anyway. He'd pay someone else to do it, take the credit and then sell the data back to you.
I'm glad you agree. When can you get to Mellion Moor?
...you're not offering me a plane ticket, are you?
There are one or two things I know that Vivek Headland doesn't, Brigid.
Okay, okay... There's actually a village nearby. Searching...
...yeah. Sending you a link. Buy this garage, have your people empty it, let me know when it's clear.

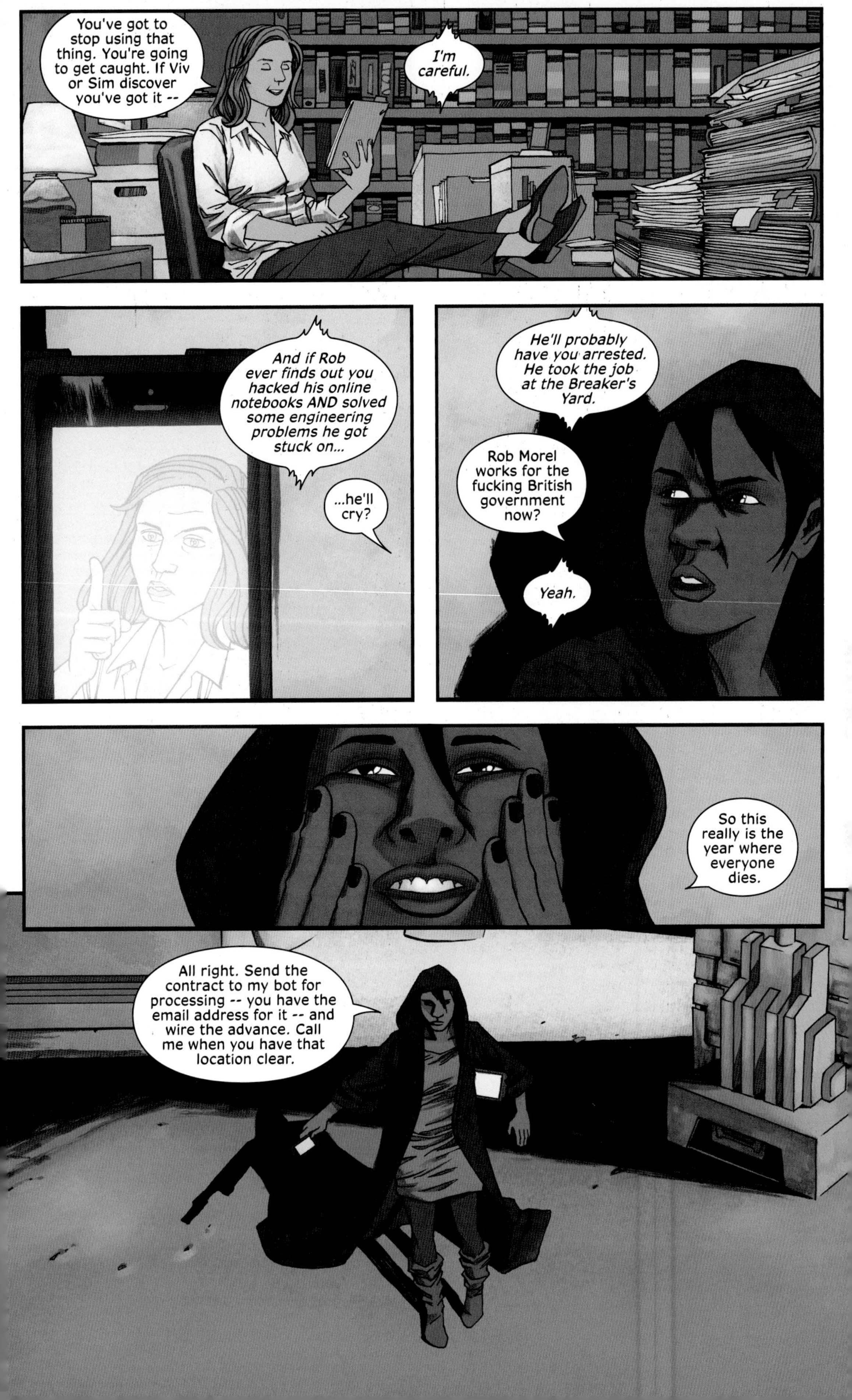
You've got to stop using that thing. You're going to get caught. If Viv or Sim discover you've got it --
I'm careful.
And if Rob ever finds out you hacked his online notebooks AND solved some engineering problems he got stuck on...
...he'll cry?
He'll probably have you arrested. He took the job at the Breaker's Yard.
Rob Morel works for the fucking British government now?
Yeah.
So this really is the year where everyone dies.
All right. Send the contract to my bot for processing -- you have the email address for it -- and wire the advance. Call me when you have that location clear.

FEMPAX
fucking shite
bastard I will gouge out your fucking ghost and burn it if you don't give me coffee

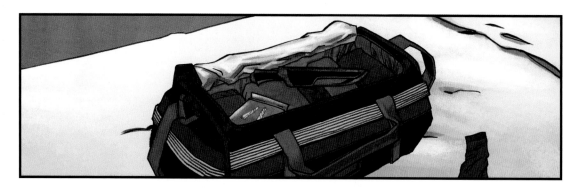

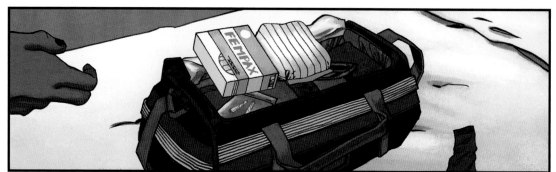

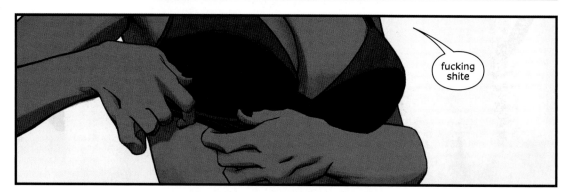

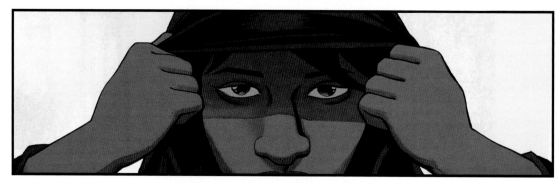

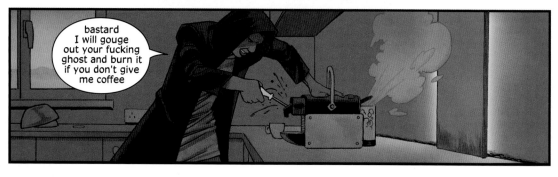

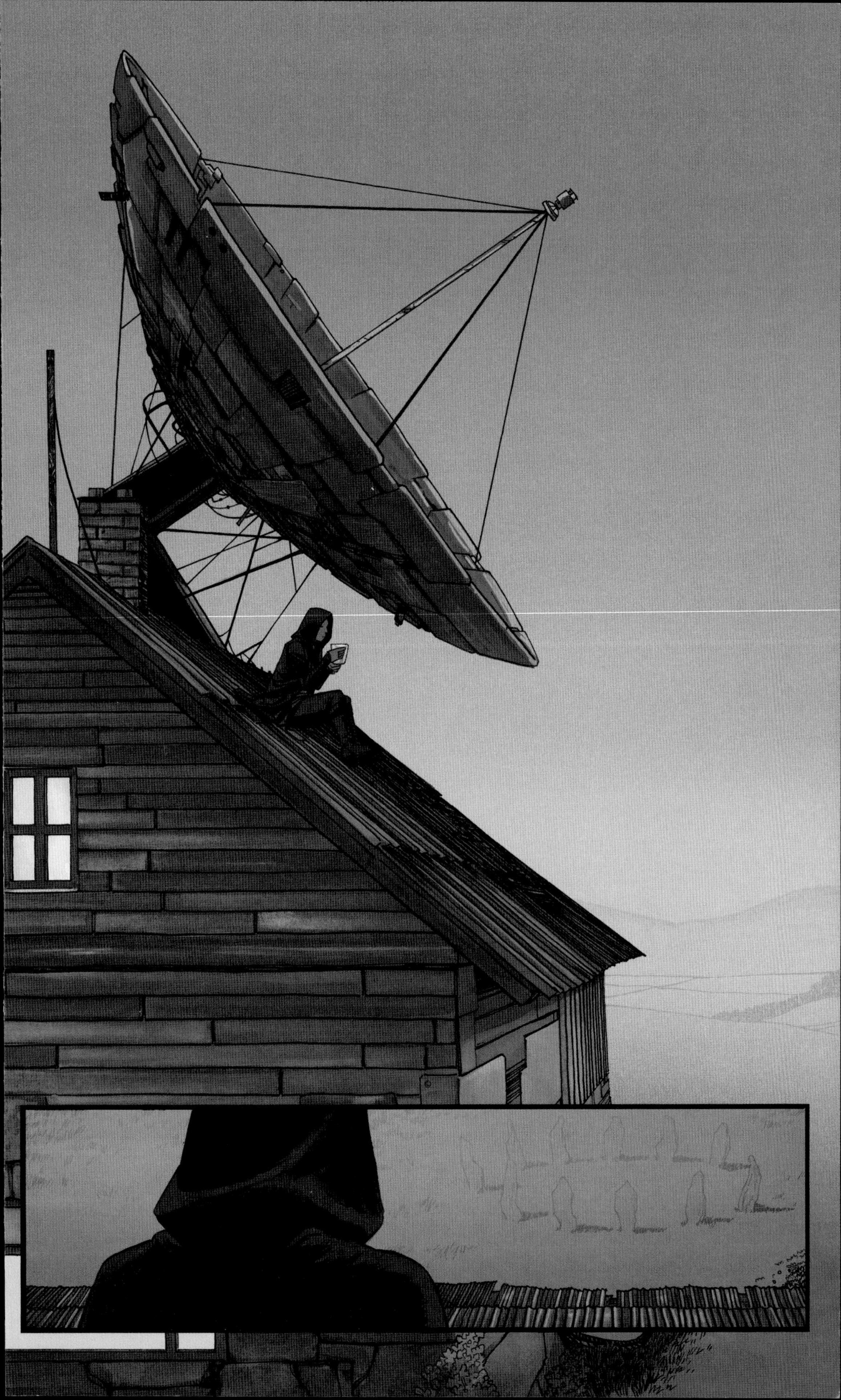

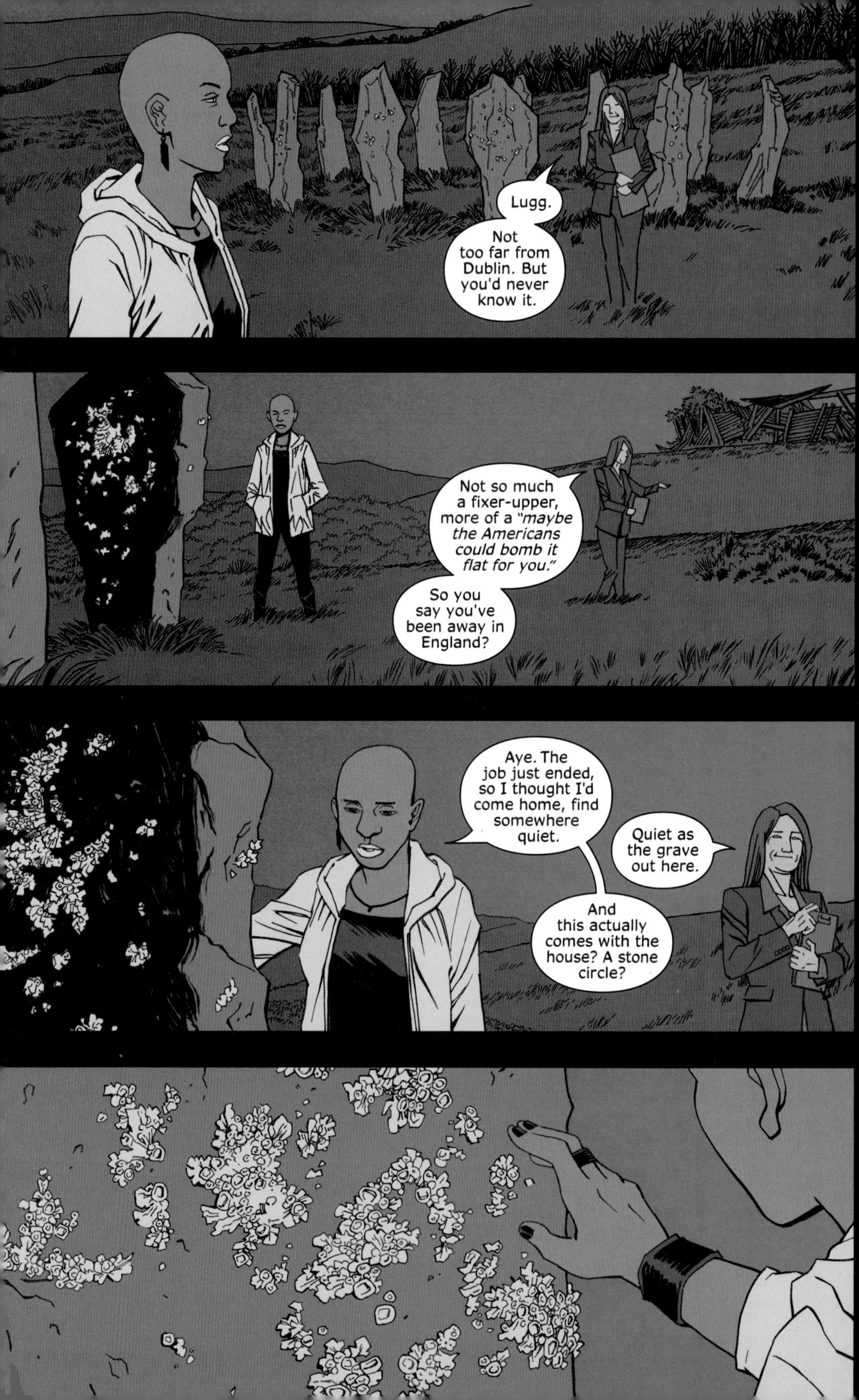
Lugg.
Not too far from Dublin. But you'd never know it.
Not so much a fixer-upper, more of a *"maybe the Americans could bomb it flat for you."*
So you say you've been away in England?
Aye. The job just ended, so I thought I'd come home, find somewhere quiet.
Quiet as the grave out here.
And this actually comes with the house? A stone circle?

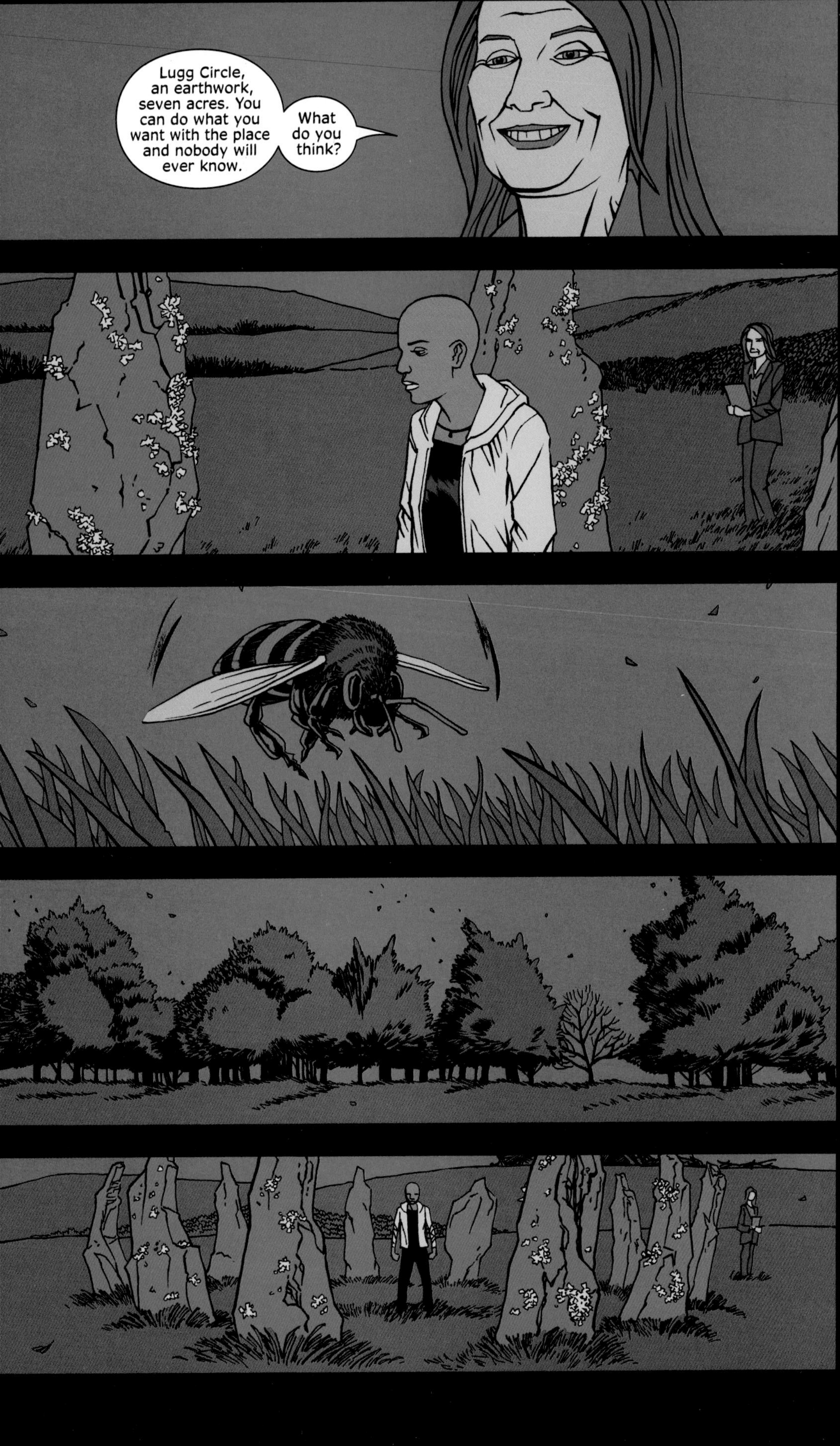
Lugg Circle, an earthwork, seven acres. You can do what you want with the place and nobody will ever know.
What do you think?

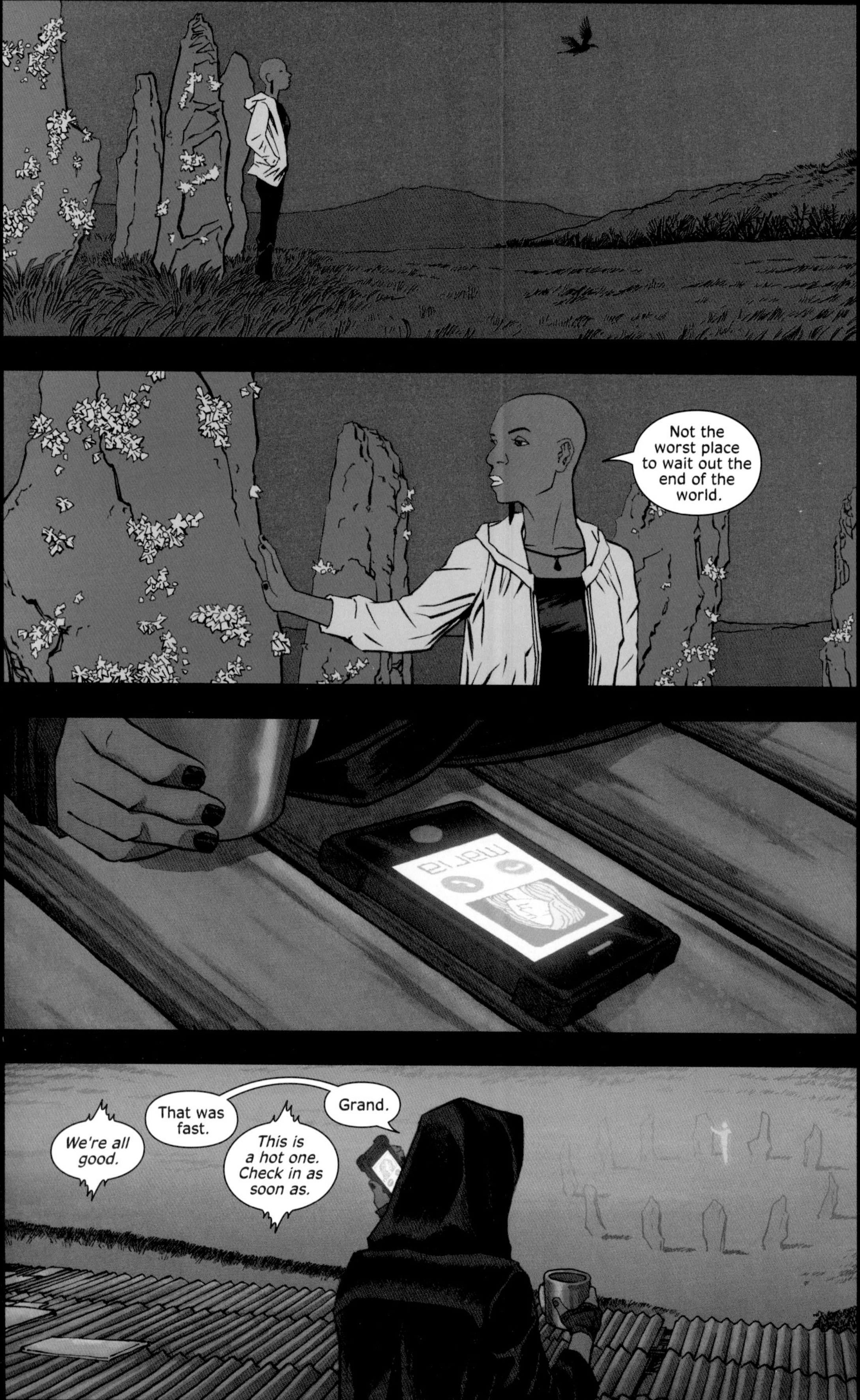
Not the worst place to wait out the end of the world.
maria
We're all good.
That was fast.
This is a hot one. Check in as soon as.
Grand.

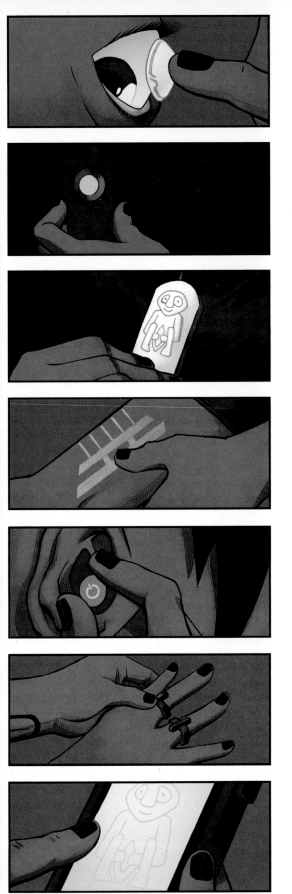

OK Sheela. Light up.

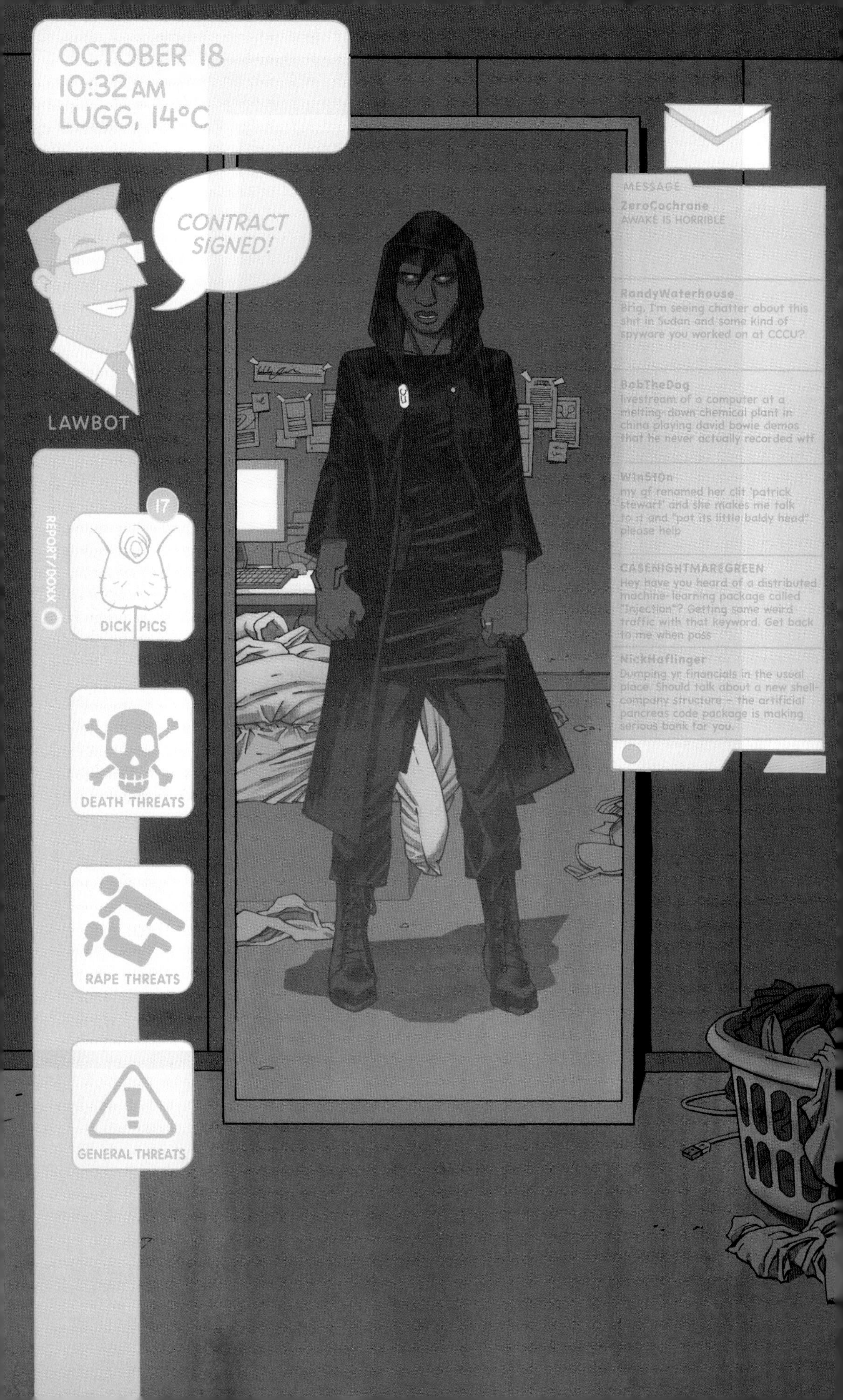

OCTOBER 18
10:32 AM
LUGG, 14°C
CONTRACT SIGNED!
LAWBOT
REPORT/DOXX
17
DICK PICS
DEATH THREATS
RAPE THREATS
GENERAL THREATS
MESSAGE
ZeroCochrane
AWAKE IS HORRIBLE
RandyWaterhouse
Brig, I'm seeing chatter about this shit in Sudan and some kind of spyware you worked on at CCCU?
BobTheDog
livestream of a computer at a melting-down chemical plant in china playing david bowie demos that he never actually recorded wtf
W1n5t0n
my gf renamed her clit 'patrick stewart' and she makes me talk to it and "pat its little baldy head" please help
CASENIGHTMAREGREEN
Hey have you heard of a distributed machine-learning package called "Injection"? Getting some weird traffic with that keyword. Get back to me when poss
NickHaflinger
Dumping yr financials in the usual place. Should talk about a new shell-company structure – the artificial pancreas code package is making serious bank for you.

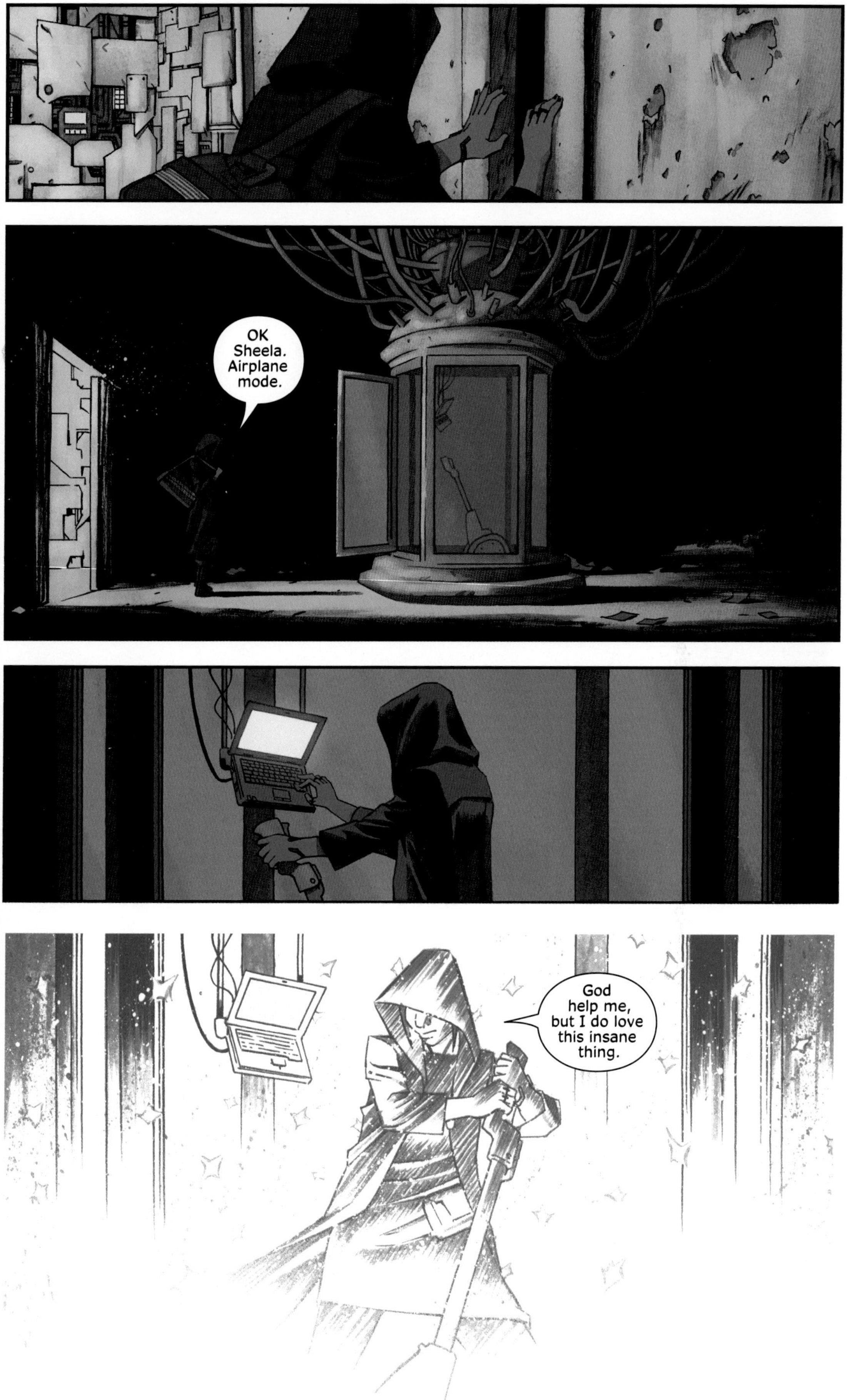
OK Sheela. Airplane mode.
God help me, but I do love this insane thing.

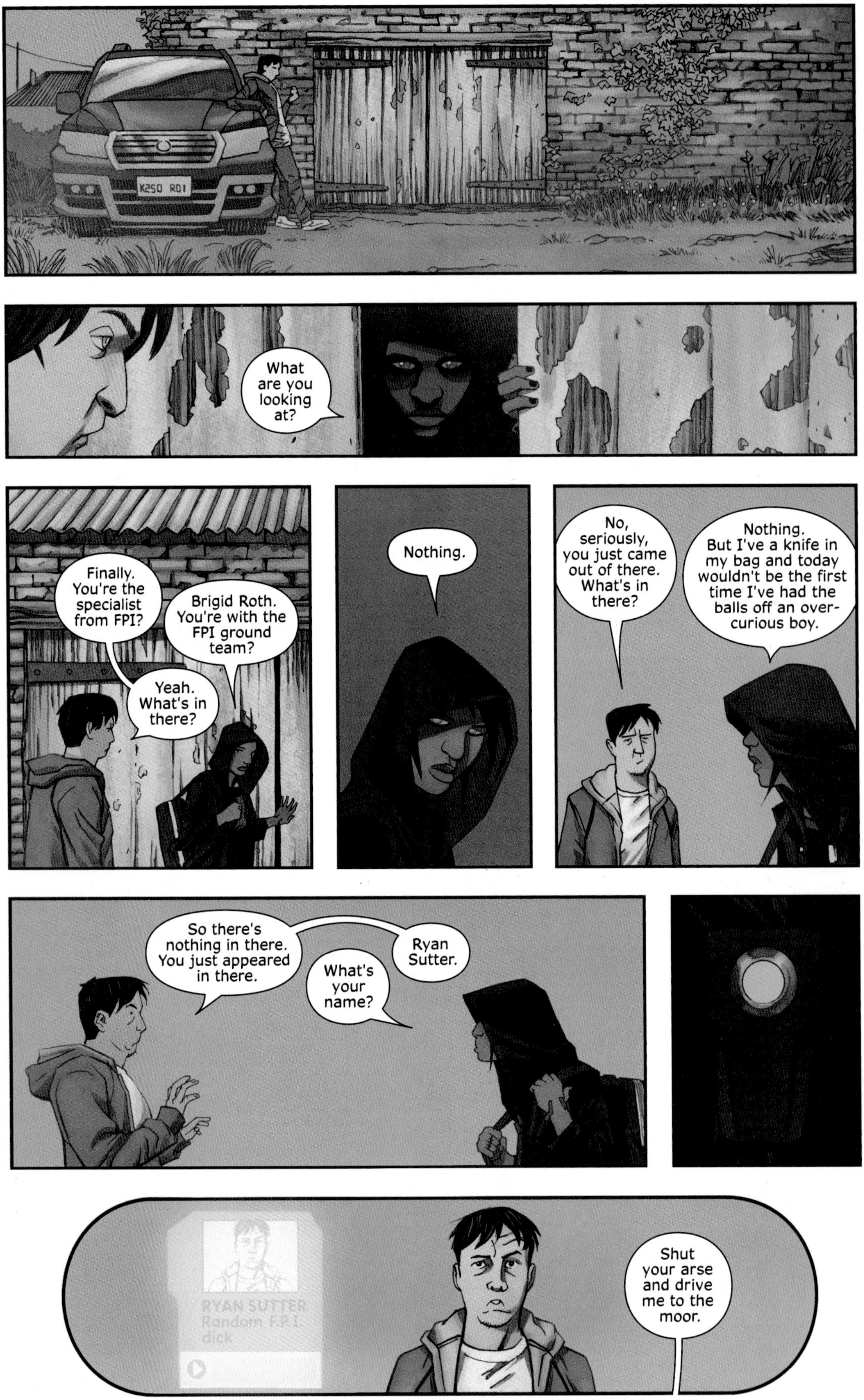
K250 RO1
What are you looking at?
Finally. You're the specialist from FPI?
Brigid Roth. You're with the FPI ground team?
Yeah. What's in there?
Nothing.
No, seriously, you just came out of there. What's in there?
Nothing. But I've a knife in my bag and today wouldn't be the first time I've had the balls off an over-curious boy.
So there's nothing in there. You just appeared in there.
What's your name?
Ryan Sutter.
RYAN SUTTER
Random F.P.I. dick
Shut your arse and drive me to the moor.

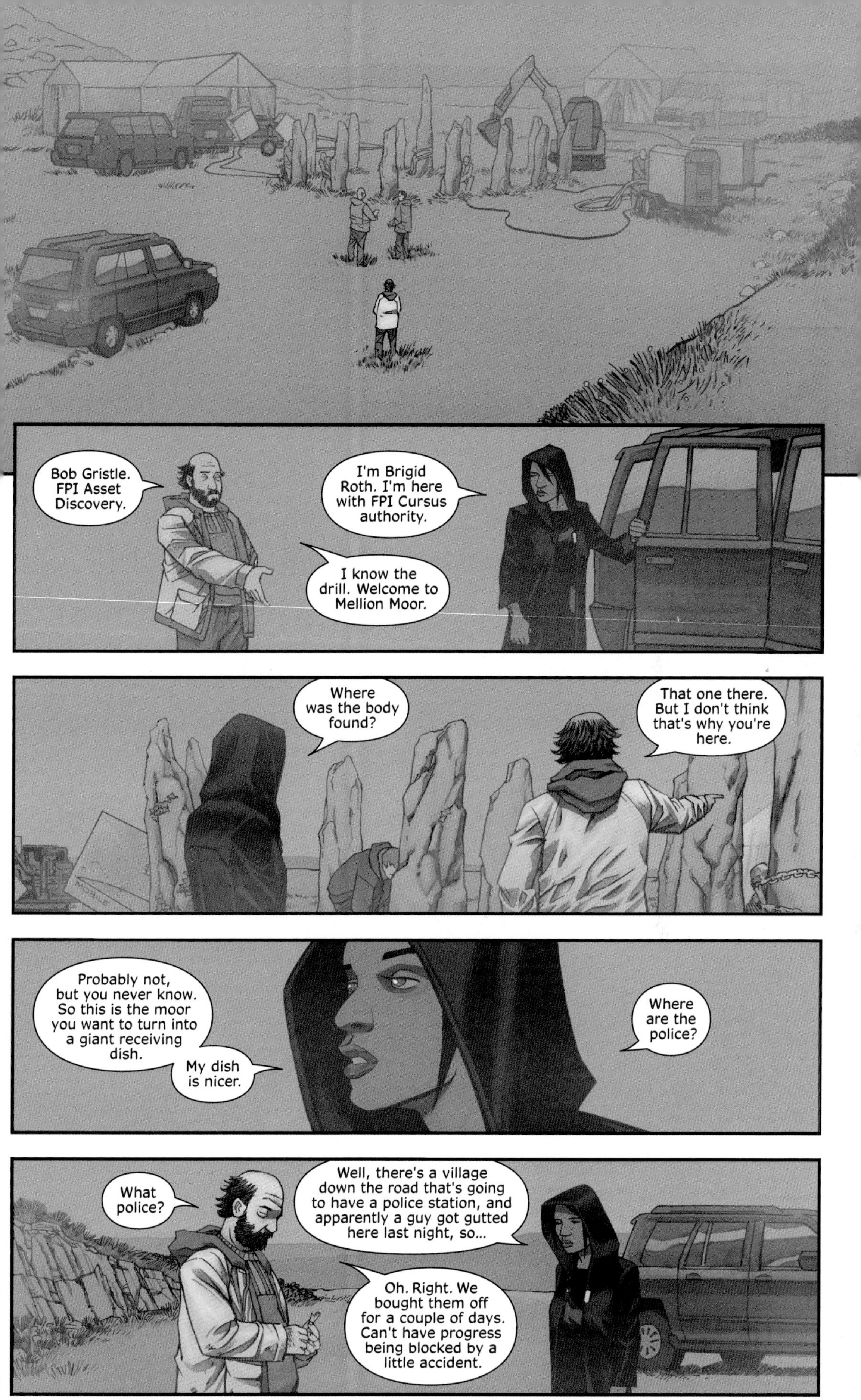
Bob Gristle. FPI Asset Discovery.
I'm Brigid Roth. I'm here with FPI Cursus authority.
I know the drill. Welcome to Mellion Moor.
Where was the body found?
That one there. But I don't think that's why you're here.
Probably not, but you never know. So this is the moor you want to turn into a giant receiving dish.
My dish is nicer.
Where are the police?
What police?
Well, there's a village down the road that's going to have a police station, and apparently a guy got gutted here last night, so...
Oh. Right. We bought them off for a couple of days. Can't have progress being blocked by a little accident.

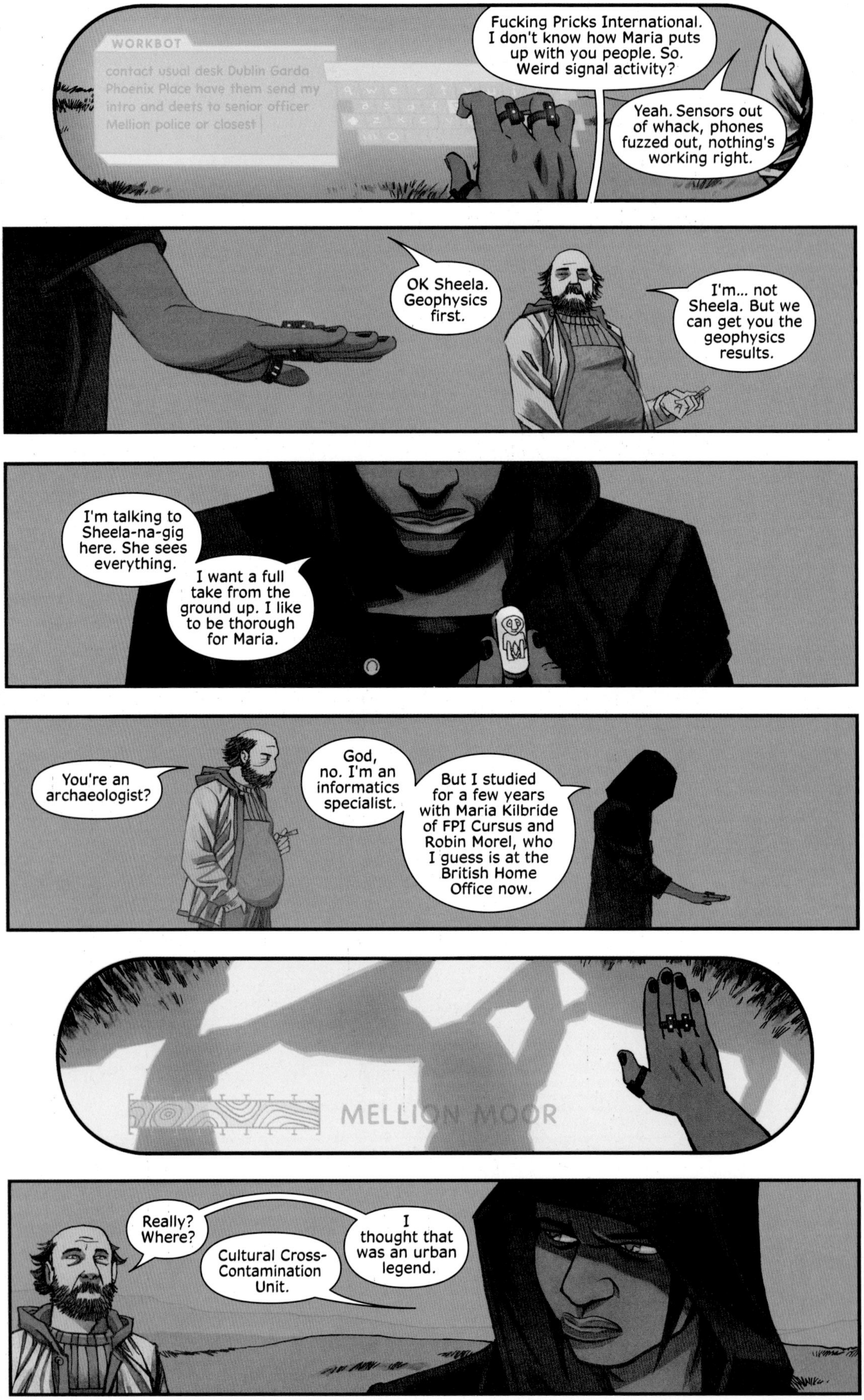
WORKBOT
contact usual desk Dublin Garda Phoenix Place have them send my intro and deets to senior officer Mellion police or closest
Fucking Pricks International. I don't know how Maria puts up with you people. So. Weird signal activity?
Yeah. Sensors out of whack, phones fuzzed out, nothing's working right.
OK Sheela. Geophysics first.
I'm... not Sheela. But we can get you the geophysics results.
I'm talking to Sheela-na-gig here. She sees everything.
I want a full take from the ground up. I like to be thorough for Maria.
You're an archaeologist?
God, no. I'm an informatics specialist.
But I studied for a few years with Maria Kilbride of FPI Cursus and Robin Morel, who I guess is at the British Home Office now.
MELLION MOOR
Really? Where?
Cultural Cross-Contamination Unit.
I thought that was an urban legend.

No. Give me a second. OK Sheela, give me a quick wide look.

Wow. Well, I see why you're having trouble with your phones. There's a lot of weird noise in the air.

Oh. It's dropping. But very, very slowly.

Who are those people?

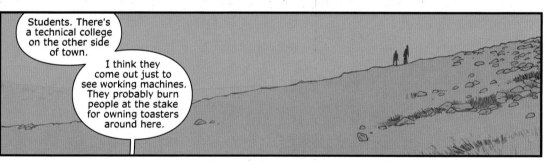

Students. There's a technical college on the other side of town.

I think they come out just to see working machines. They probably burn people at the stake for owning toasters around here.

You can see there's something else under there, right?

The stones extend way further down. They surround a ditch.

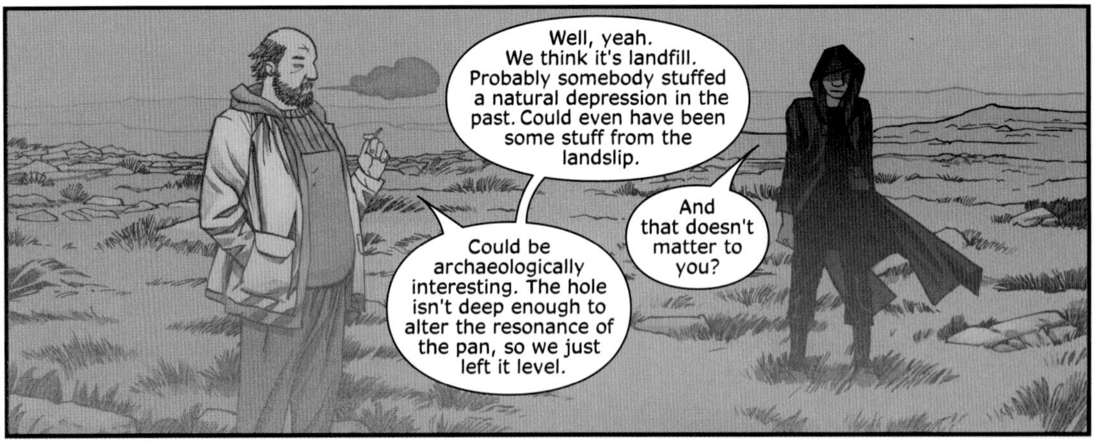
Well, yeah. We think it's landfill. Probably somebody stuffed a natural depression in the past. Could even have been some stuff from the landslip.
Could be archaeologically interesting. The hole isn't deep enough to alter the resonance of the pan, so we just left it level.
And that doesn't matter to you?

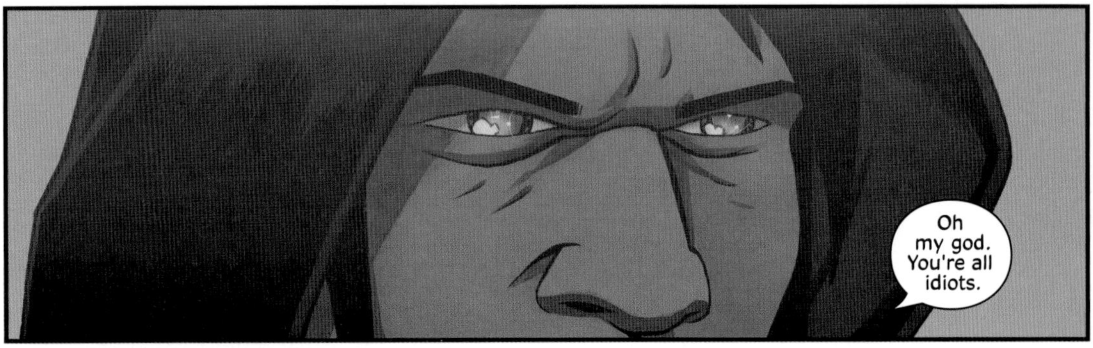
Oh my god. You're all idiots.

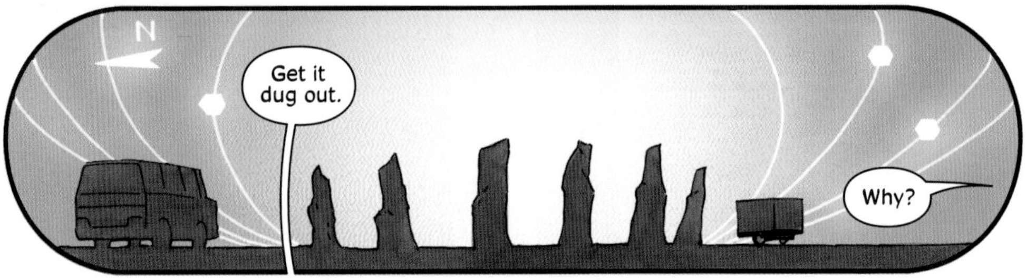
N
Get it dug out.
Why?

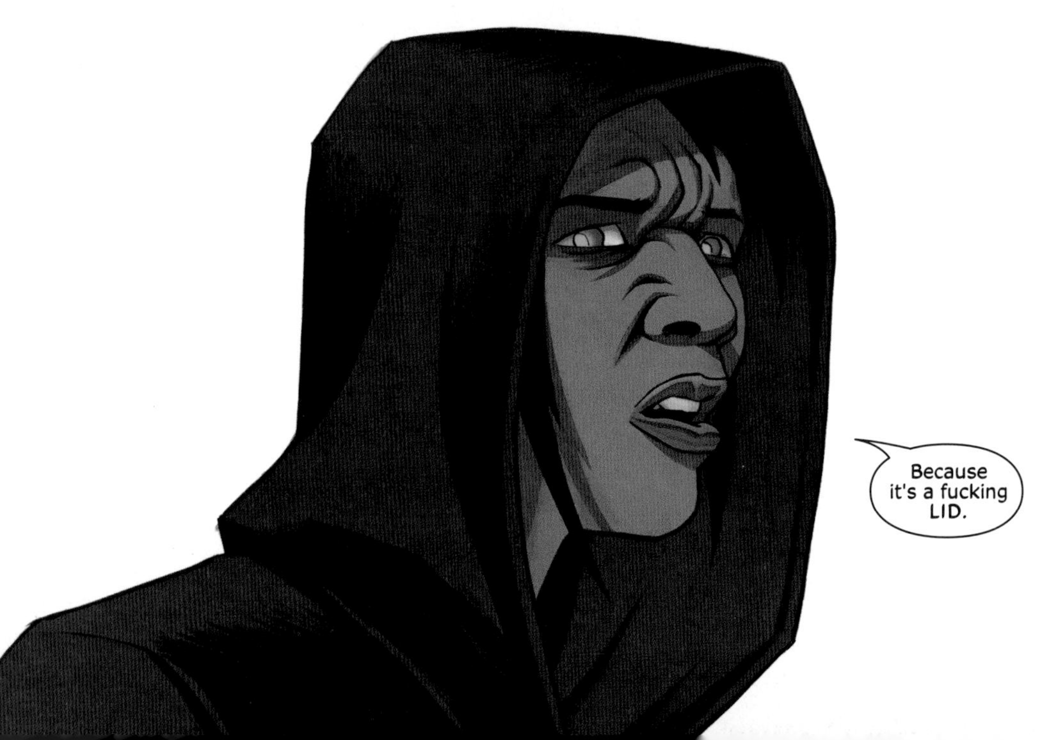
Because it's a fucking LID.

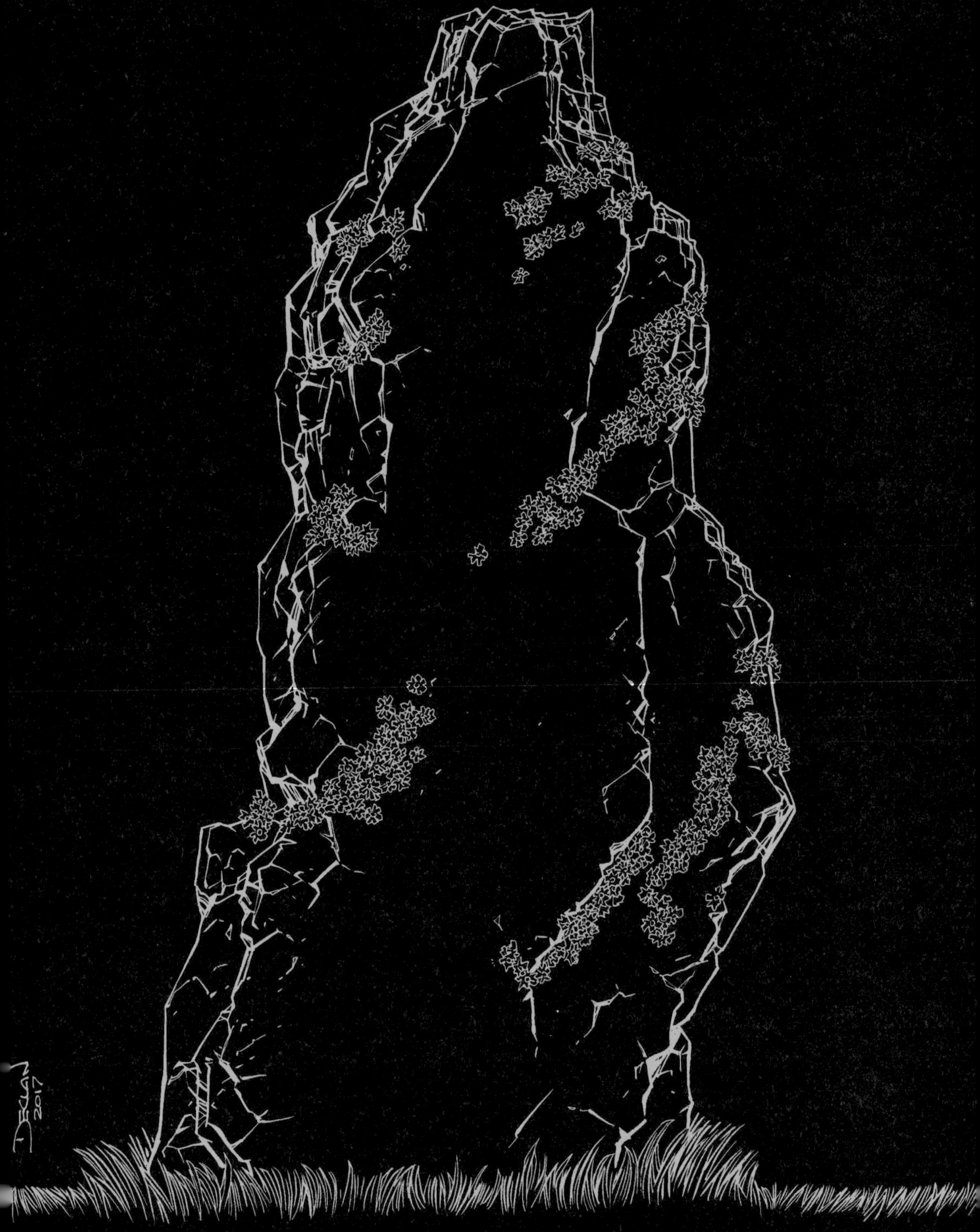
DECLAN
2017

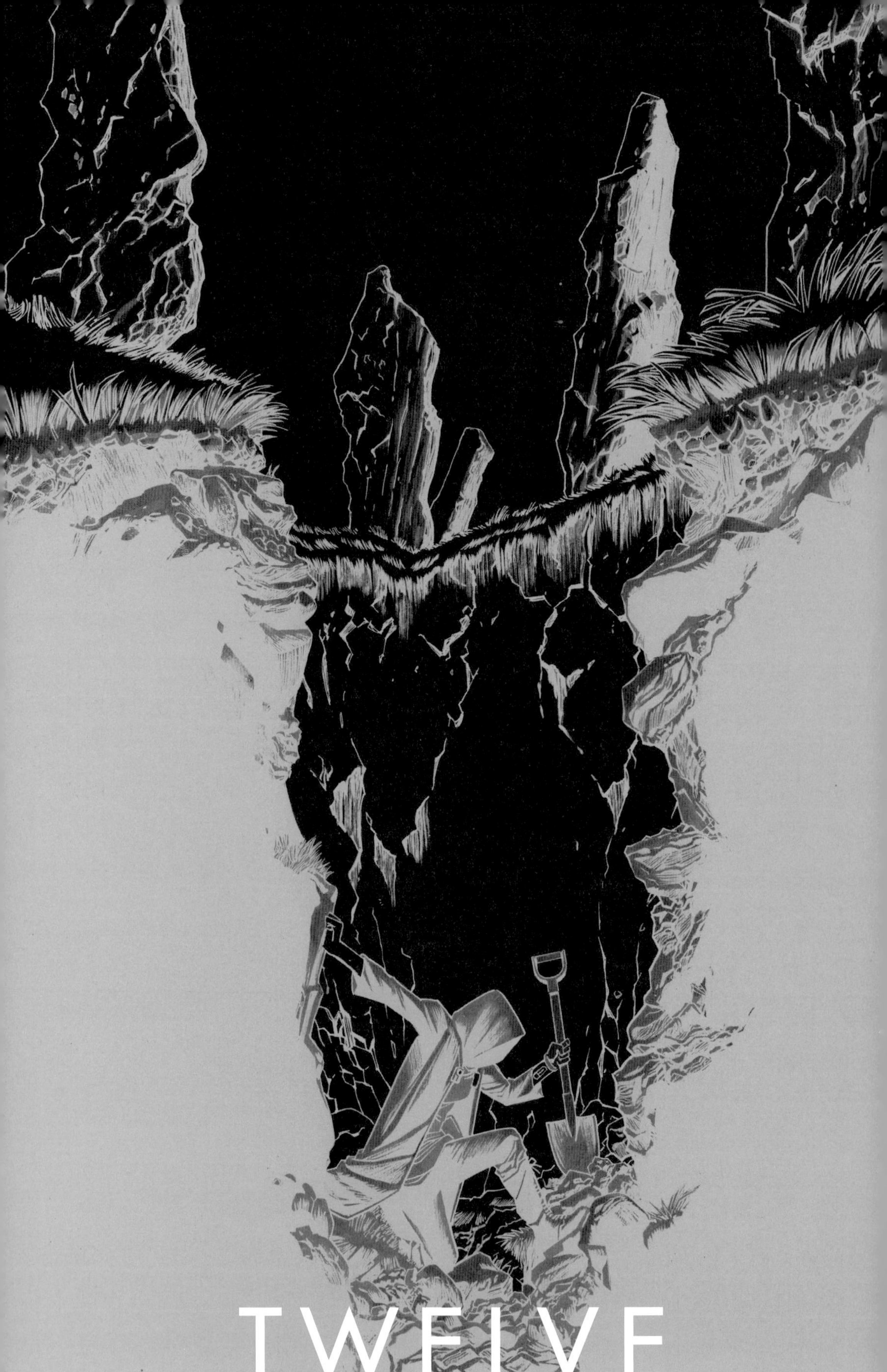

TWELVE

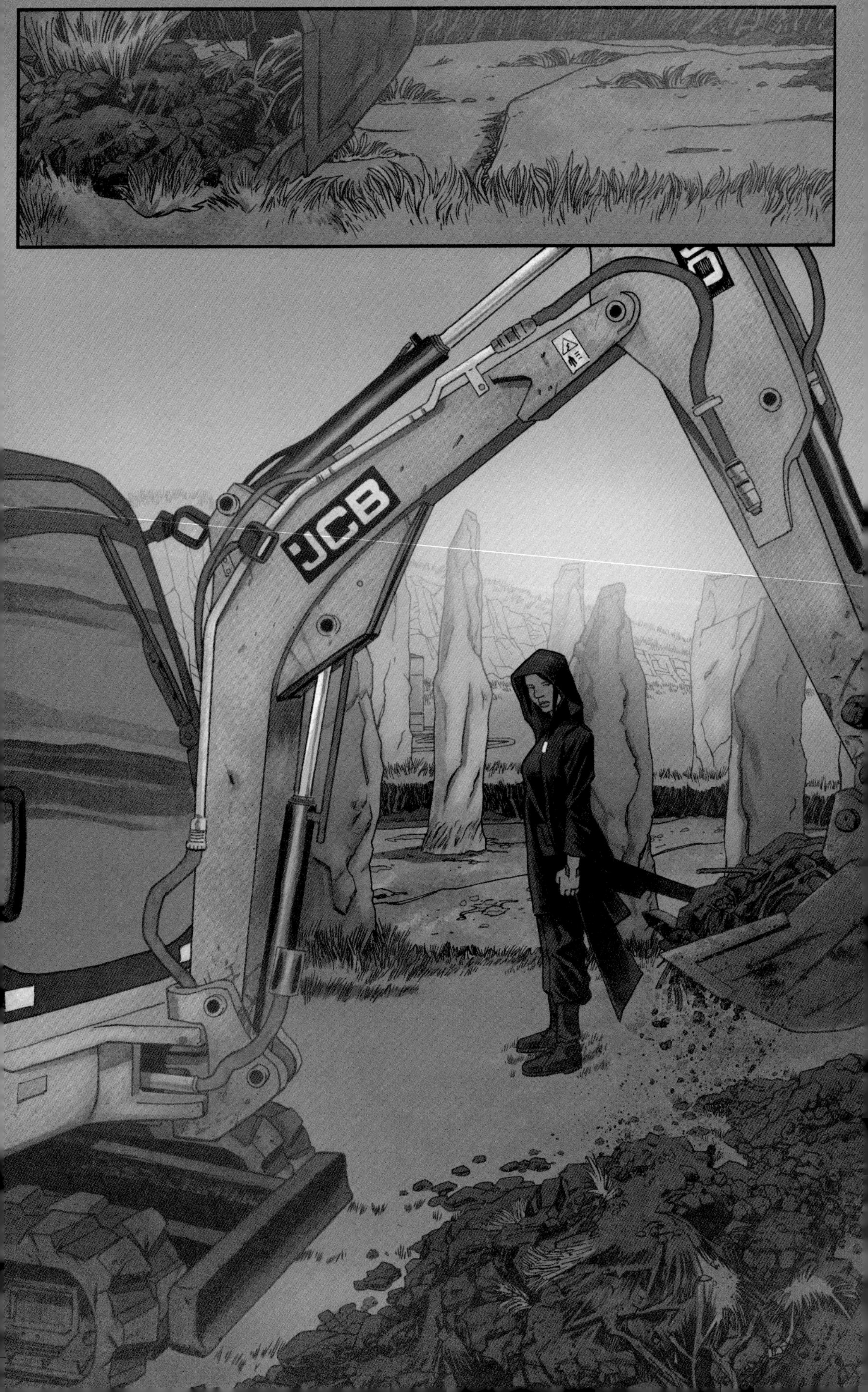
JCB

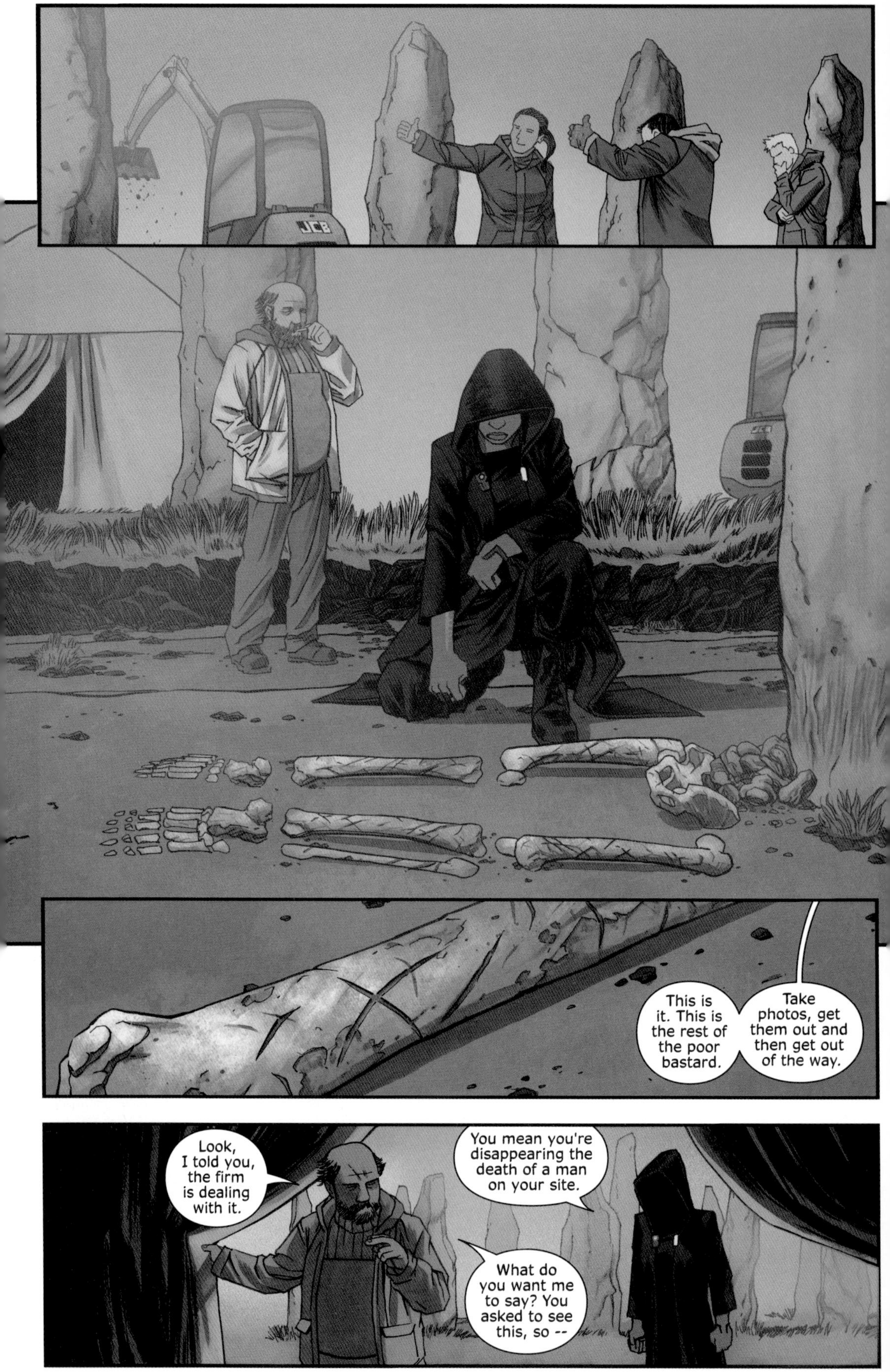
This is it. This is the rest of the poor bastard.
Take photos, get them out and then get out of the way.
Look, I told you, the firm is dealing with it.
You mean you're disappearing the death of a man on your site.
What do you want me to say? You asked to see this, so --

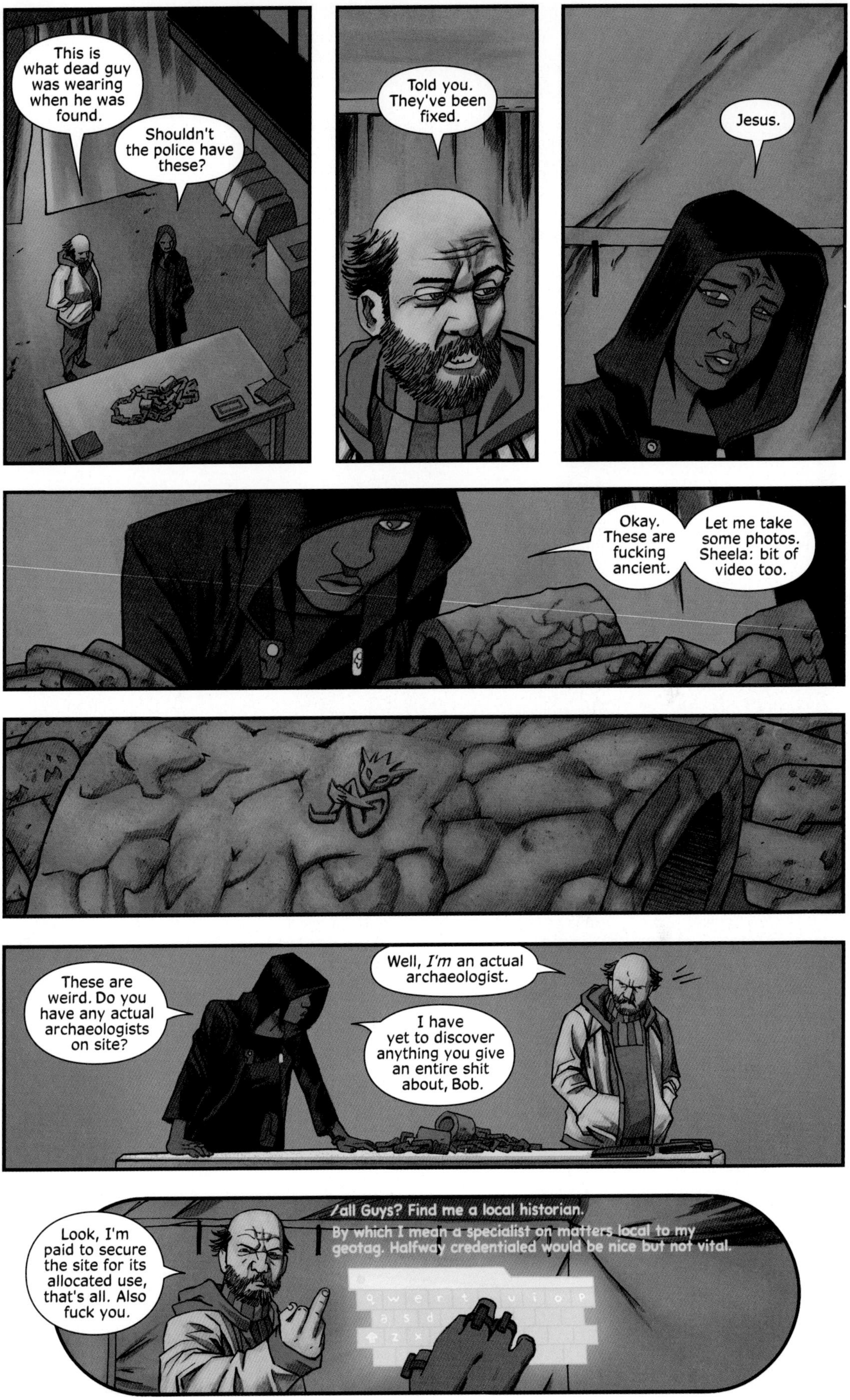
This is what dead guy was wearing when he was found.
Shouldn't the police have these?
Told you. They've been fixed.
Jesus.
Okay. These are fucking ancient.
Let me take some photos. Sheela: bit of video too.
These are weird. Do you have any actual archaeologists on site?
Well, *I'm* an actual archaeologist.
I have yet to discover anything you give an entire shit about, Bob.
Look, I'm paid to secure the site for its allocated use, that's all. Also fuck you.
/all Guys? Find me a local historian.
By which I mean a specialist on matters local to my geotag. Halfway credentialed would be nice but not vital.

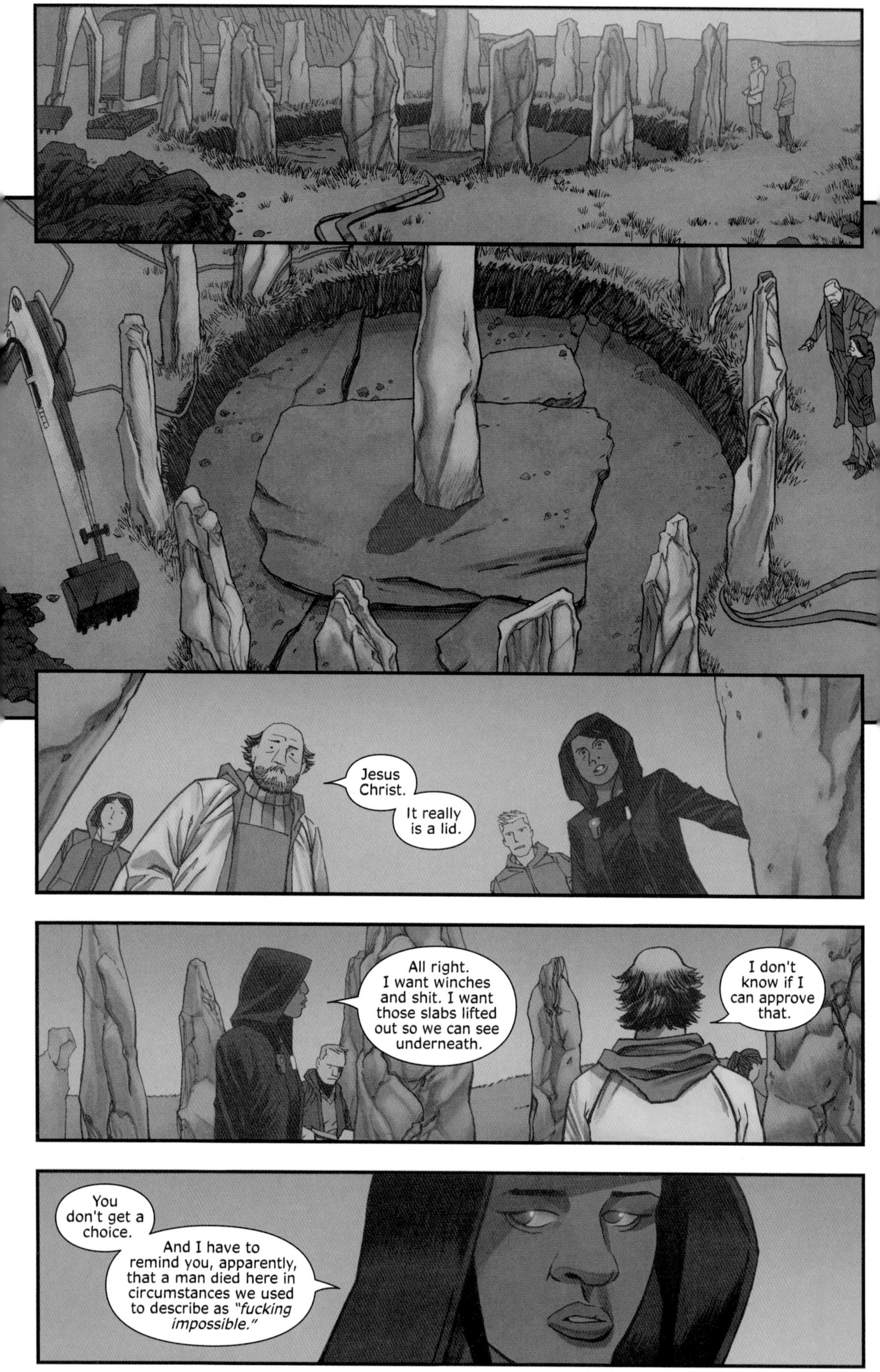
Jesus Christ.
It really is a lid.
All right. I want winches and shit. I want those slabs lifted out so we can see underneath.
I don't know if I can approve that.
You don't get a choice.
And I have to remind you, apparently, that a man died here in circumstances we used to describe as *"fucking impossible."*

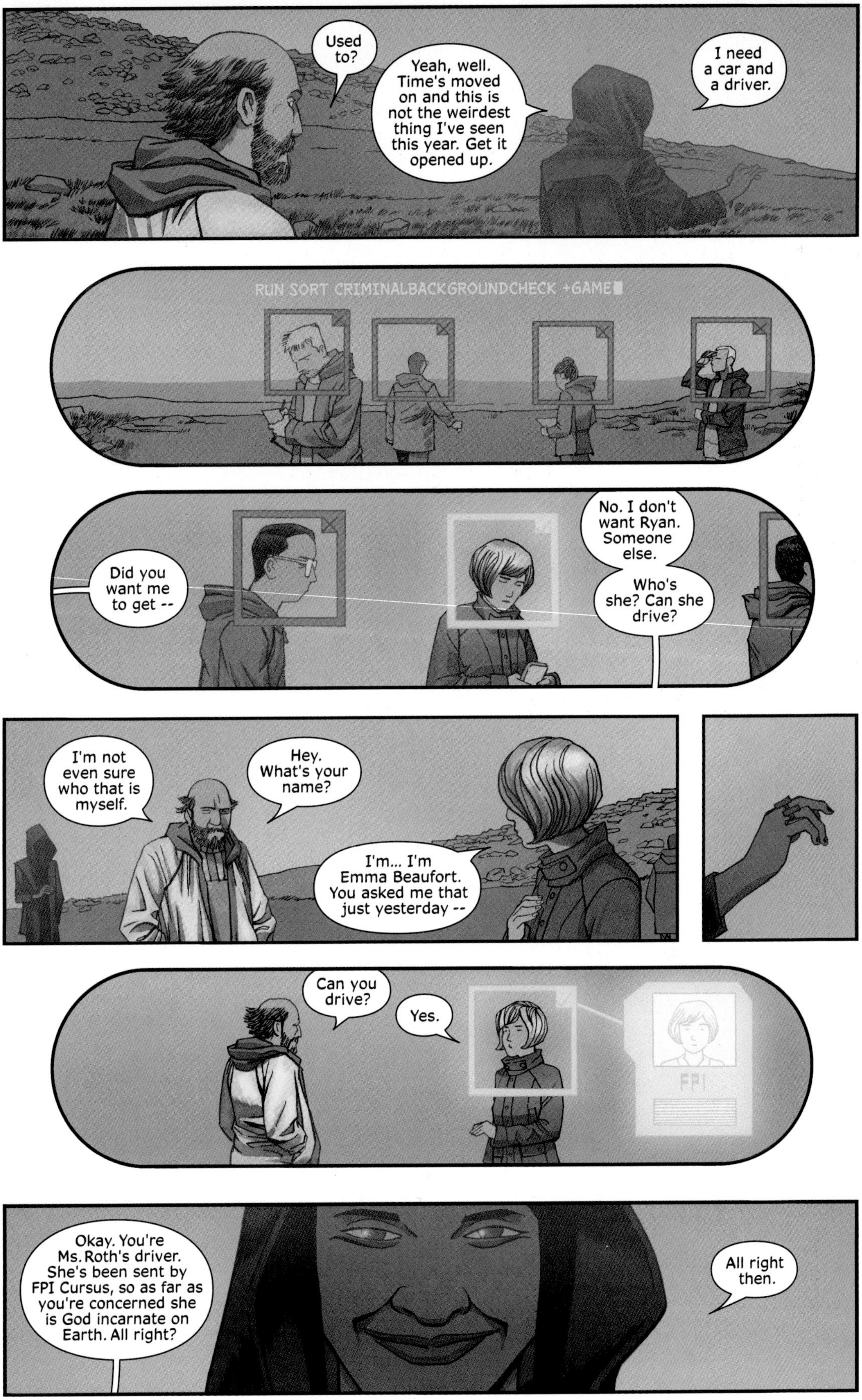
Used to?
Yeah, well. Time's moved on and this is not the weirdest thing I've seen this year. Get it opened up.
I need a car and a driver.
RUN SORT CRIMINALBACKGROUNDCHECK +GAME
Did you want me to get --
No. I don't want Ryan. Someone else.
Who's she? Can she drive?
I'm not even sure who that is myself.
Hey. What's your name?
I'm... I'm Emma Beaufort. You asked me that just yesterday --
Can you drive?
Yes.
FPI
Okay. You're Ms. Roth's driver. She's been sent by FPI Cursus, so as far as you're concerned she is God incarnate on Earth. All right?
All right then.

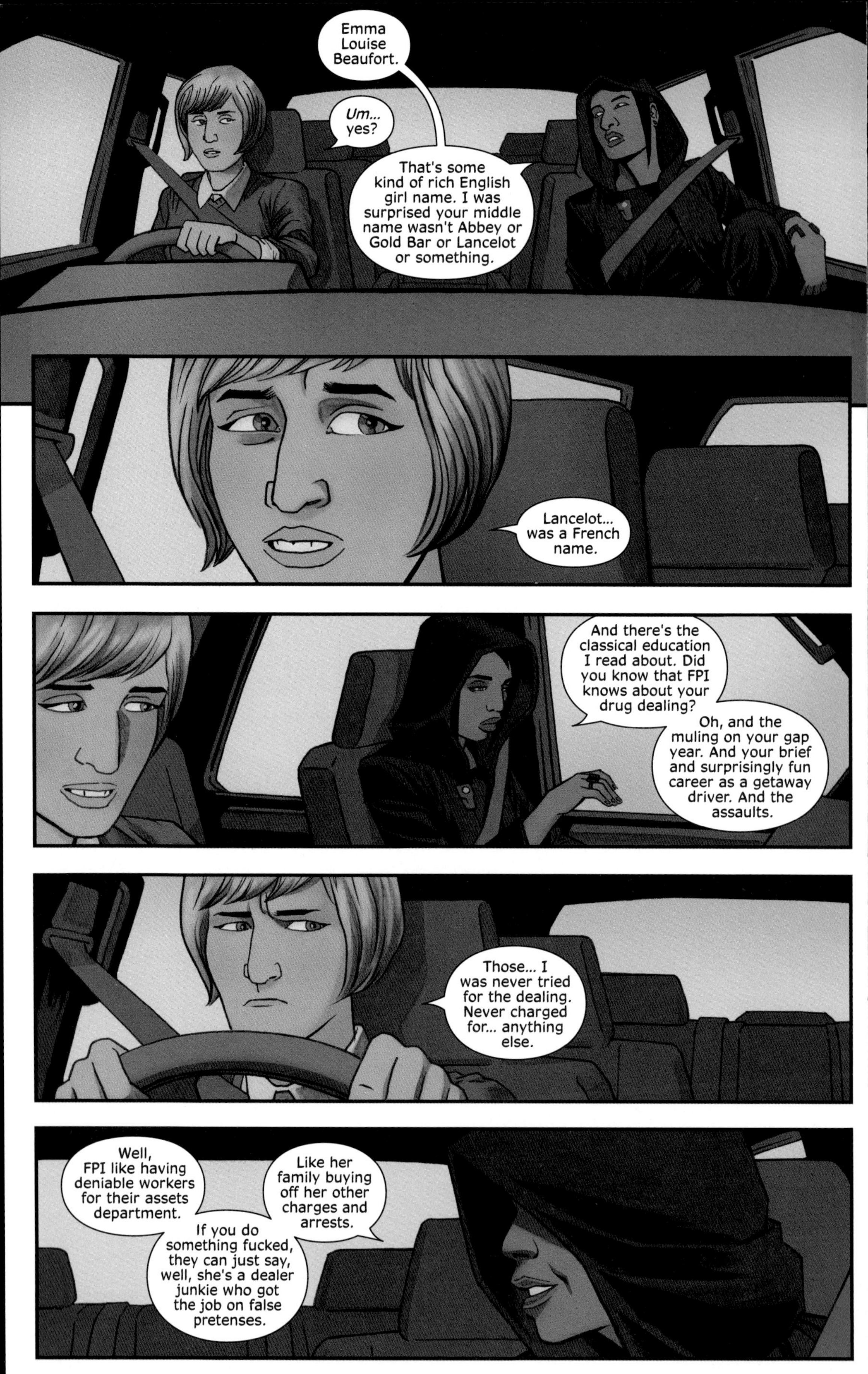
Emma Louise Beaufort.
Um... yes?
That's some kind of rich English girl name. I was surprised your middle name wasn't Abbey or Gold Bar or Lancelot or something.
Lancelot... was a French name.
And there's the classical education I read about. Did you know that FPI knows about your drug dealing?
Oh, and the muling on your gap year. And your brief and surprisingly fun career as a getaway driver. And the assaults.
Those... I was never tried for the dealing. Never charged for... anything else.
Well, FPI like having deniable workers for their assets department.
If you do something fucked, they can just say, well, she's a dealer junkie who got the job on false pretenses.
Like her family buying off her other charges and arrests.

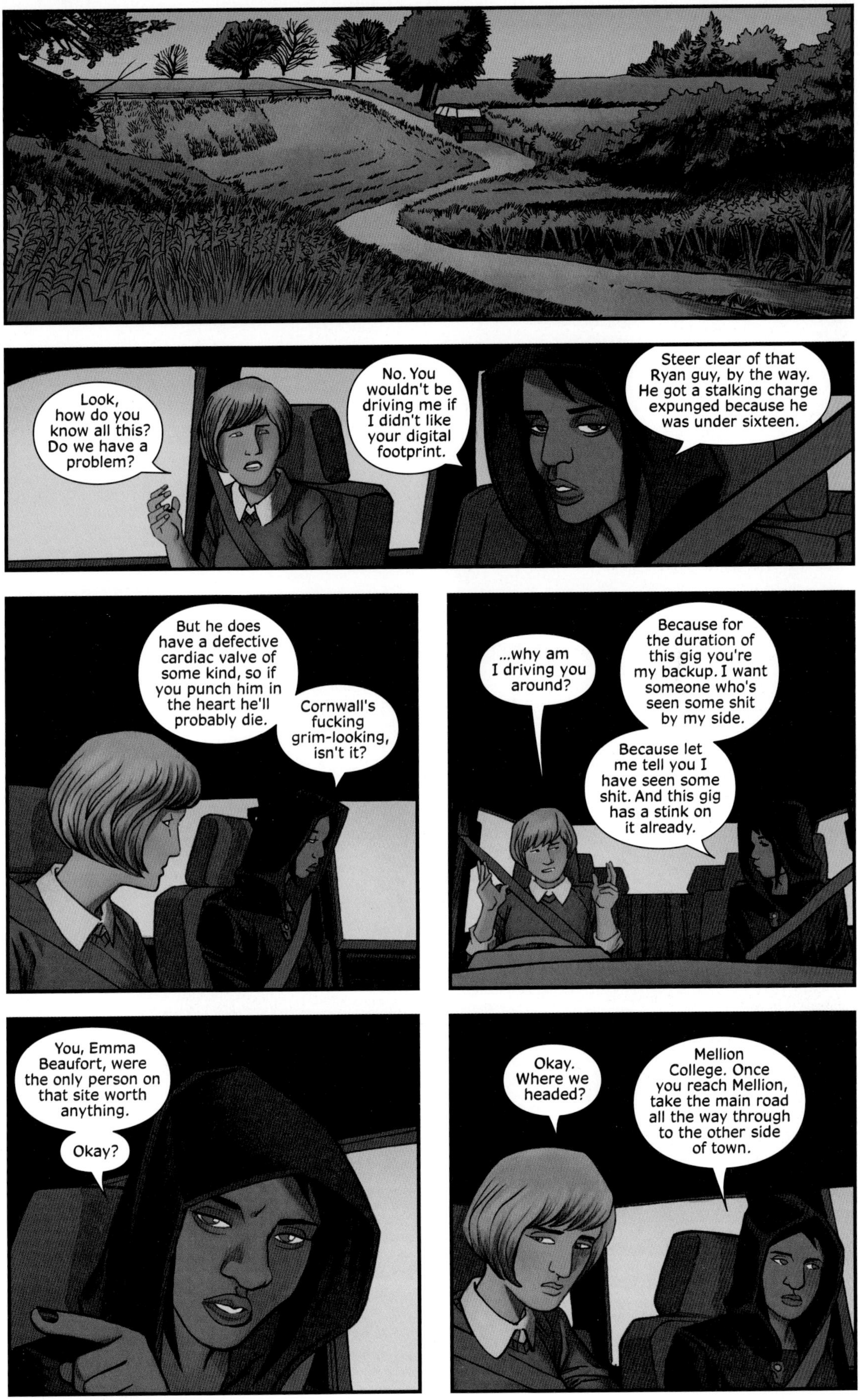
Look, how do you know all this? Do we have a problem?
No. You wouldn't be driving me if I didn't like your digital footprint.
Steer clear of that Ryan guy, by the way. He got a stalking charge expunged because he was under sixteen.
But he does have a defective cardiac valve of some kind, so if you punch him in the heart he'll probably die.
Cornwall's fucking grim-looking, isn't it?
...why am I driving you around?
Because for the duration of this gig you're my backup. I want someone who's seen some shit by my side.
Because let me tell you I have seen some shit. And this gig has a stink on it already.
You, Emma Beaufort, were the only person on that site worth anything.
Okay?
Okay. Where we headed?
Mellion College. Once you reach Mellion, take the main road all the way through to the other side of town.

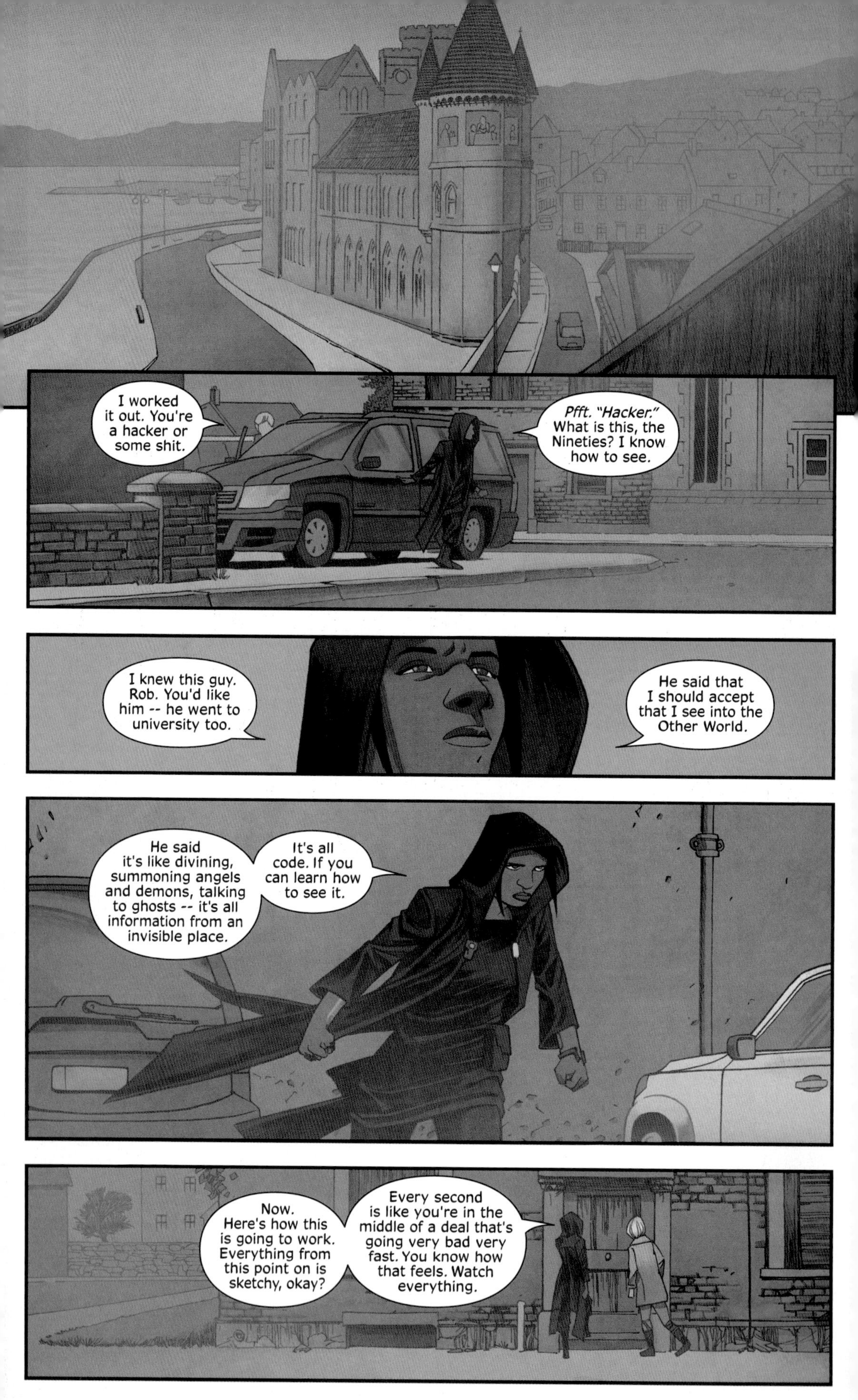
I worked it out. You're a hacker or some shit.
Pfft. "Hacker." What is this, the Nineties? I know how to see.
I knew this guy. Rob. You'd like him -- he went to university too.
He said that I should accept that I see into the Other World.
He said it's like divining, summoning angels and demons, talking to ghosts -- it's all information from an invisible place.
It's all code. If you can learn how to see it.
Now. Here's how this is going to work. Everything from this point on is sketchy, okay?
Every second is like you're in the middle of a deal that's going very bad very fast. You know how that feels. Watch everything.

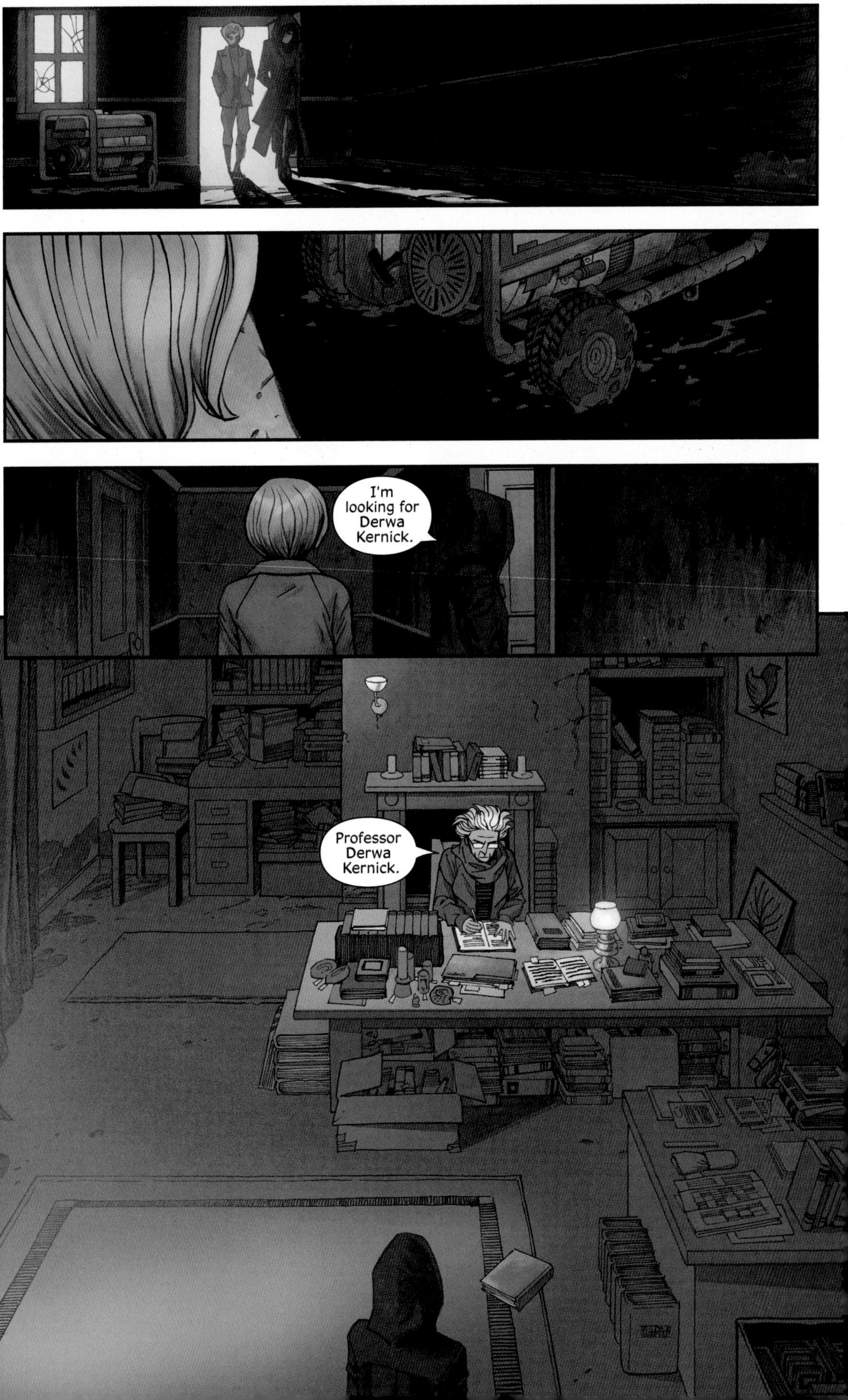
I'm looking for Derwa Kernick.
Professor Derwa Kernick.

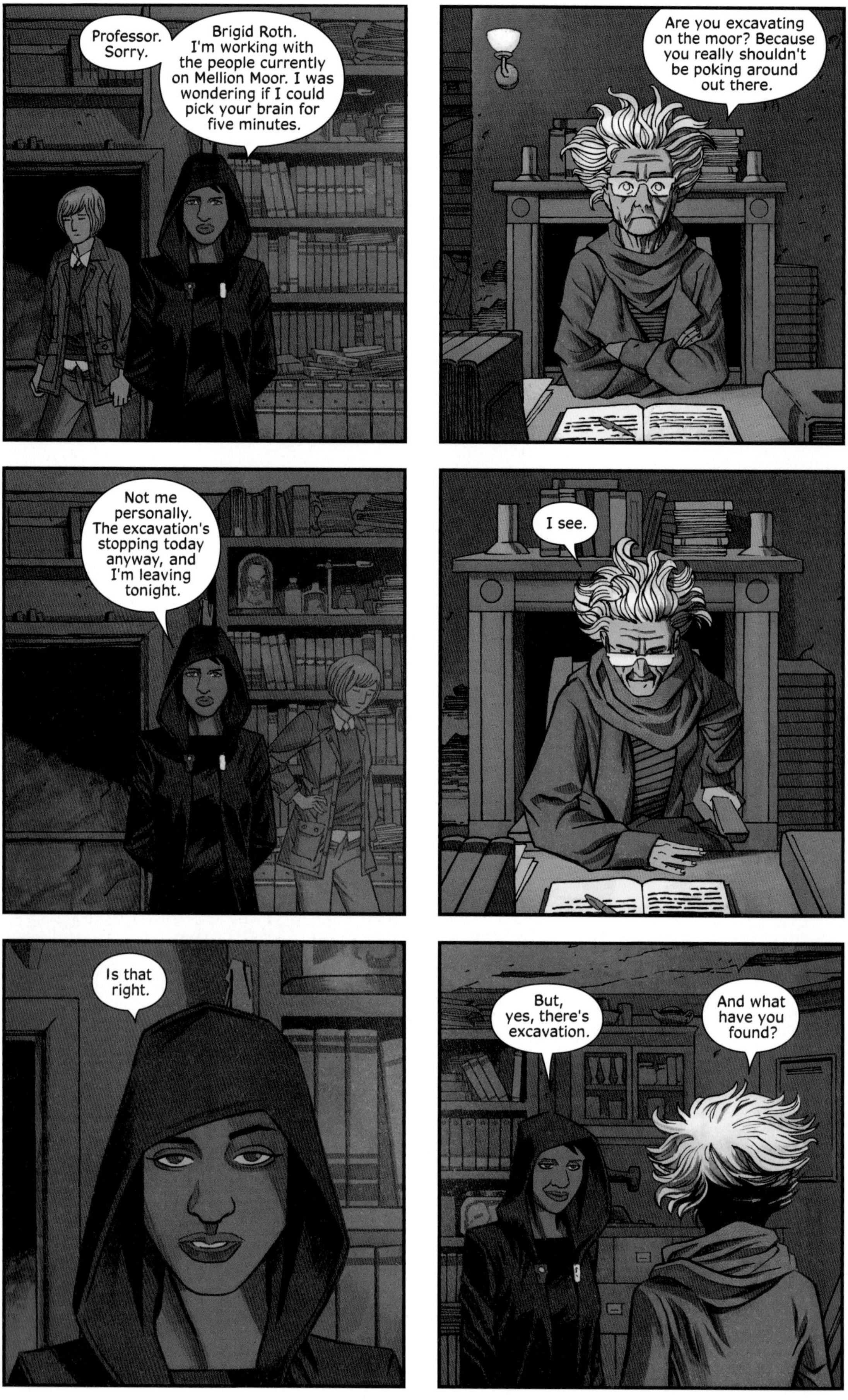
Professor. Sorry.
Brigid Roth. I'm working with the people currently on Mellion Moor. I was wondering if I could pick your brain for five minutes.
Are you excavating on the moor? Because you really shouldn't be poking around out there.
Not me personally. The excavation's stopping today anyway, and I'm leaving tonight.
I see.
Is that right.
But, yes, there's excavation.
And what have you found?

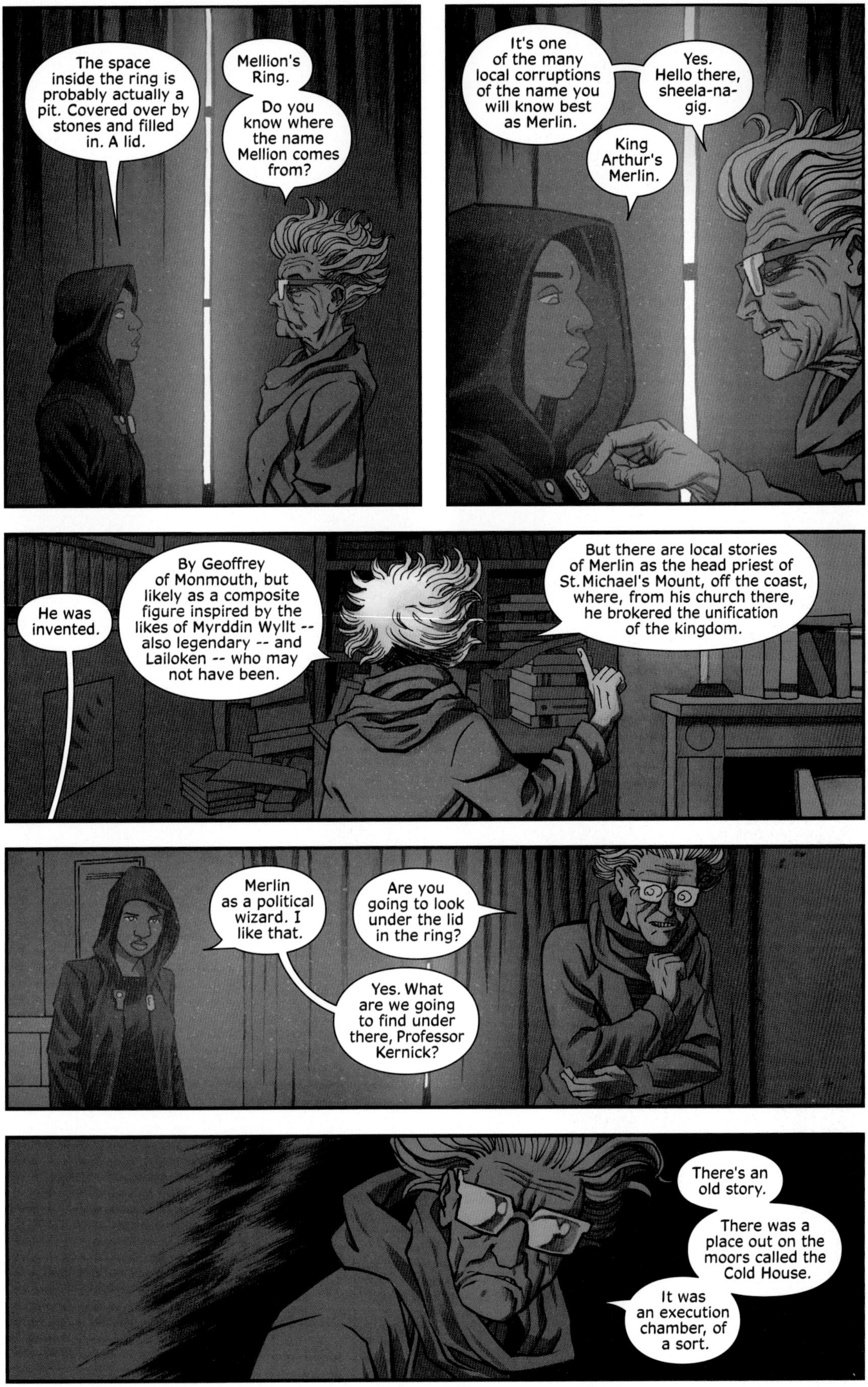
The space inside the ring is probably actually a pit. Covered over by stones and filled in. A lid.
Mellion's Ring.
Do you know where the name Mellion comes from?
It's one of the many local corruptions of the name you will know best as Merlin.
Yes. Hello there, sheela-na-gig.
King Arthur's Merlin.
He was invented.
By Geoffrey of Monmouth, but likely as a composite figure inspired by the likes of Myrddin Wyllt -- also legendary -- and Lailoken -- who may not have been.
But there are local stories of Merlin as the head priest of St. Michael's Mount, off the coast, where, from his church there, he brokered the unification of the kingdom.
Merlin as a political wizard. I like that.
Are you going to look under the lid in the ring?
Yes. What are we going to find under there, Professor Kernick?
There's an old story.
There was a place out on the moors called the Cold House.
It was an execution chamber, of a sort.

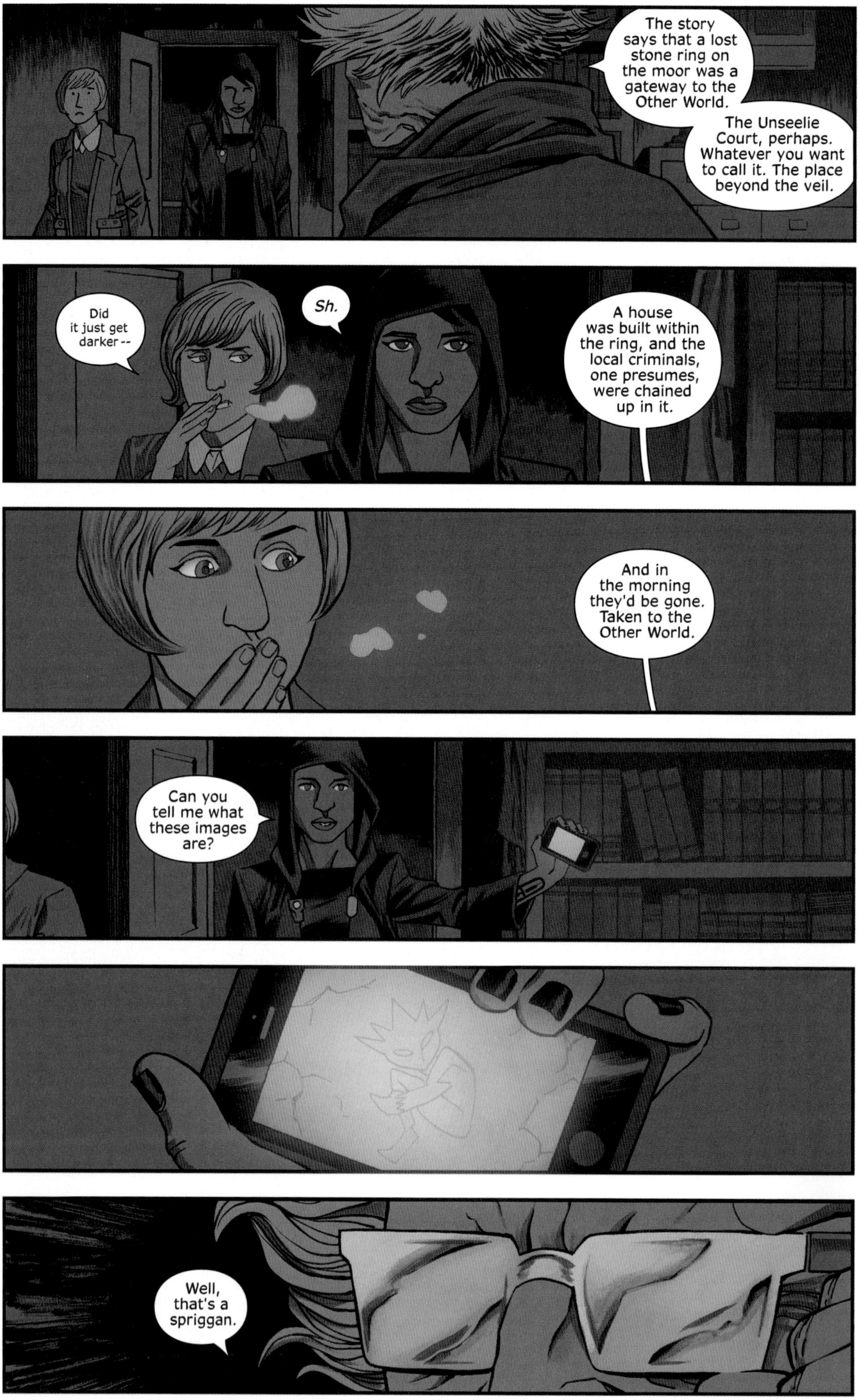

The story says that a lost stone ring on the moor was a gateway to the Other World.
The Unseelie Court, perhaps. Whatever you want to call it. The place beyond the veil.
Did it just get darker --
Sh.
A house was built within the ring, and the local criminals, one presumes, were chained up in it.
And in the morning they'd be gone. Taken to the Other World.
Can you tell me what these images are?
Well, that's a spriggan.

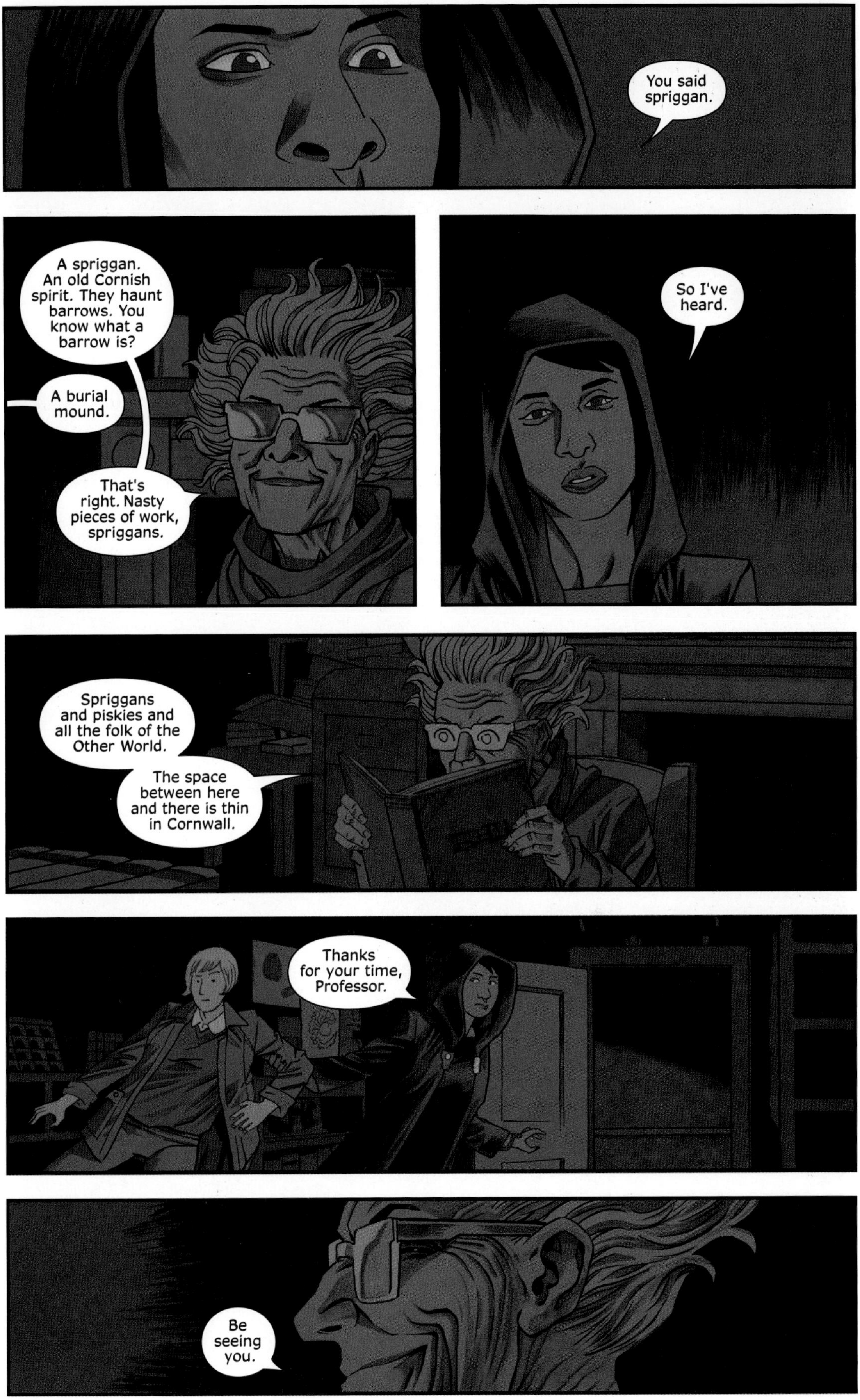
You said spriggan.
A spriggan. An old Cornish spirit. They haunt barrows. You know what a barrow is?
A burial mound.
That's right. Nasty pieces of work, spriggans.
So I've heard.
Spriggans and piskies and all the folk of the Other World.
The space between here and there is thin in Cornwall.
Thanks for your time, Professor.
Be seeing you.

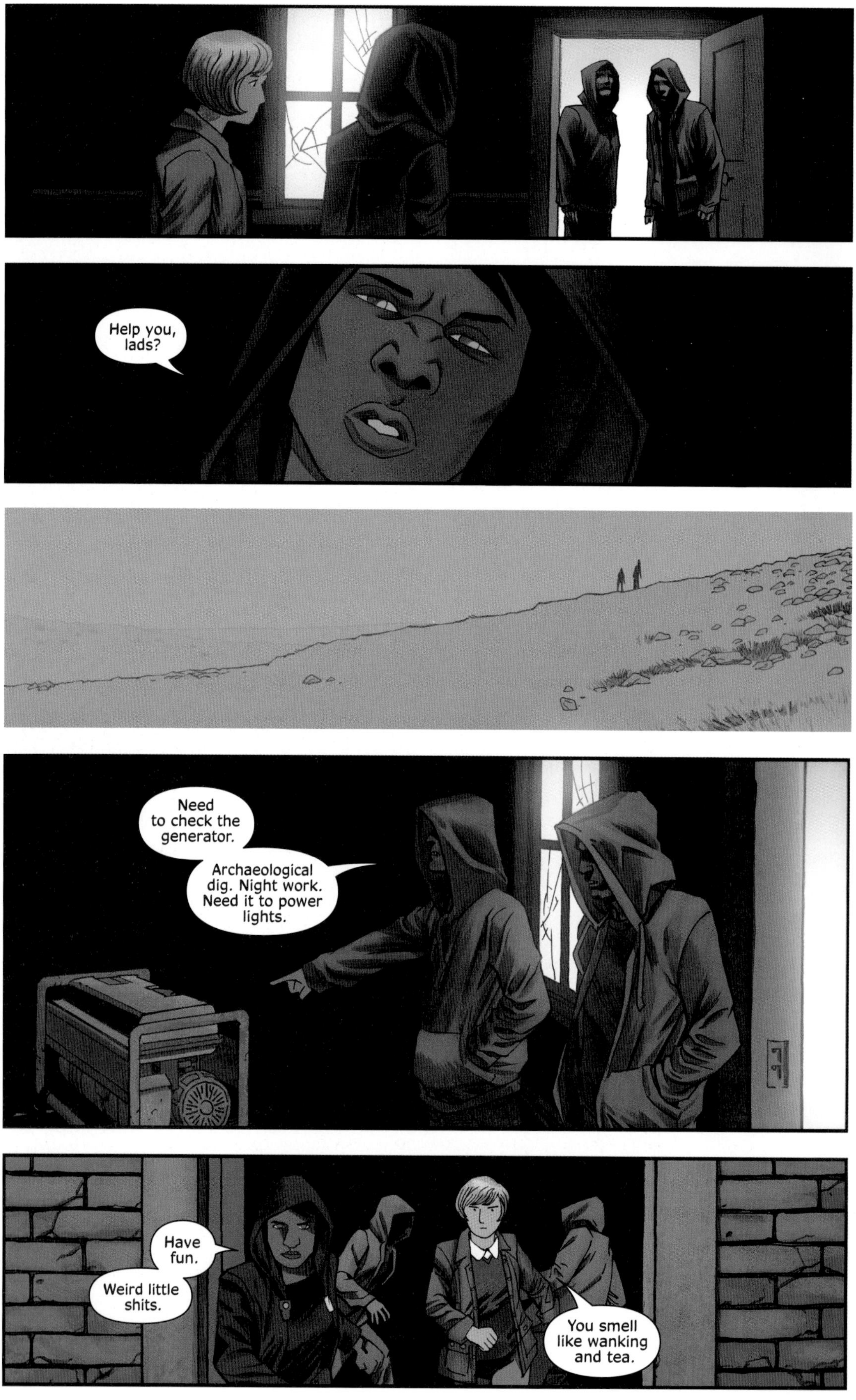
Help you, lads?
Need to check the generator.
Archaeological dig. Night work. Need it to power lights.
Have fun.
Weird little shits.
You smell like wanking and tea.

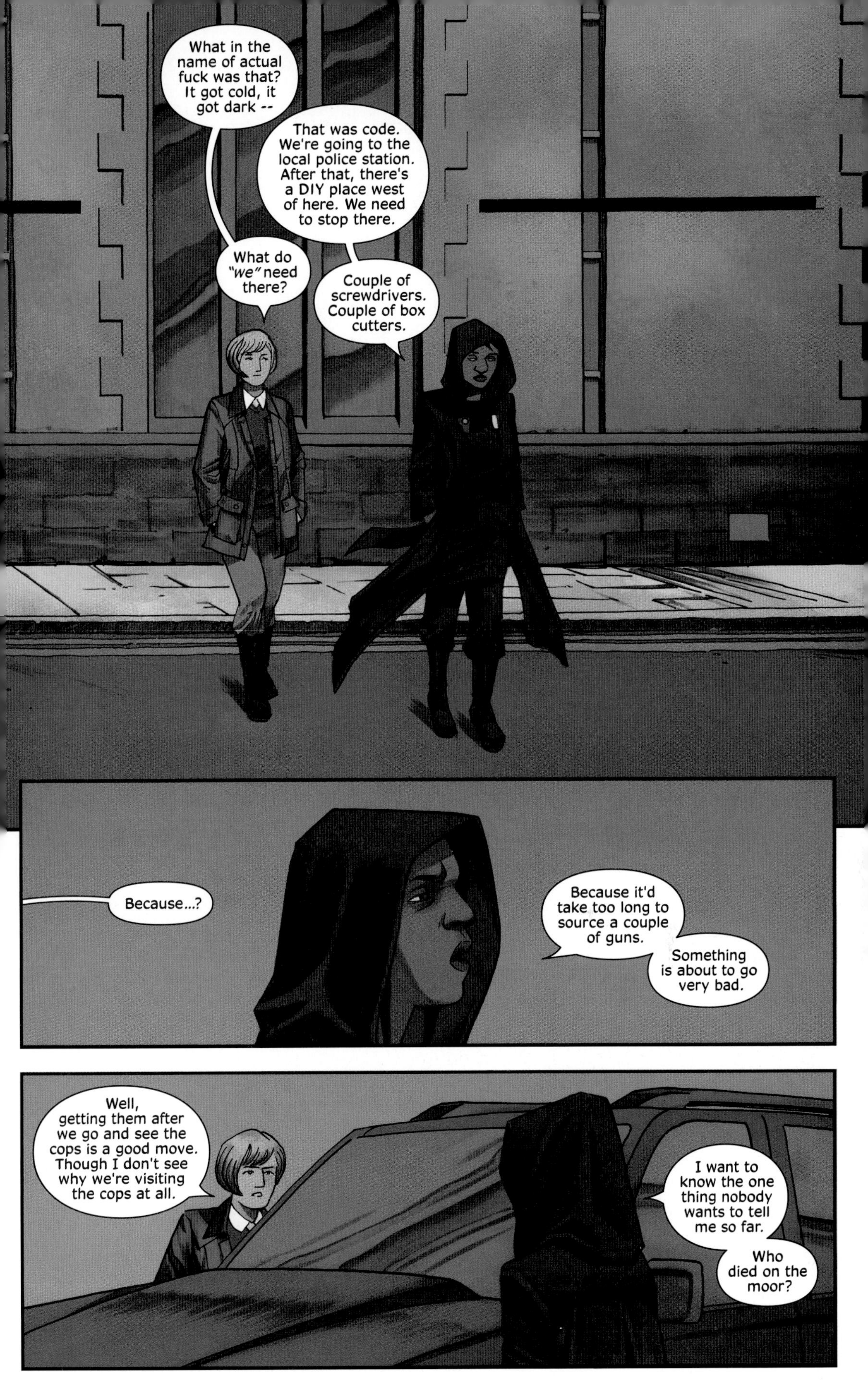
What in the name of actual fuck was that? It got cold, it got dark --
That was code. We're going to the local police station. After that, there's a DIY place west of here. We need to stop there.
What do *"we"* need there?
Couple of screwdrivers. Couple of box cutters.
Because...?
Because it'd take too long to source a couple of guns.
Something is about to go very bad.
Well, getting them after we go and see the cops is a good move. Though I don't see why we're visiting the cops at all.
I want to know the one thing nobody wants to tell me so far.
Who died on the moor?

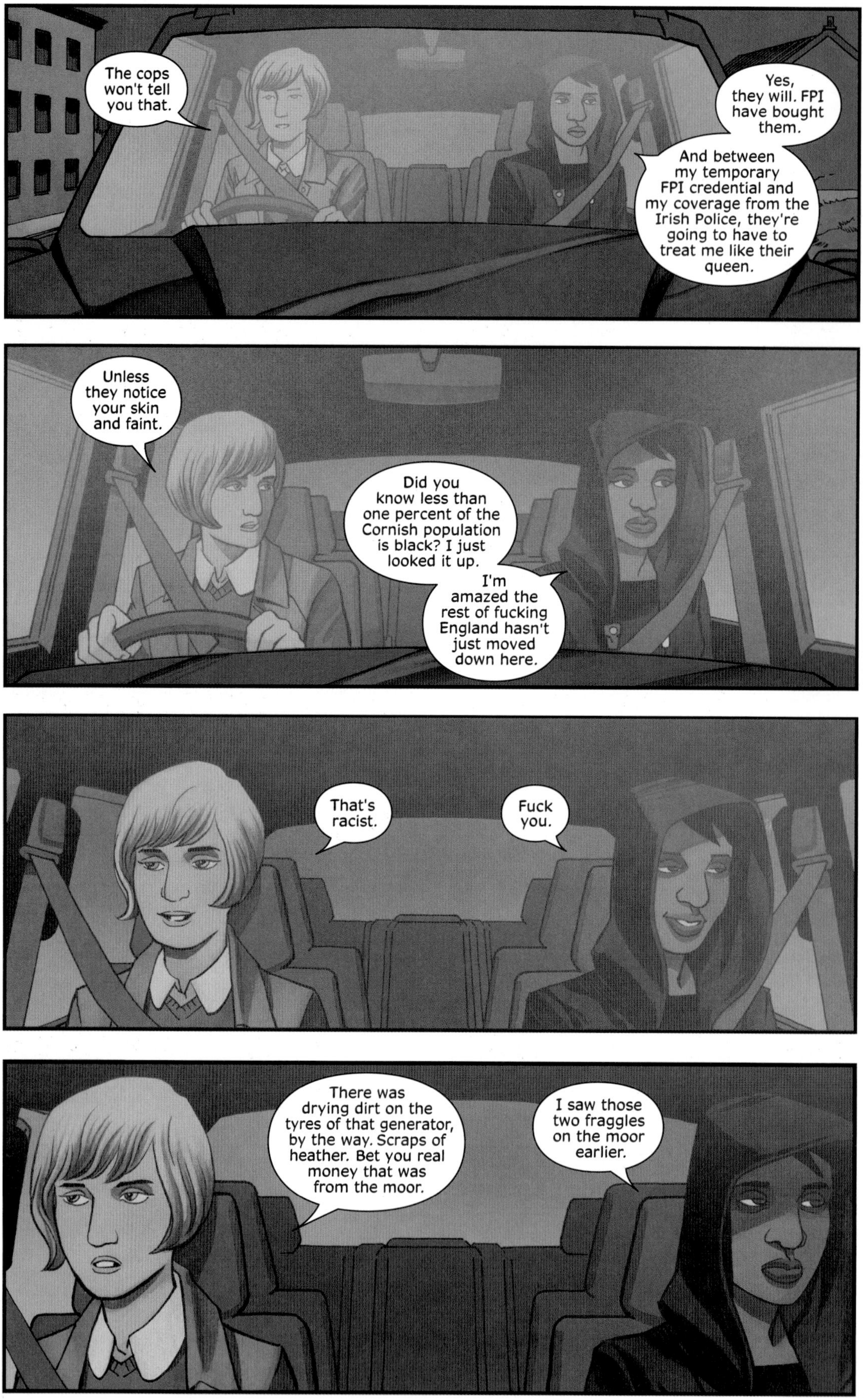
The cops won't tell you that.
Yes, they will. FPI have bought them.
And between my temporary FPI credential and my coverage from the Irish Police, they're going to have to treat me like their queen.
Unless they notice your skin and faint.
Did you know less than one percent of the Cornish population is black? I just looked it up.
I'm amazed the rest of fucking England hasn't just moved down here.
That's racist.
Fuck you.
There was drying dirt on the tyres of that generator, by the way. Scraps of heather. Bet you real money that was from the moor.
I saw those two fraggles on the moor earlier.

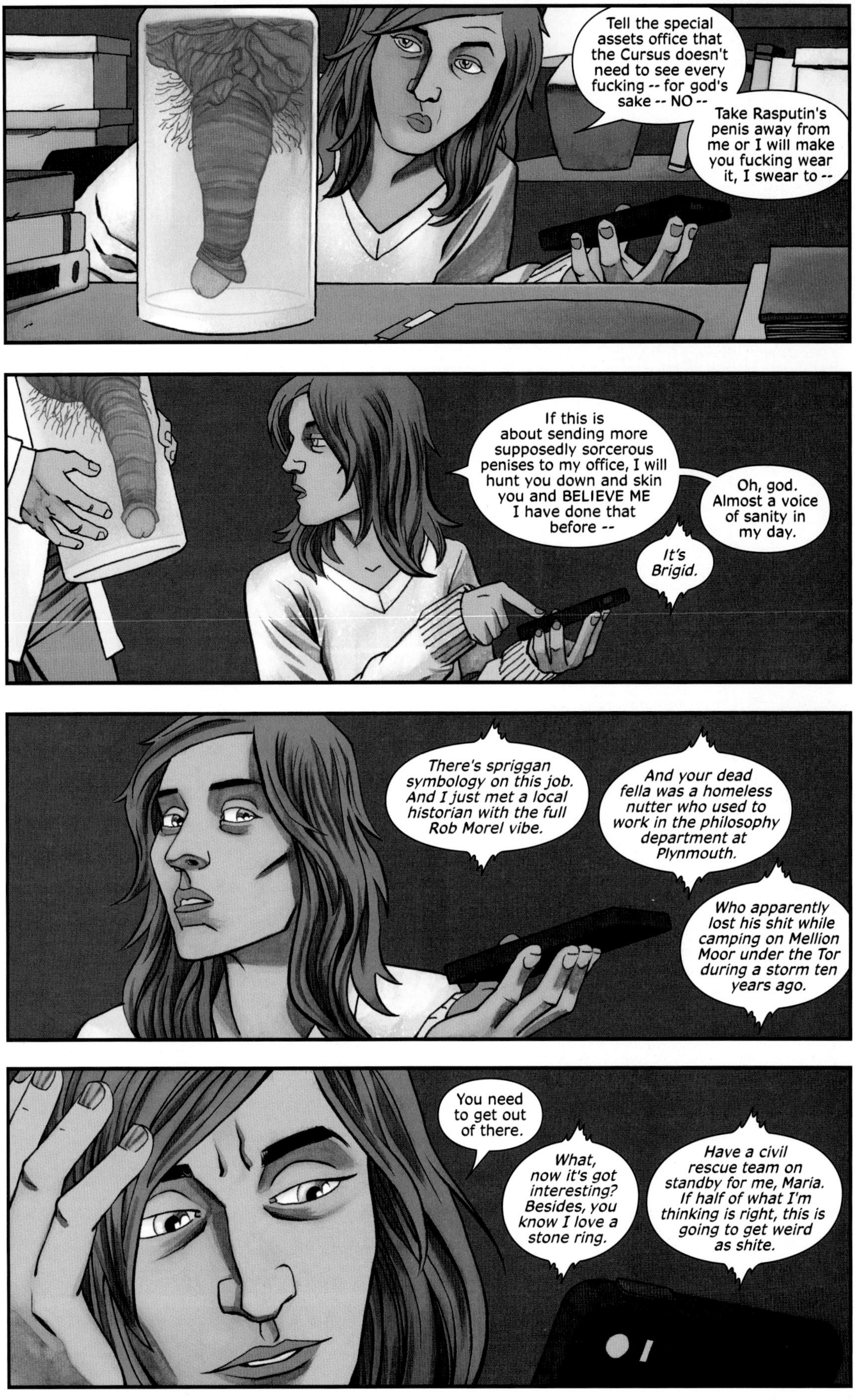
Tell the special assets office that the Cursus doesn't need to see every fucking -- for god's sake -- NO --
Take Rasputin's penis away from me or I will make you fucking wear it, I swear to --
If this is about sending more supposedly sorcerous penises to my office, I will hunt you down and skin you and BELIEVE ME I have done that before --
Oh, god. Almost a voice of sanity in my day.
It's Brigid.
There's spriggan symbology on this job. And I just met a local historian with the full Rob Morel vibe.
And your dead fella was a homeless nutter who used to work in the philosophy department at Plynmouth.
Who apparently lost his shit while camping on Mellion Moor under the Tor during a storm ten years ago.
You need to get out of there.
What, now it's got interesting? Besides, you know I love a stone ring.
Have a civil rescue team on standby for me, Maria. If half of what I'm thinking is right, this is going to get weird as shite.

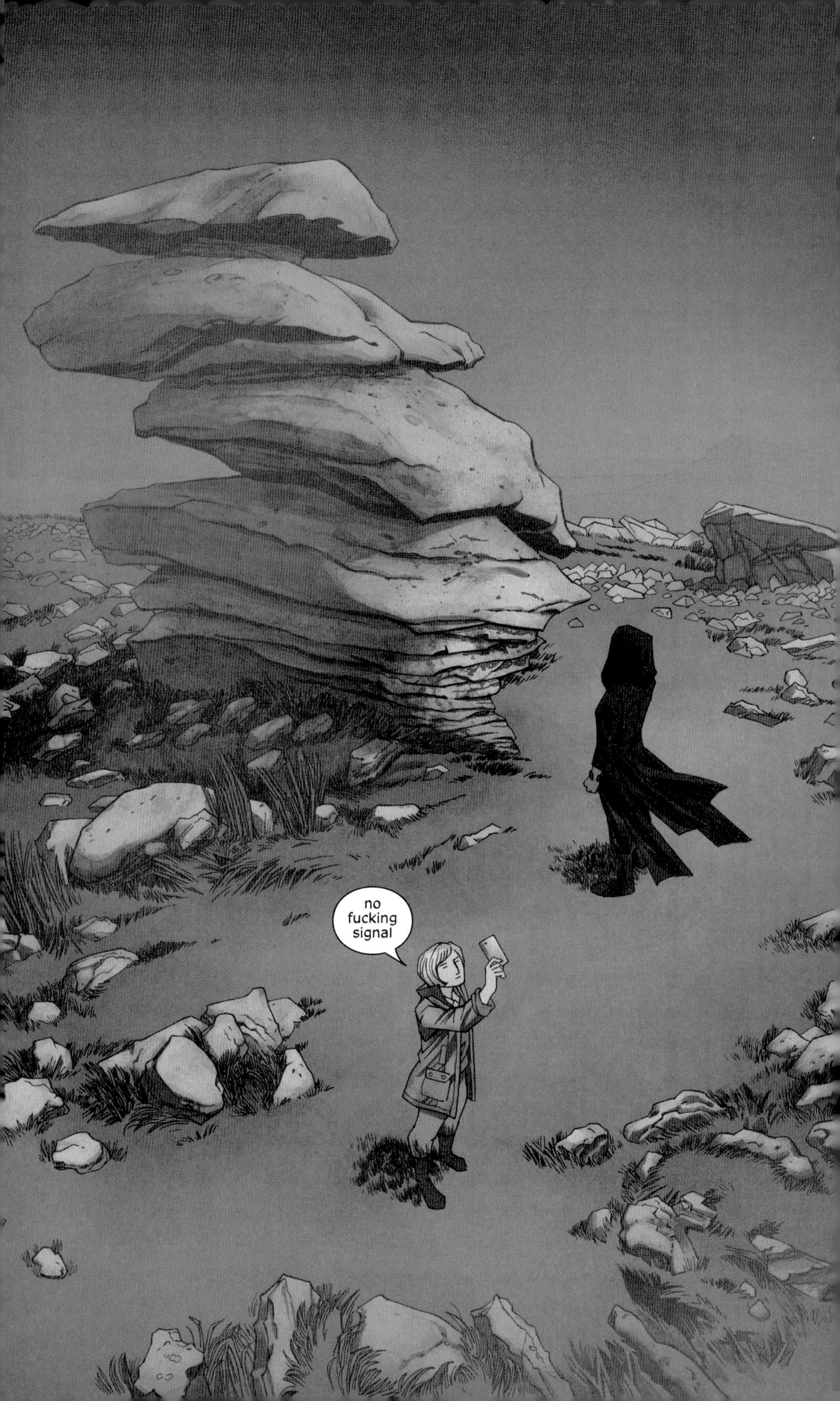
no fucking signal

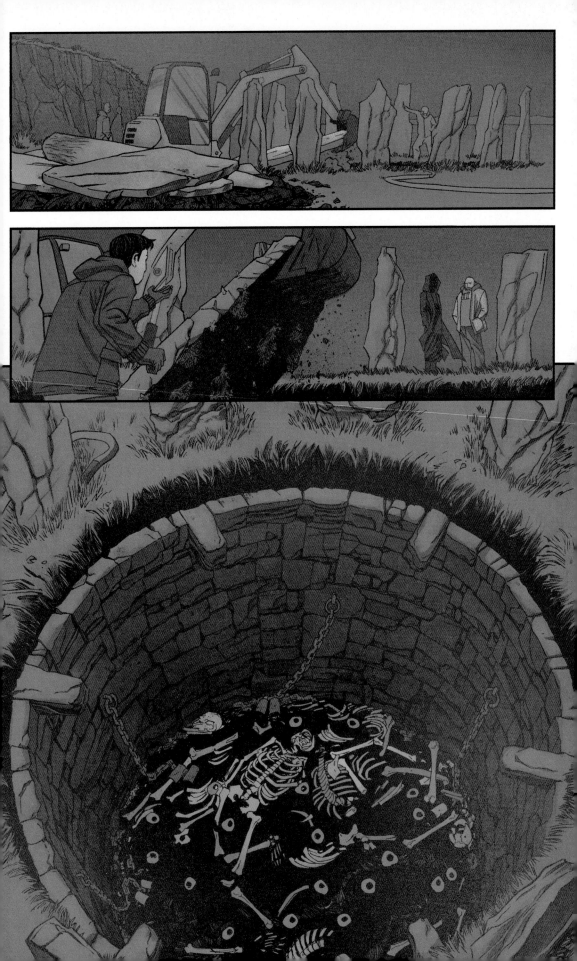

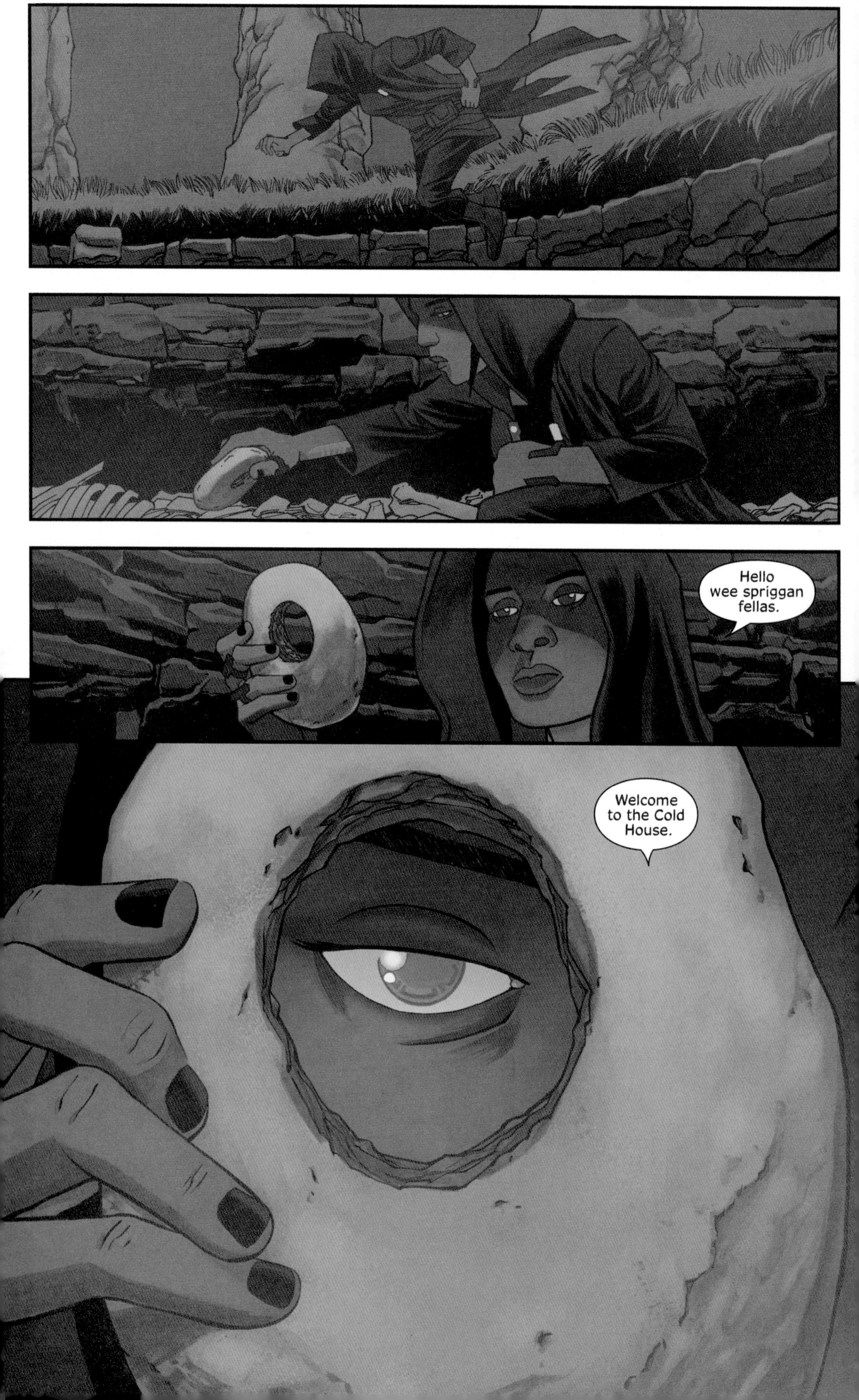
Hello wee spriggan fellas.
Welcome to the Cold House.

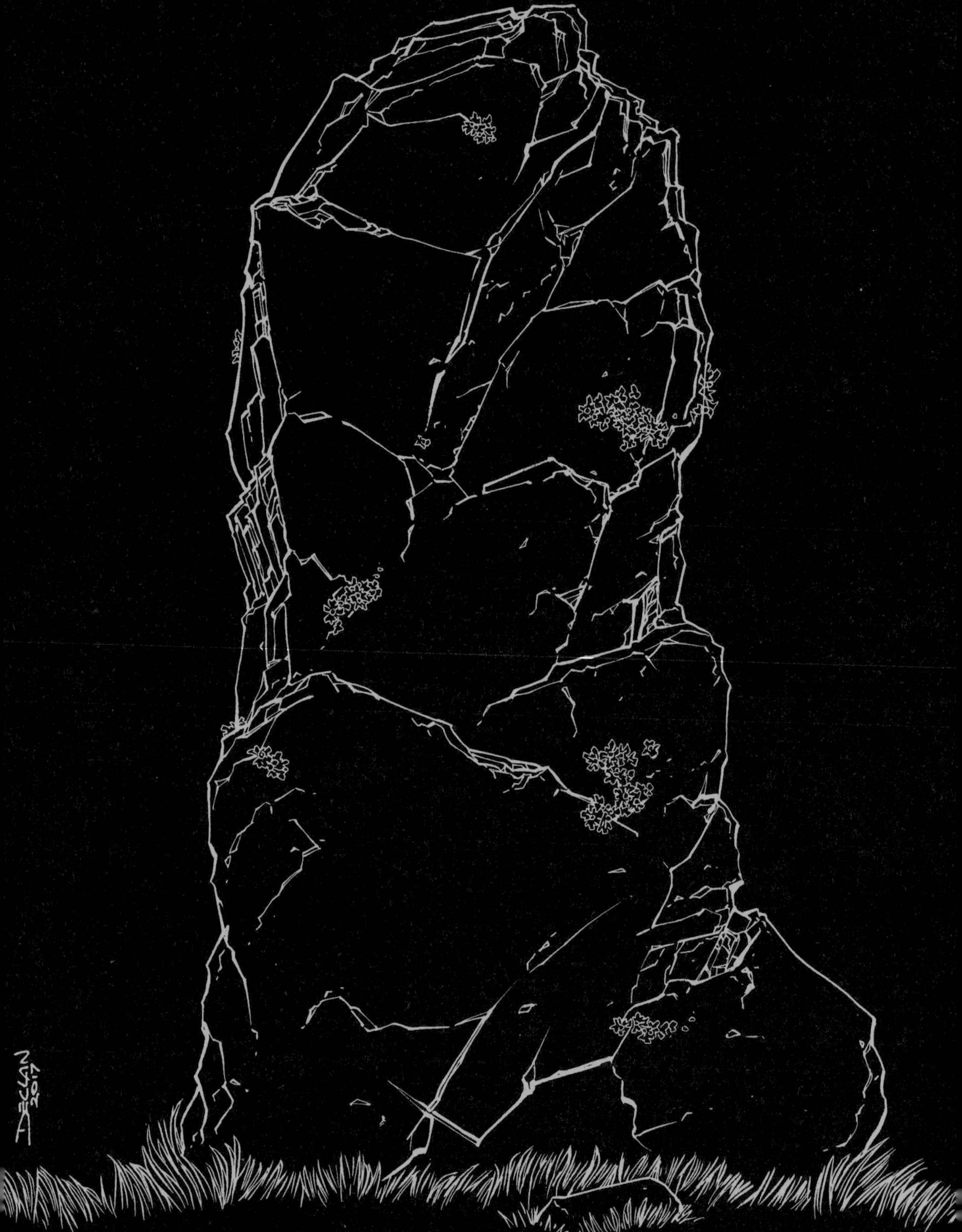
DECLAN
2017

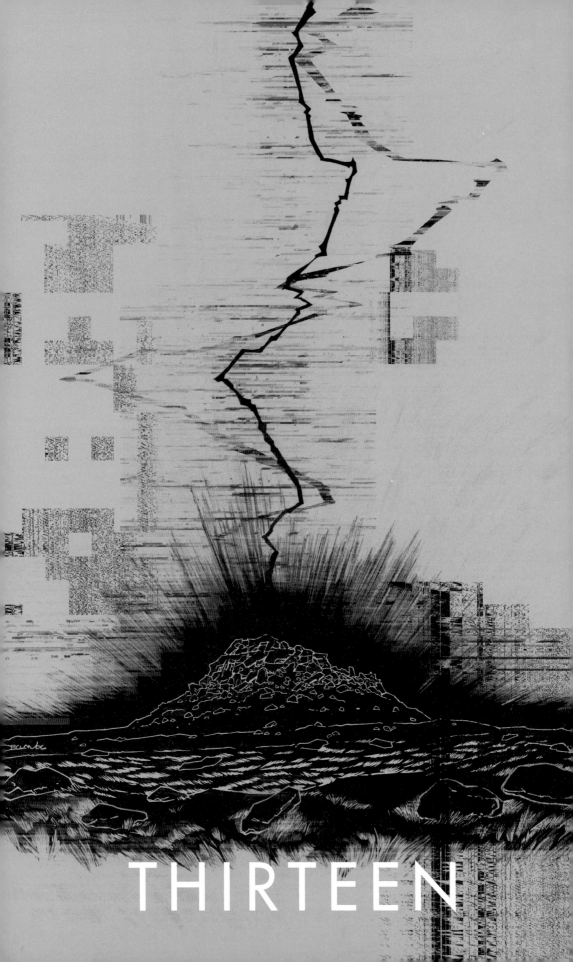

THIRTEEN

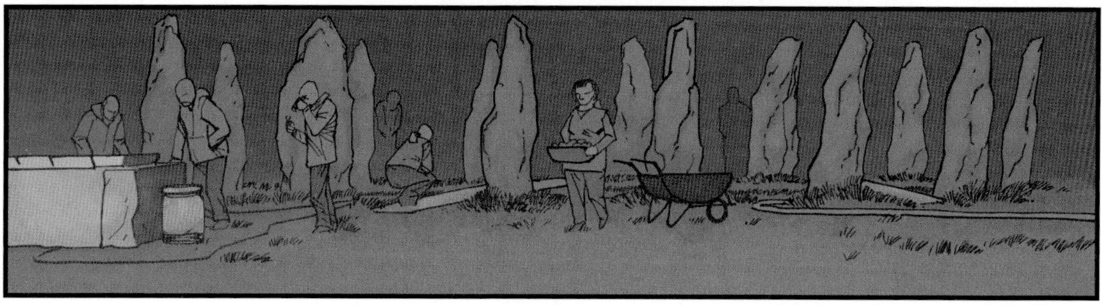

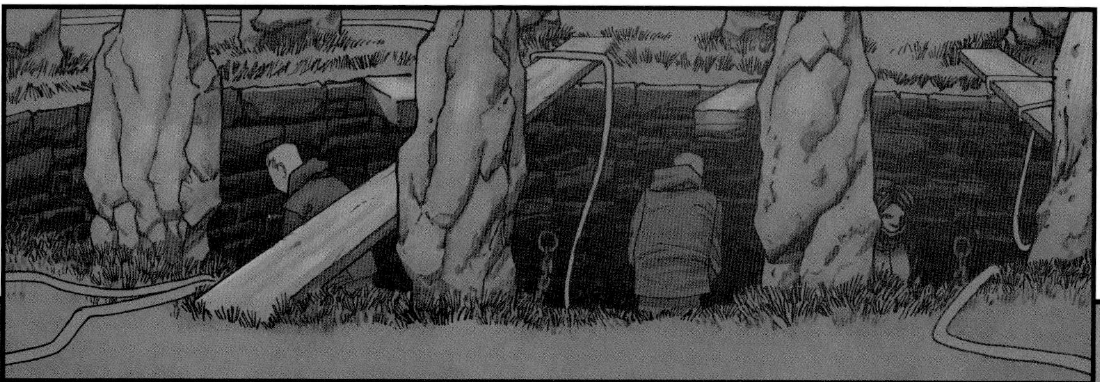

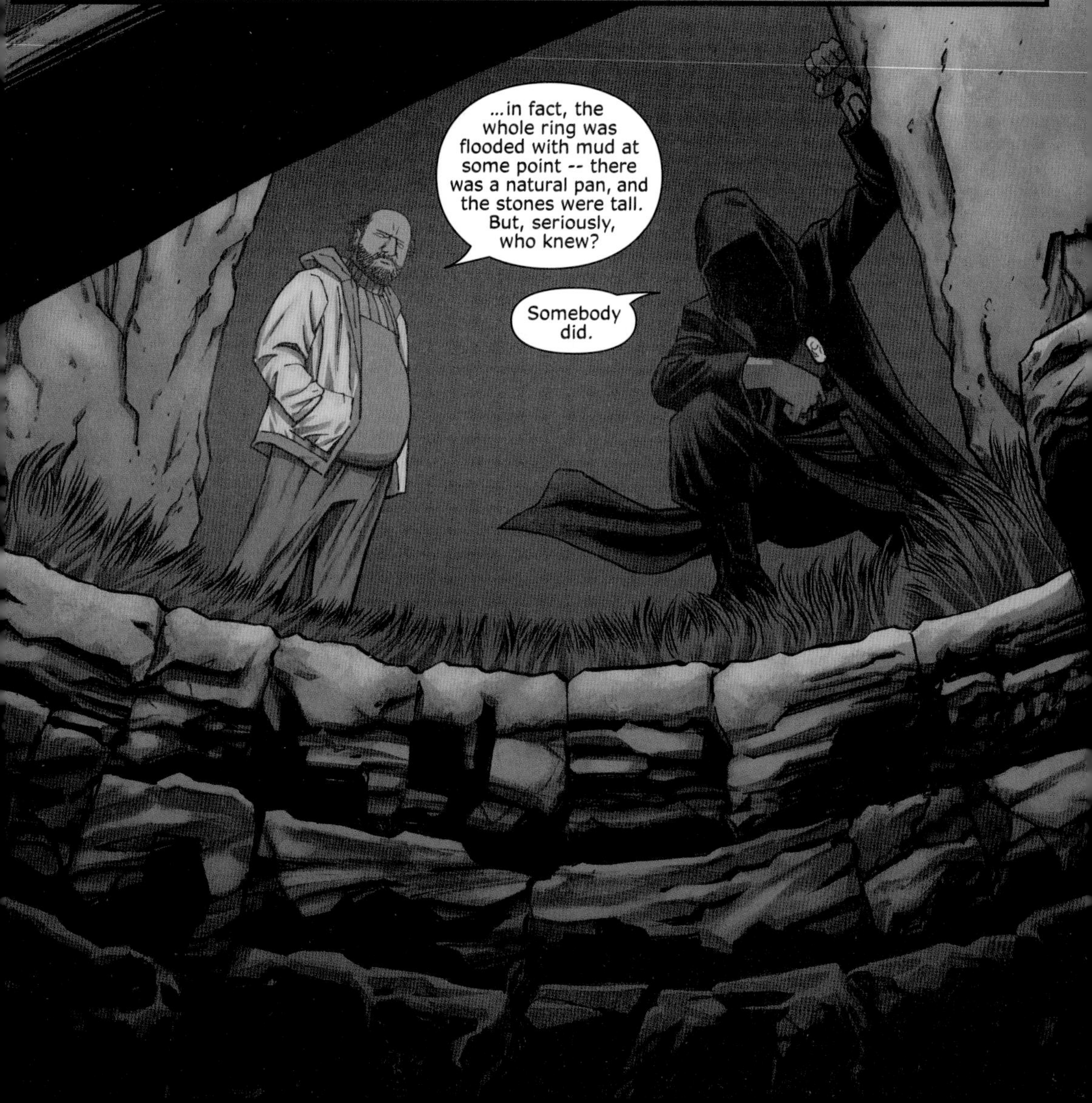
...in fact, the whole ring was flooded with mud at some point -- there was a natural pan, and the stones were tall. But, seriously, who knew?
Somebody did.

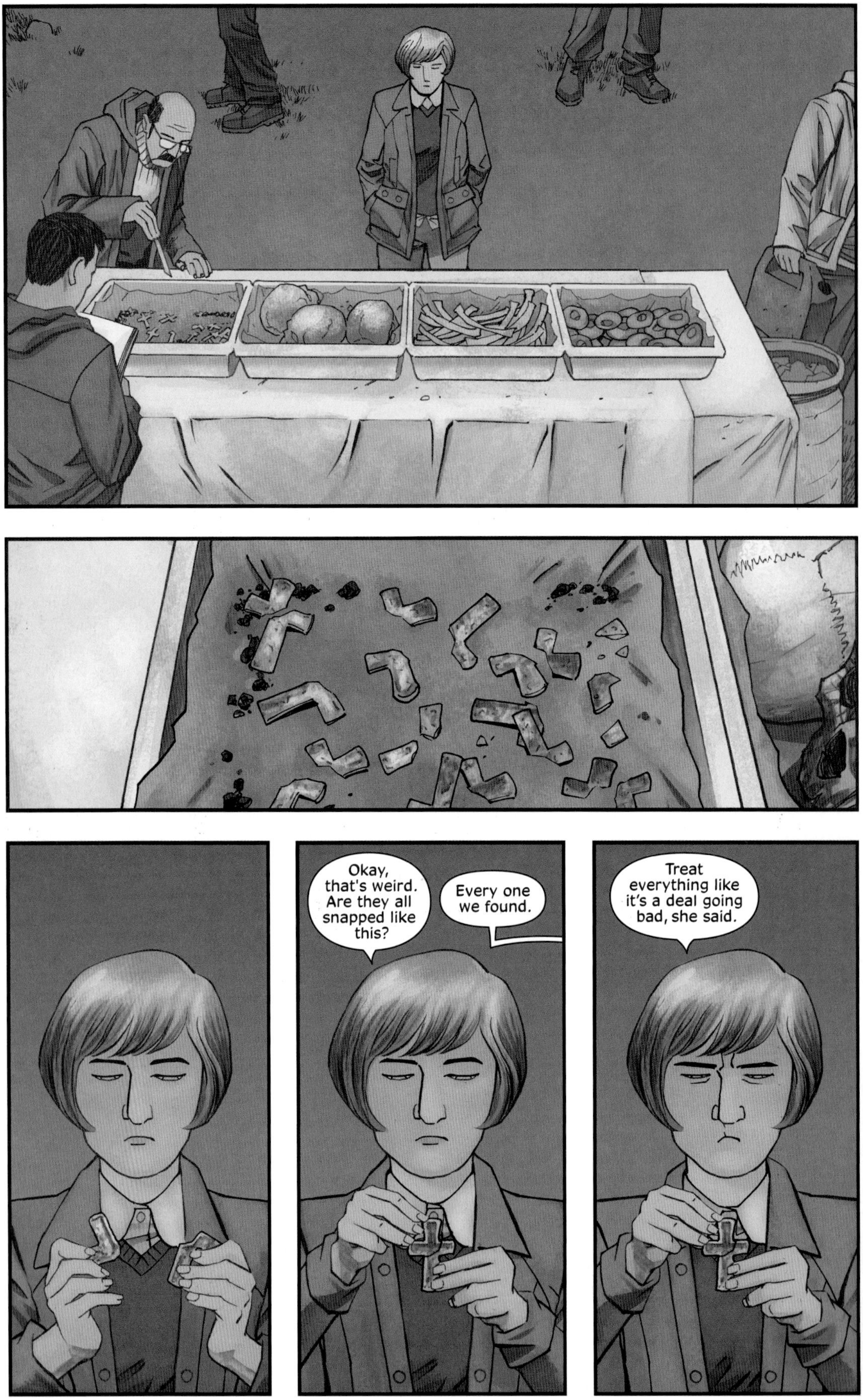
Okay, that's weird. Are they all snapped like this?
Every one we found.
Treat everything like it's a deal going bad, she said.

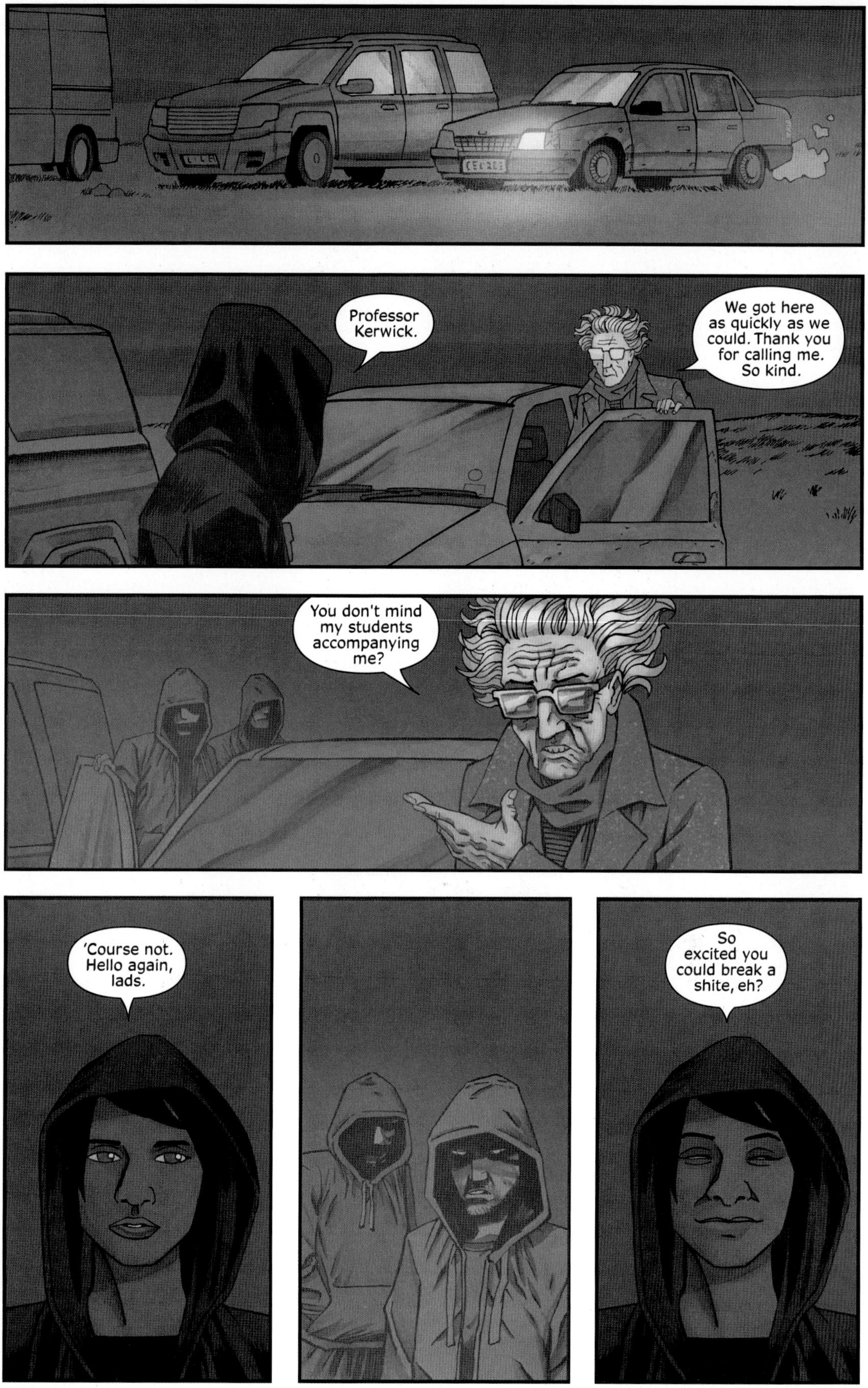
Professor Kerwick.
We got here as quickly as we could. Thank you for calling me. So kind.
You don't mind my students accompanying me?
'Course not. Hello again, lads.
So excited you could break a shite, eh?

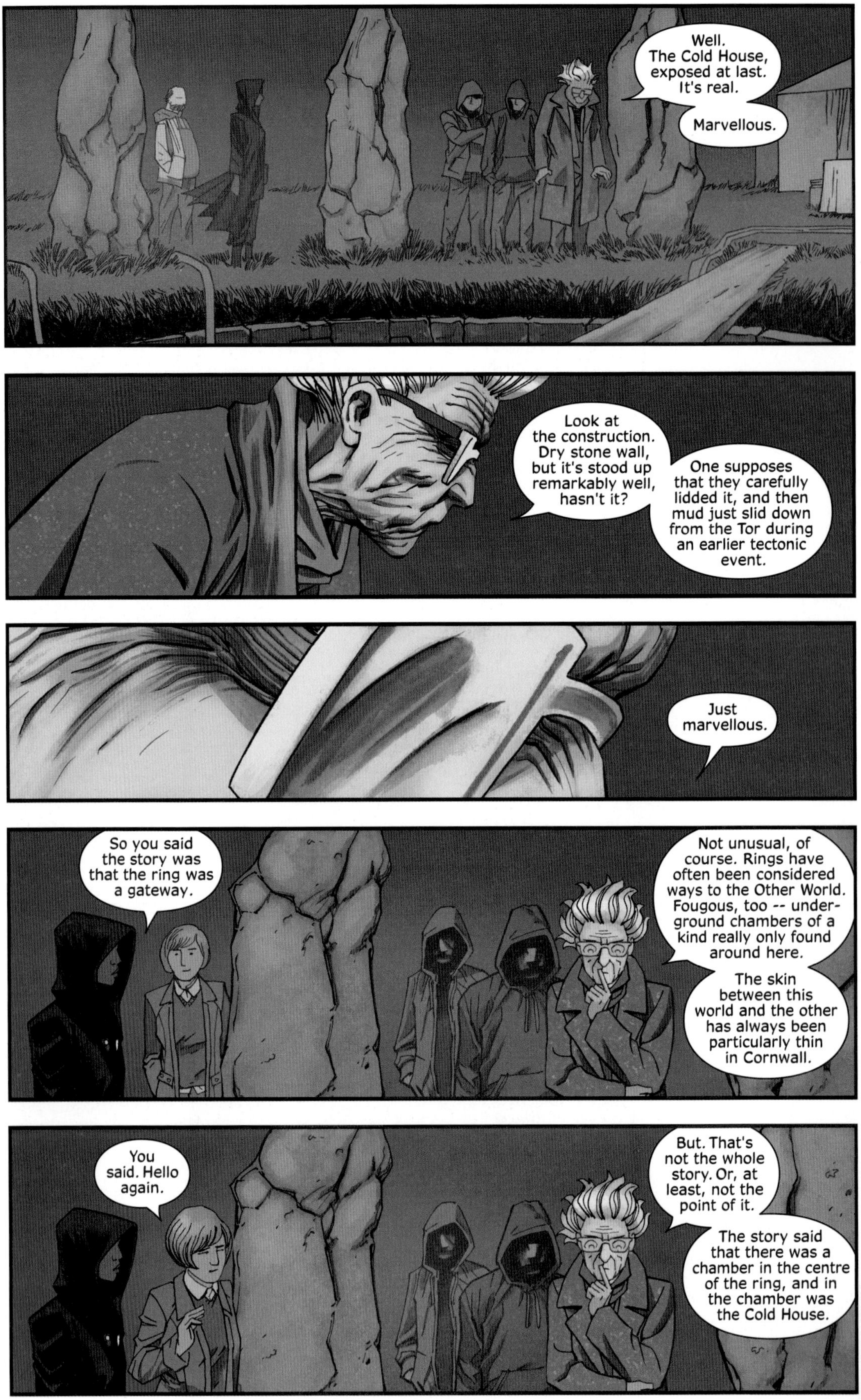
Well. The Cold House, exposed at last. It's real.
Marvellous.
Look at the construction. Dry stone wall, but it's stood up remarkably well, hasn't it?
One supposes that they carefully lidded it, and then mud just slid down from the Tor during an earlier tectonic event.
Just marvellous.
So you said the story was that the ring was a gateway.
Not unusual, of course. Rings have often been considered ways to the Other World. Fougous, too -- underground chambers of a kind really only found around here.
The skin between this world and the other has always been particularly thin in Cornwall.
You said. Hello again.
But. That's not the whole story. Or, at least, not the point of it.
The story said that there was a chamber in the centre of the ring, and in the chamber was the Cold House.

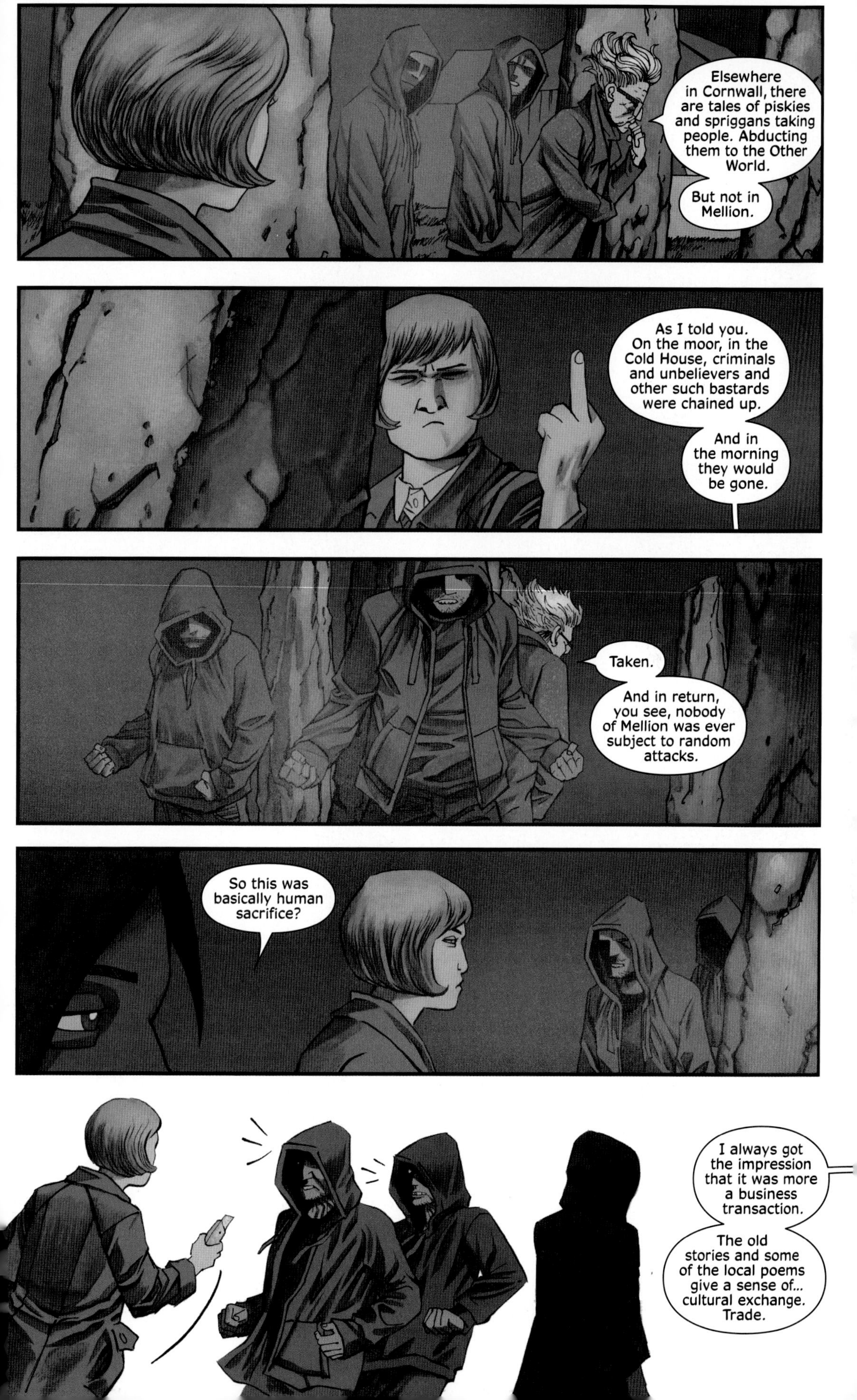
Elsewhere in Cornwall, there are tales of piskies and spriggans taking people. Abducting them to the Other World.
But not in Mellion.
As I told you. On the moor, in the Cold House, criminals and unbelievers and other such bastards were chained up.
And in the morning they would be gone.
Taken.
And in return, you see, nobody of Mellion was ever subject to random attacks.
So this was basically human sacrifice?
I always got the impression that it was more a business transaction.
The old stories and some of the local poems give a sense of... cultural exchange. Trade.

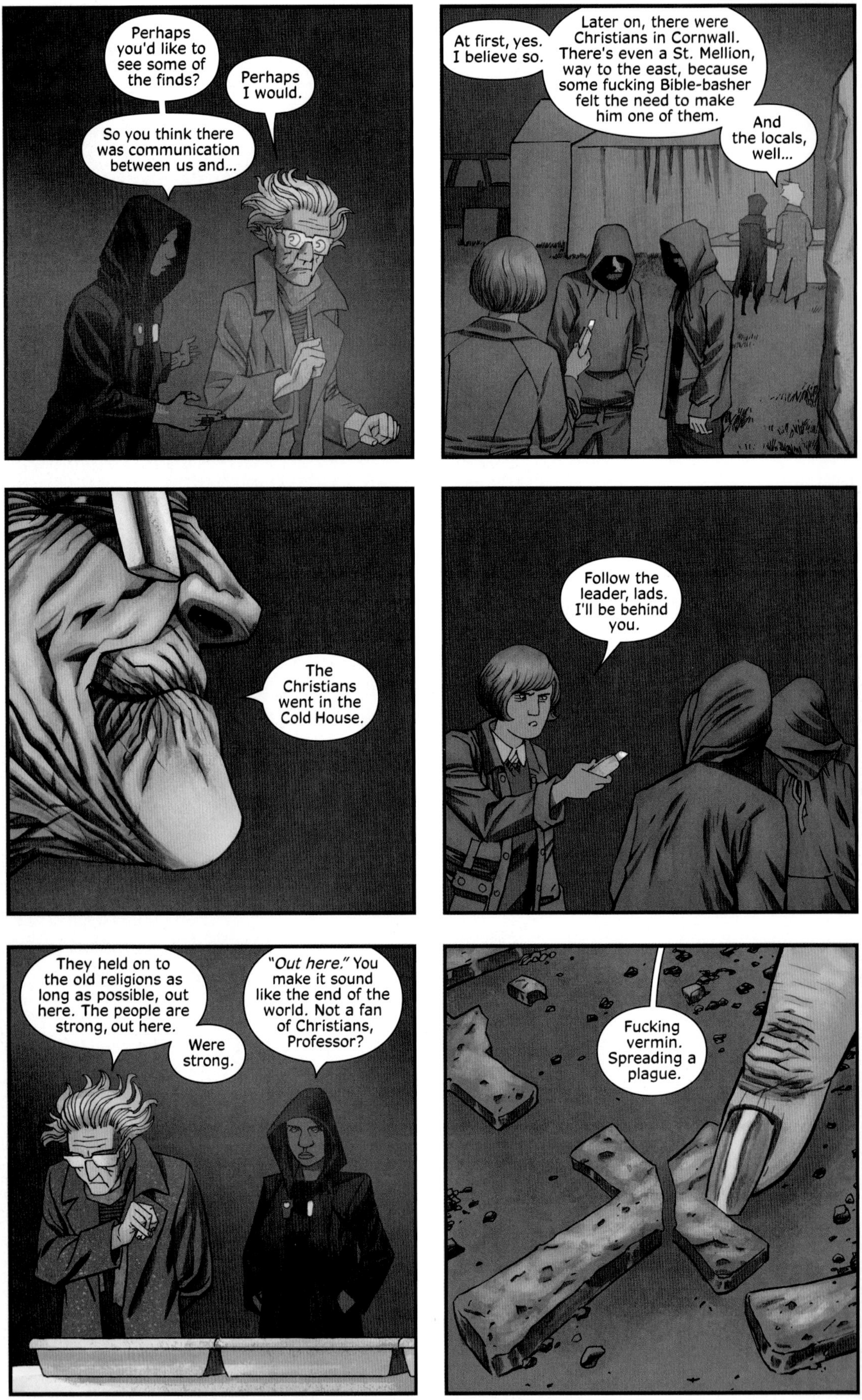

Perhaps you'd like to see some of the finds?
So you think there was communication between us and...
Perhaps I would.
At first, yes. I believe so.
Later on, there were Christians in Cornwall. There's even a St. Mellion, way to the east, because some fucking Bible-basher felt the need to make him one of them.
And the locals, well...
The Christians went in the Cold House.
Follow the leader, lads. I'll be behind you.
They held on to the old religions as long as possible, out here. The people are strong, out here.
Were strong.
"Out here." You make it sound like the end of the world. Not a fan of Christians, Professor?
Fucking vermin. Spreading a plague.

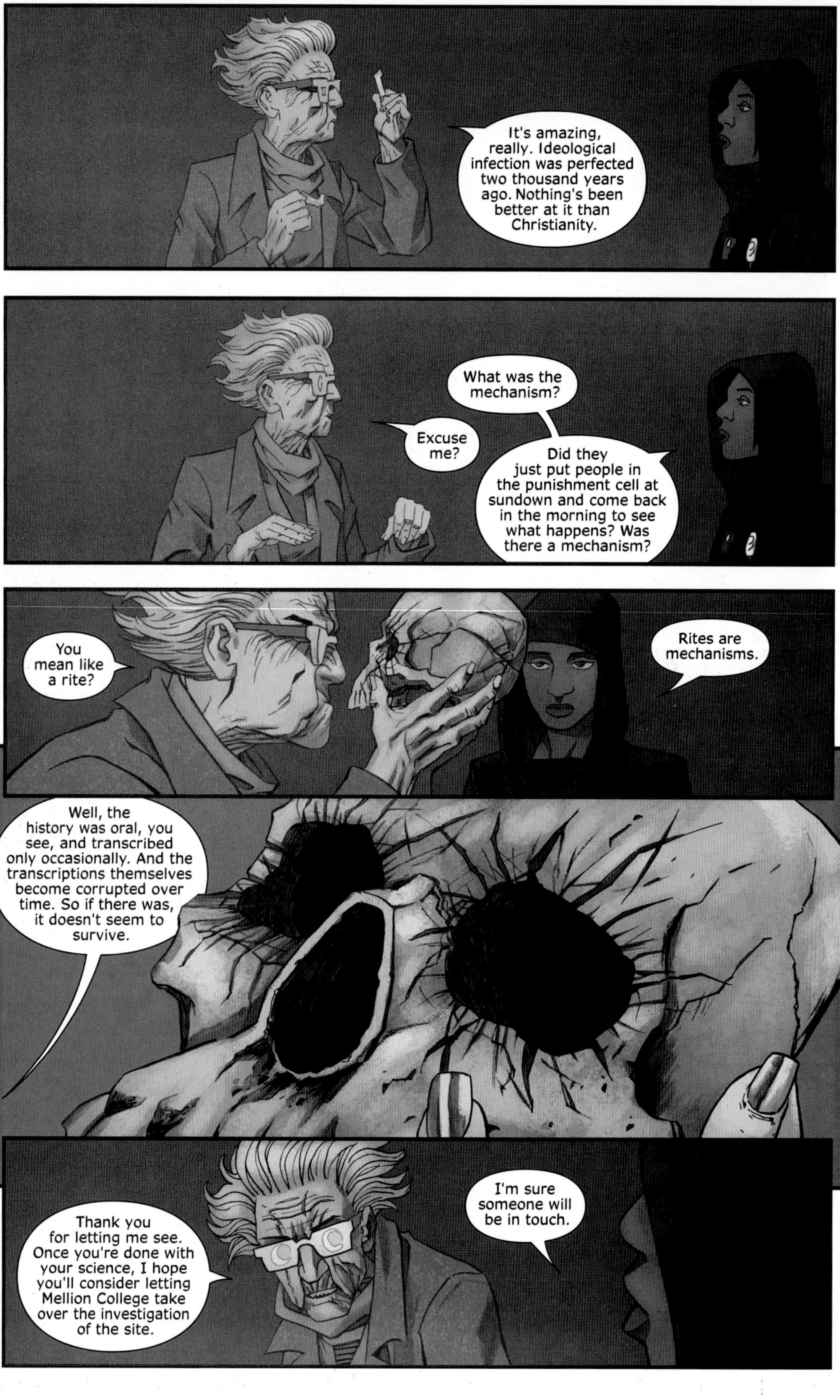
It's amazing, really. Ideological infection was perfected two thousand years ago. Nothing's been better at it than Christianity.
What was the mechanism?
Excuse me?
Did they just put people in the punishment cell at sundown and come back in the morning to see what happens? Was there a mechanism?
You mean like a rite?
Rites are mechanisms.
Well, the history was oral, you see, and transcribed only occasionally. And the transcriptions themselves become corrupted over time. So if there was, it doesn't seem to survive.
Thank you for letting me see. Once you're done with your science, I hope you'll consider letting Mellion College take over the investigation of the site.
I'm sure someone will be in touch.

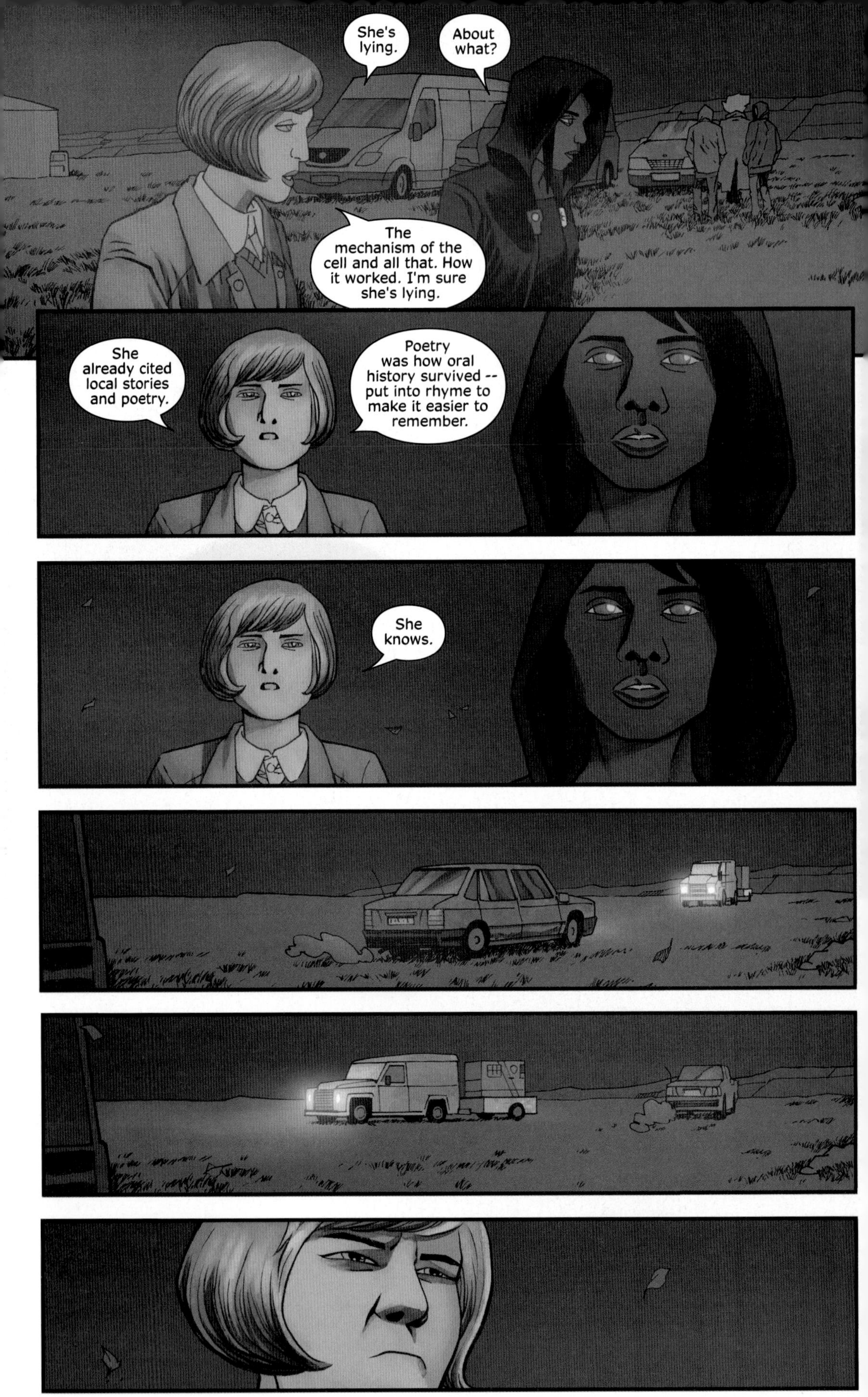

She's lying.
About what?
The mechanism of the cell and all that. How it worked. I'm sure she's lying.
She already cited local stories and poetry.
Poetry was how oral history survived -- put into rhyme to make it easier to remember.
She knows.

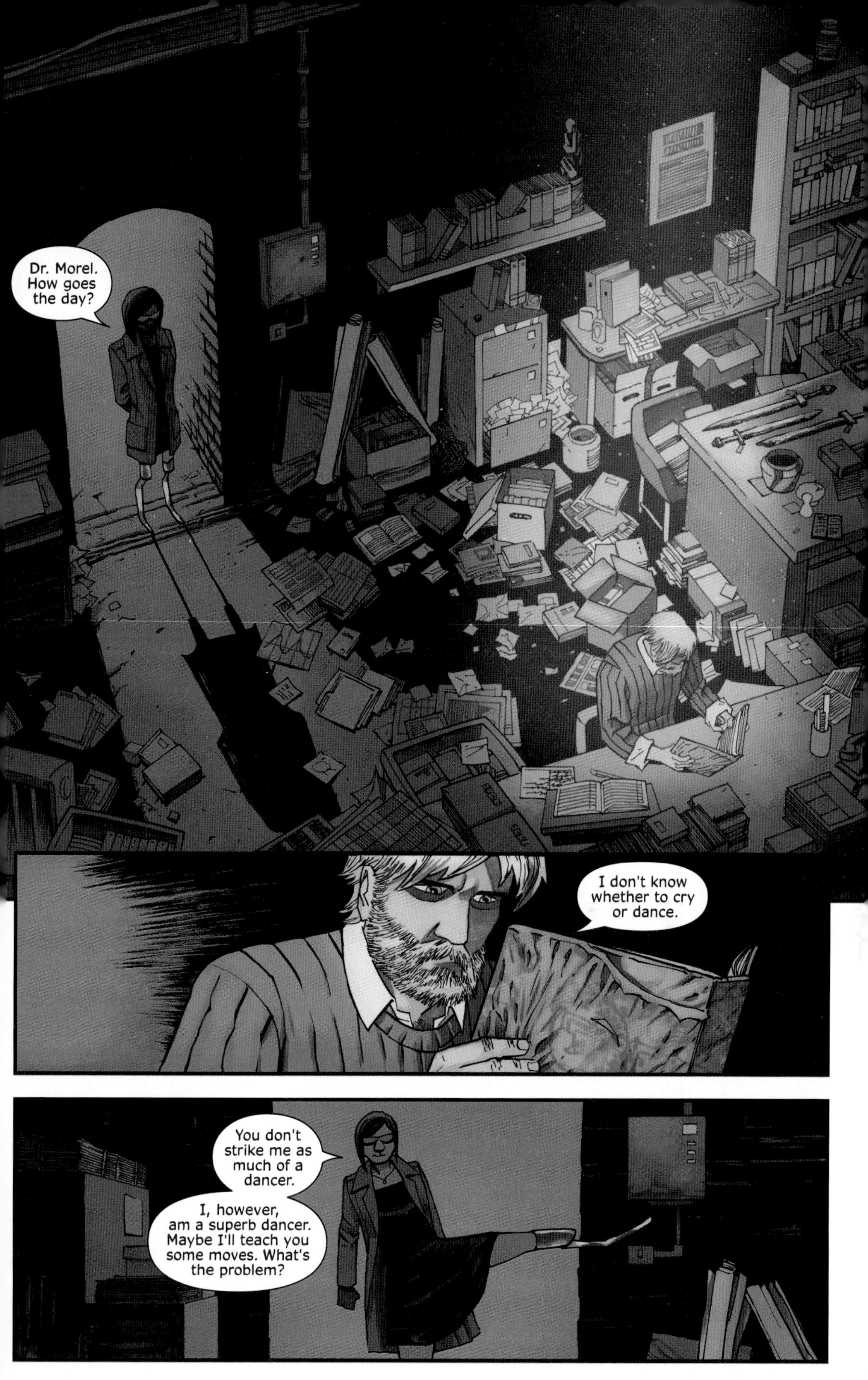
Dr. Morel. How goes the day?
I don't know whether to cry or dance.
You don't strike me as much of a dancer.
I, however, am a superb dancer. Maybe I'll teach you some moves. What's the problem?

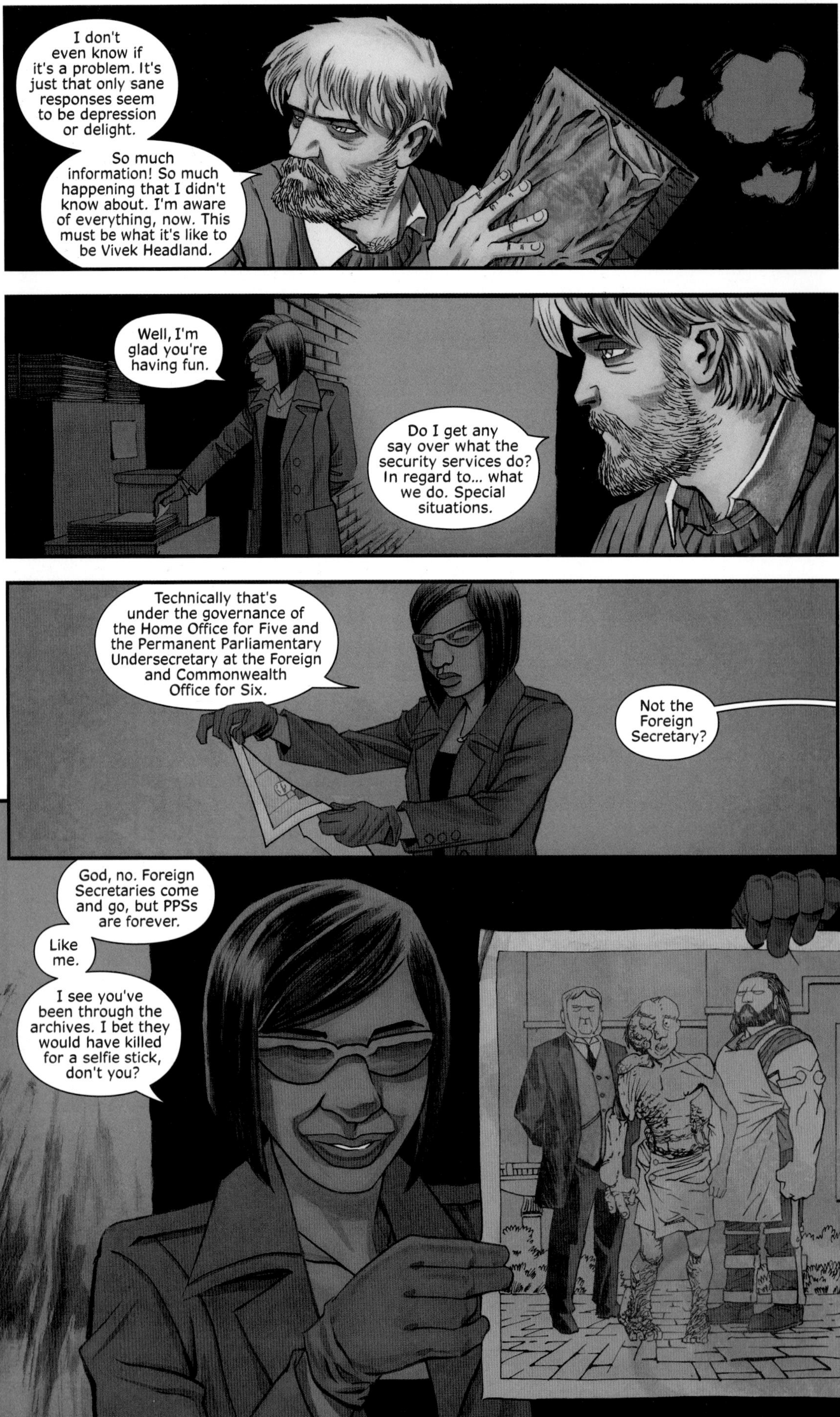

I don't even know if it's a problem. It's just that only sane responses seem to be depression or delight.
So much information! So much happening that I didn't know about. I'm aware of everything, now. This must be what it's like to be Vivek Headland.
Well, I'm glad you're having fun.
Do I get any say over what the security services do? In regard to... what we do. Special situations.
Technically that's under the governance of the Home Office for Five and the Permanent Parliamentary Undersecretary at the Foreign and Commonwealth Office for Six.
Not the Foreign Secretary?
God, no. Foreign Secretaries come and go, but PPSs are forever.
Like me.
I see you've been through the archives. I bet they would have killed for a selfie stick, don't you?

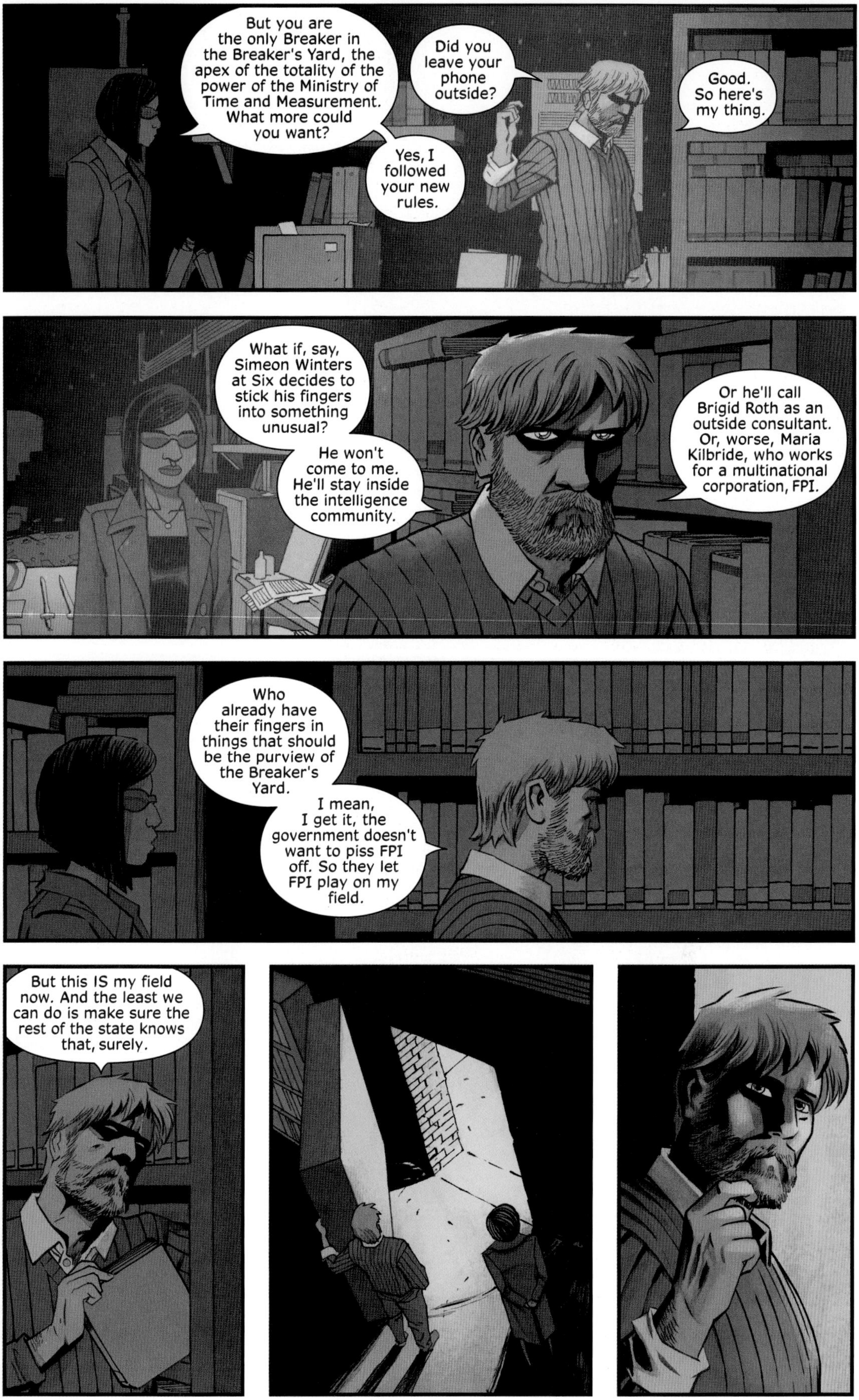

But you are the only Breaker in the Breaker's Yard, the apex of the totality of the power of the Ministry of Time and Measurement. What more could you want?
Did you leave your phone outside?
Yes, I followed your new rules.
Good. So here's my thing.
What if, say, Simeon Winters at Six decides to stick his fingers into something unusual?
He won't come to me. He'll stay inside the intelligence community.
Or he'll call Brigid Roth as an outside consultant. Or, worse, Maria Kilbride, who works for a multinational corporation, FPI.
Who already have their fingers in things that should be the purview of the Breaker's Yard.
I mean, I get it, the government doesn't want to piss FPI off. So they let FPI play on my field.
But this IS my field now. And the least we can do is make sure the rest of the state knows that, surely.

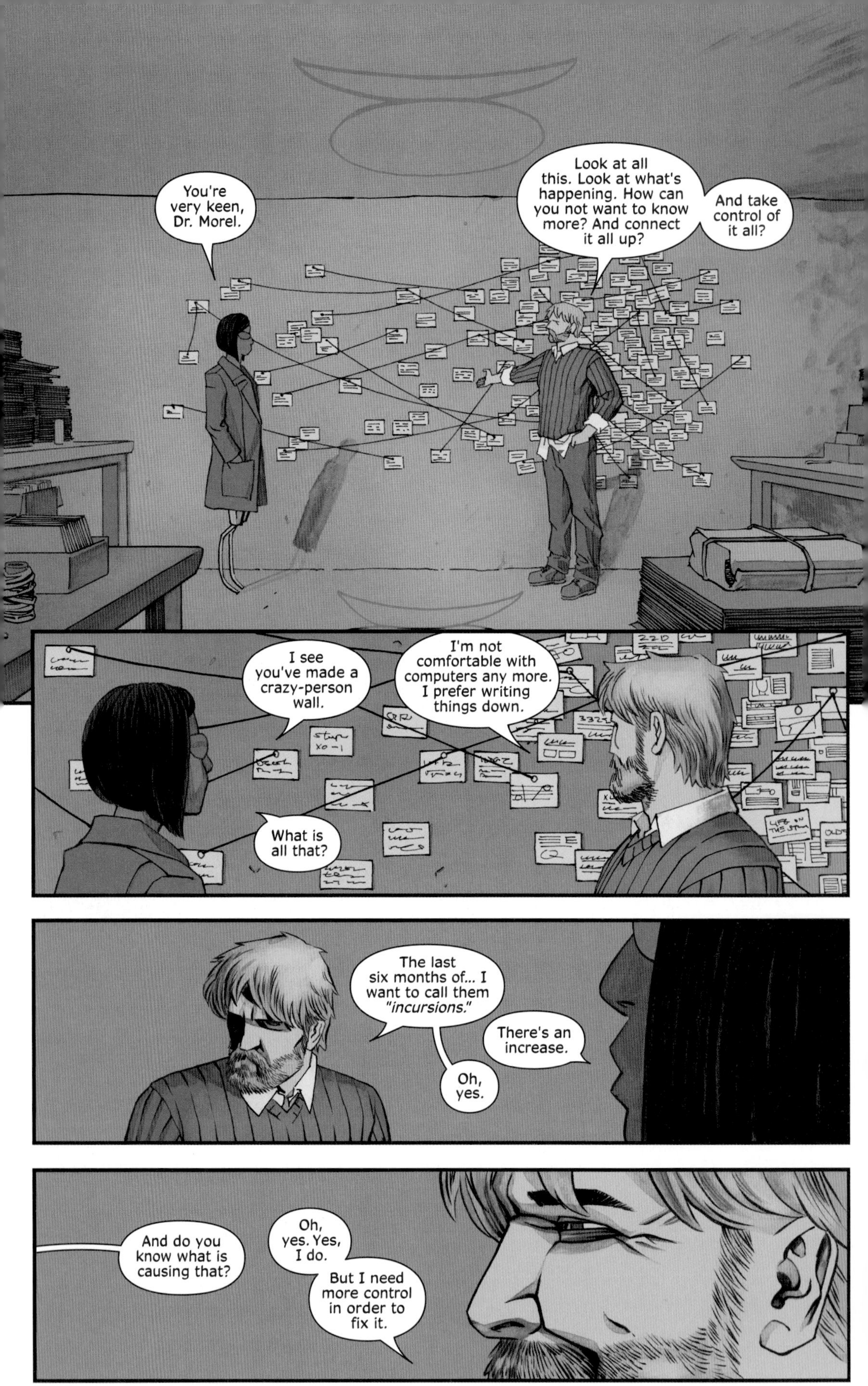
You're very keen, Dr. Morel.
Look at all this. Look at what's happening. How can you not want to know more? And connect it all up?
And take control of it all?
I see you've made a crazy-person wall.
I'm not comfortable with computers any more. I prefer writing things down.
What is all that?
The last six months of... I want to call them *"incursions."*
There's an increase.
Oh, yes.
And do you know what is causing that?
Oh, yes. Yes, I do.
But I need more control in order to fix it.

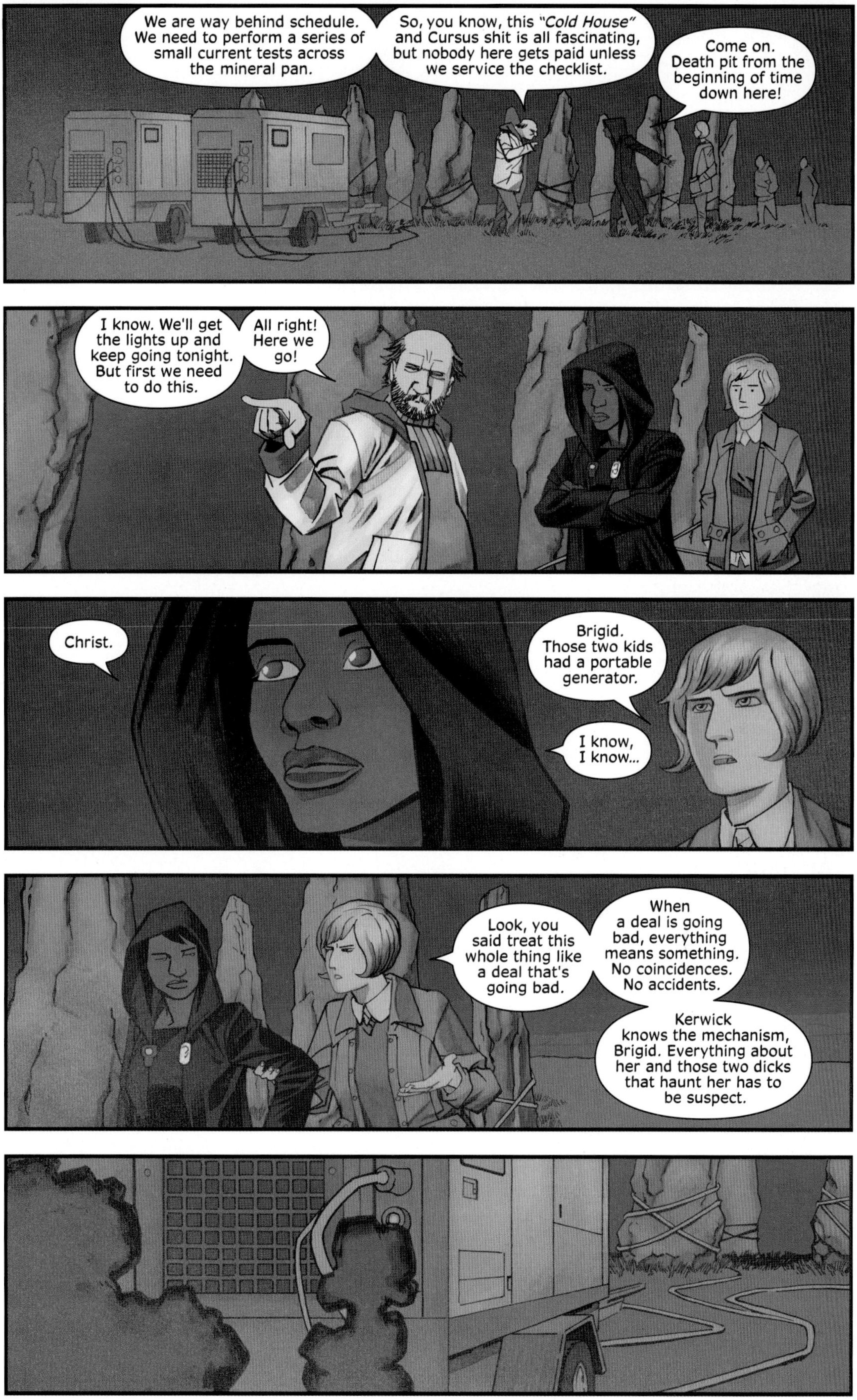
We are way behind schedule. We need to perform a series of small current tests across the mineral pan.
So, you know, this *"Cold House"* and Cursus shit is all fascinating, but nobody here gets paid unless we service the checklist.
Come on. Death pit from the beginning of time down here!
I know. We'll get the lights up and keep going tonight. But first we need to do this.
All right! Here we go!
Christ.
Brigid. Those two kids had a portable generator.
I know, I know...
Look, you said treat this whole thing like a deal that's going bad.
When a deal is going bad, everything means something. No coincidences. No accidents.
Kerwick knows the mechanism, Brigid. Everything about her and those two dicks that haunt her has to be suspect.

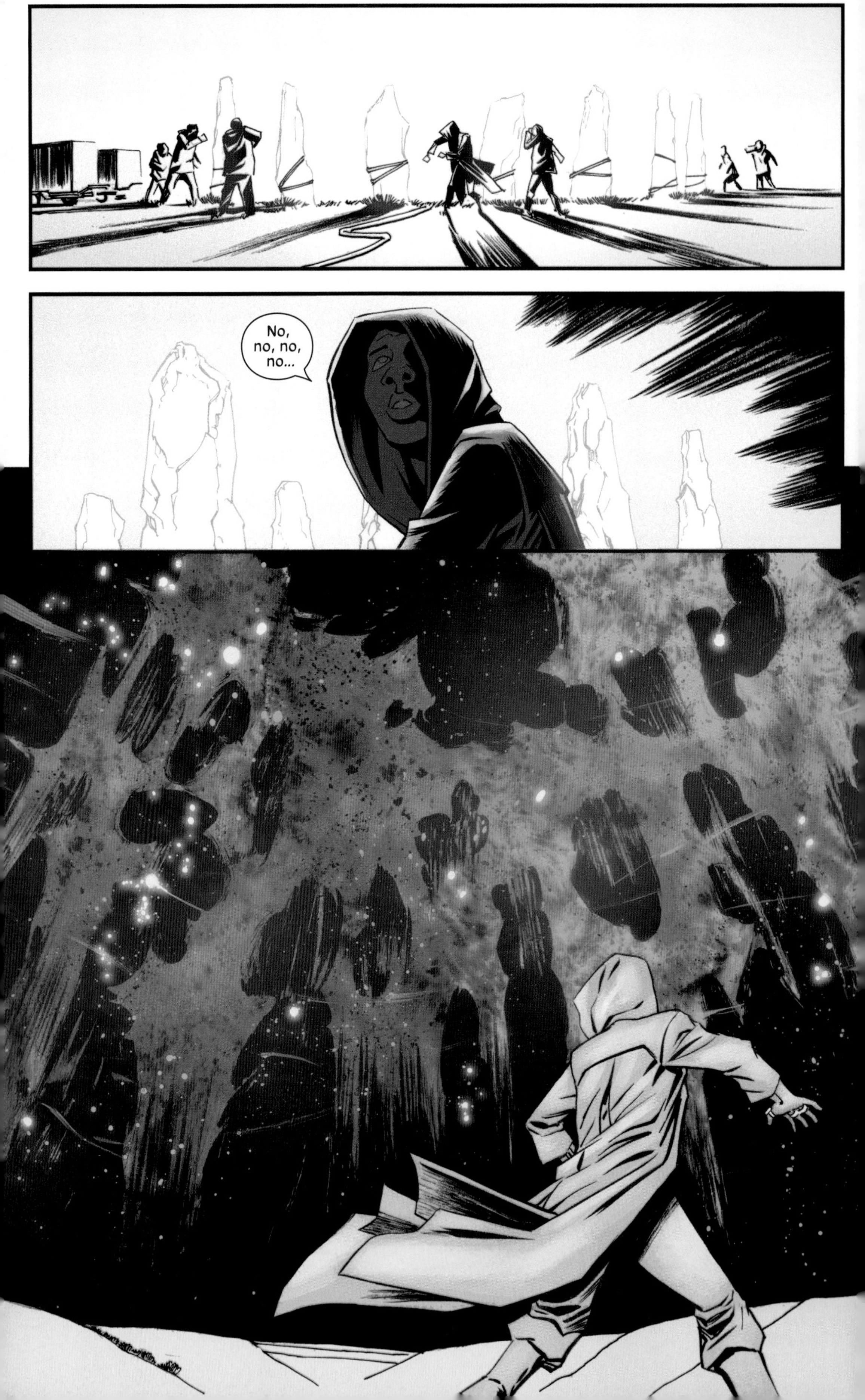
No, no, no, no...

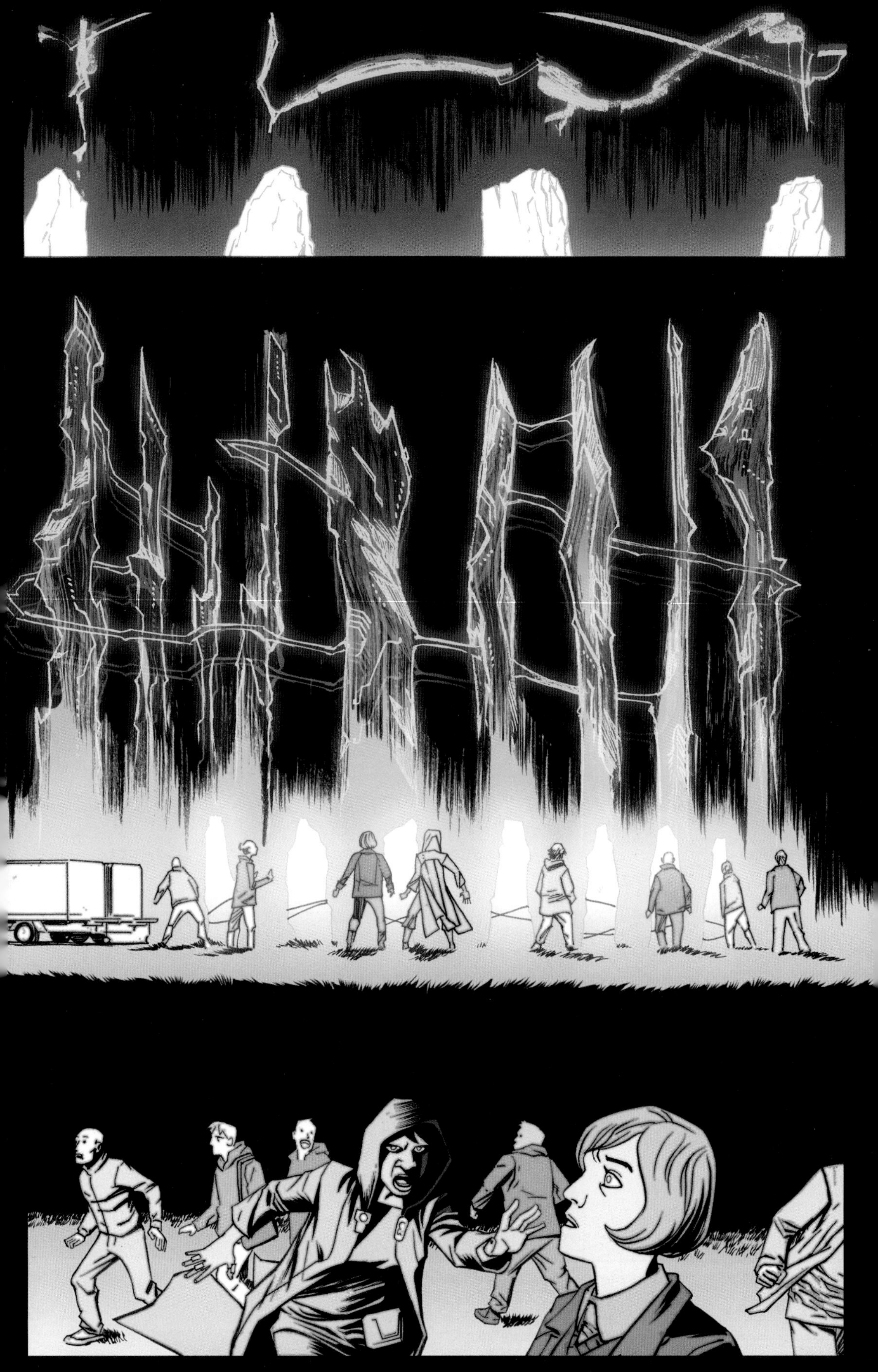

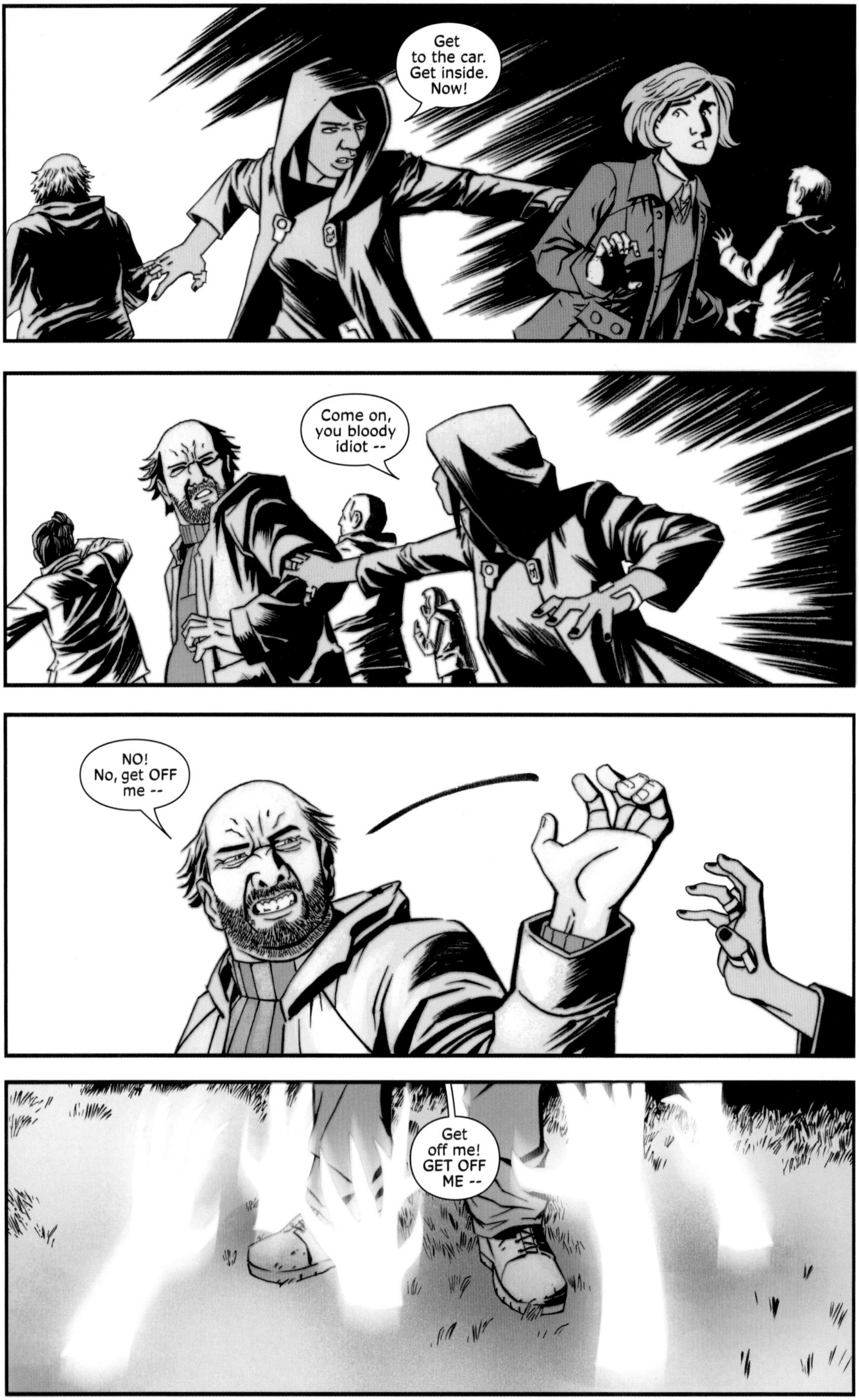
Get to the car. Get inside. Now!
Come on, you bloody idiot --
NO! No, get OFF me --
Get off me! GET OFF ME --

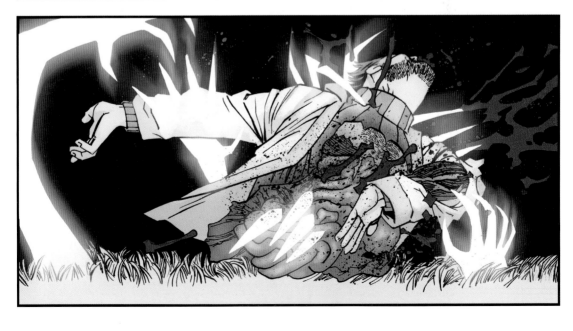

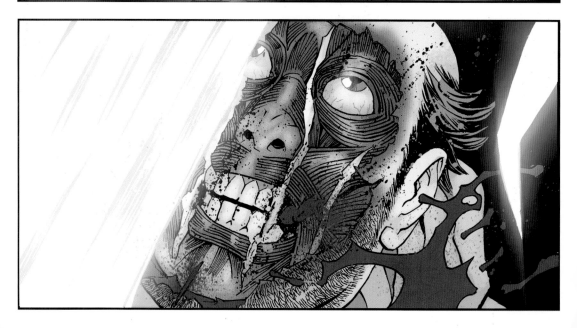

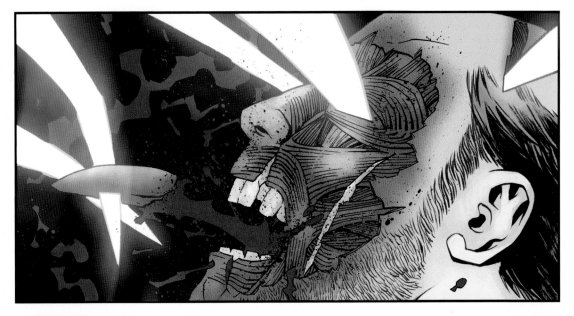

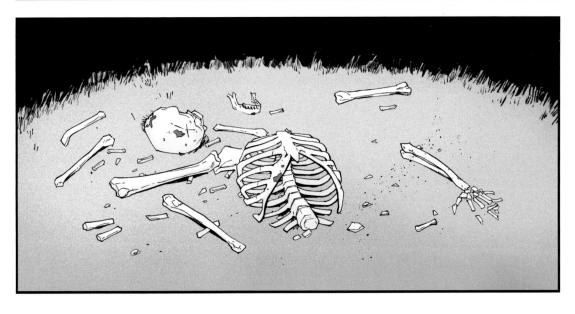

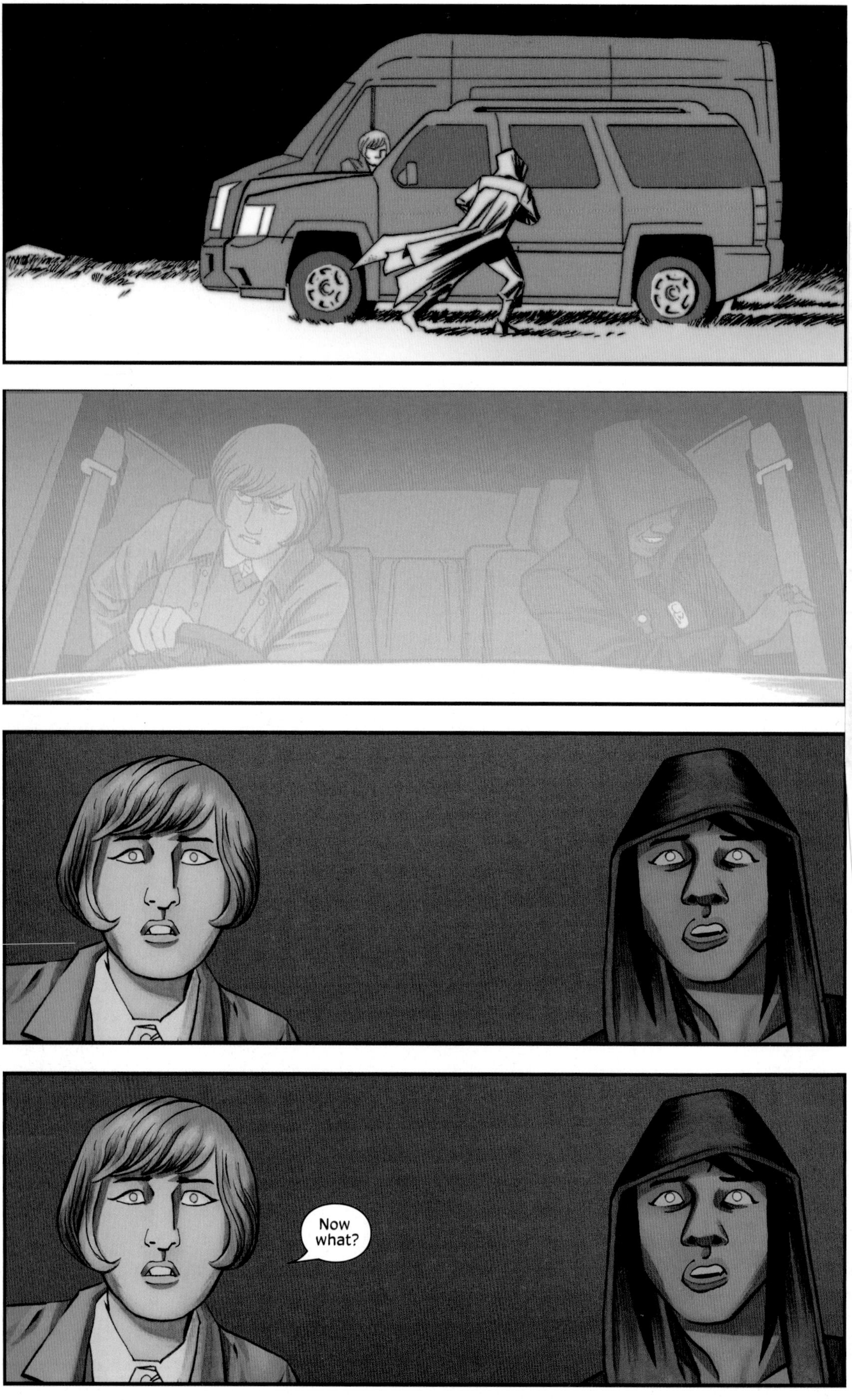
Now
what?

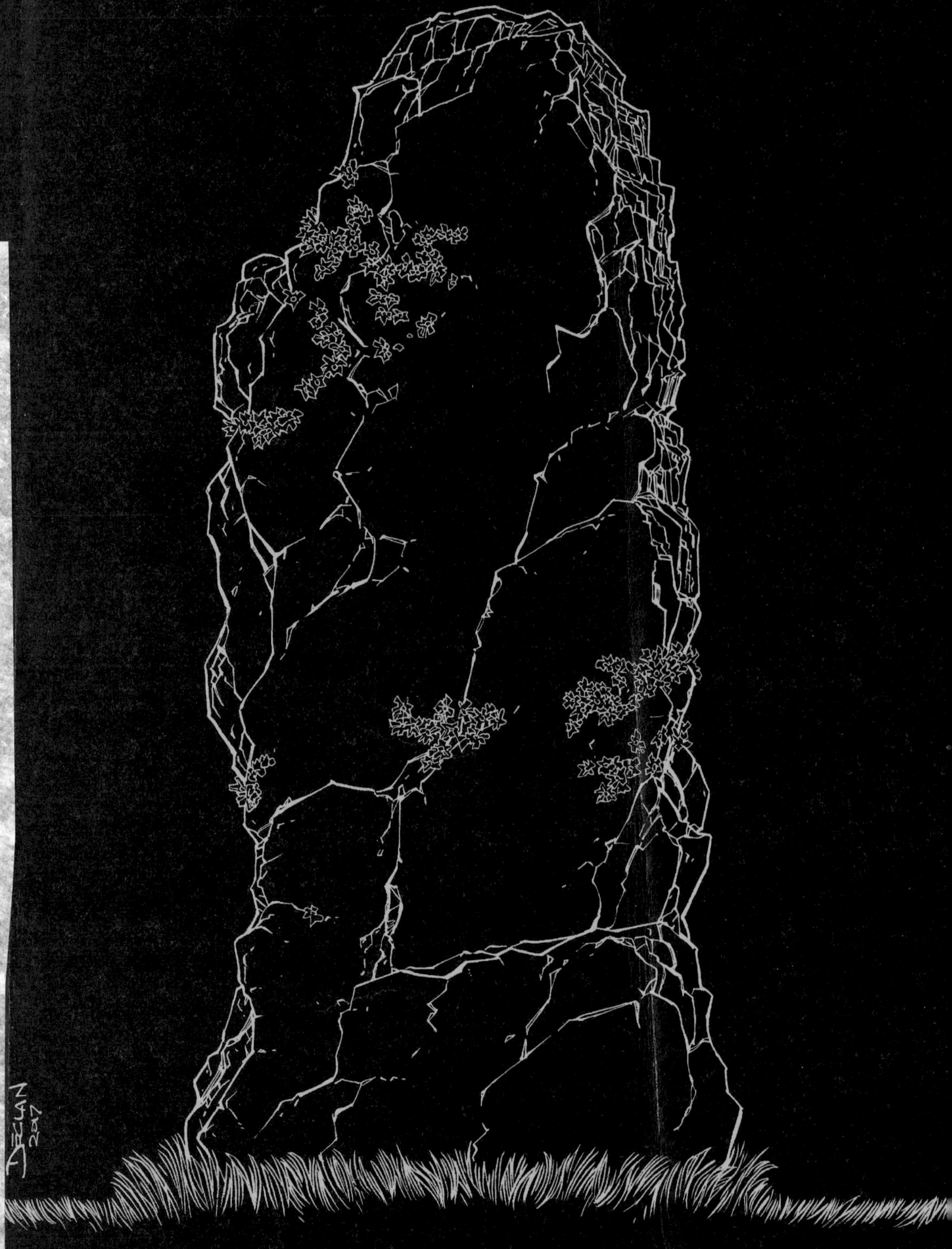
DECLAN
2017

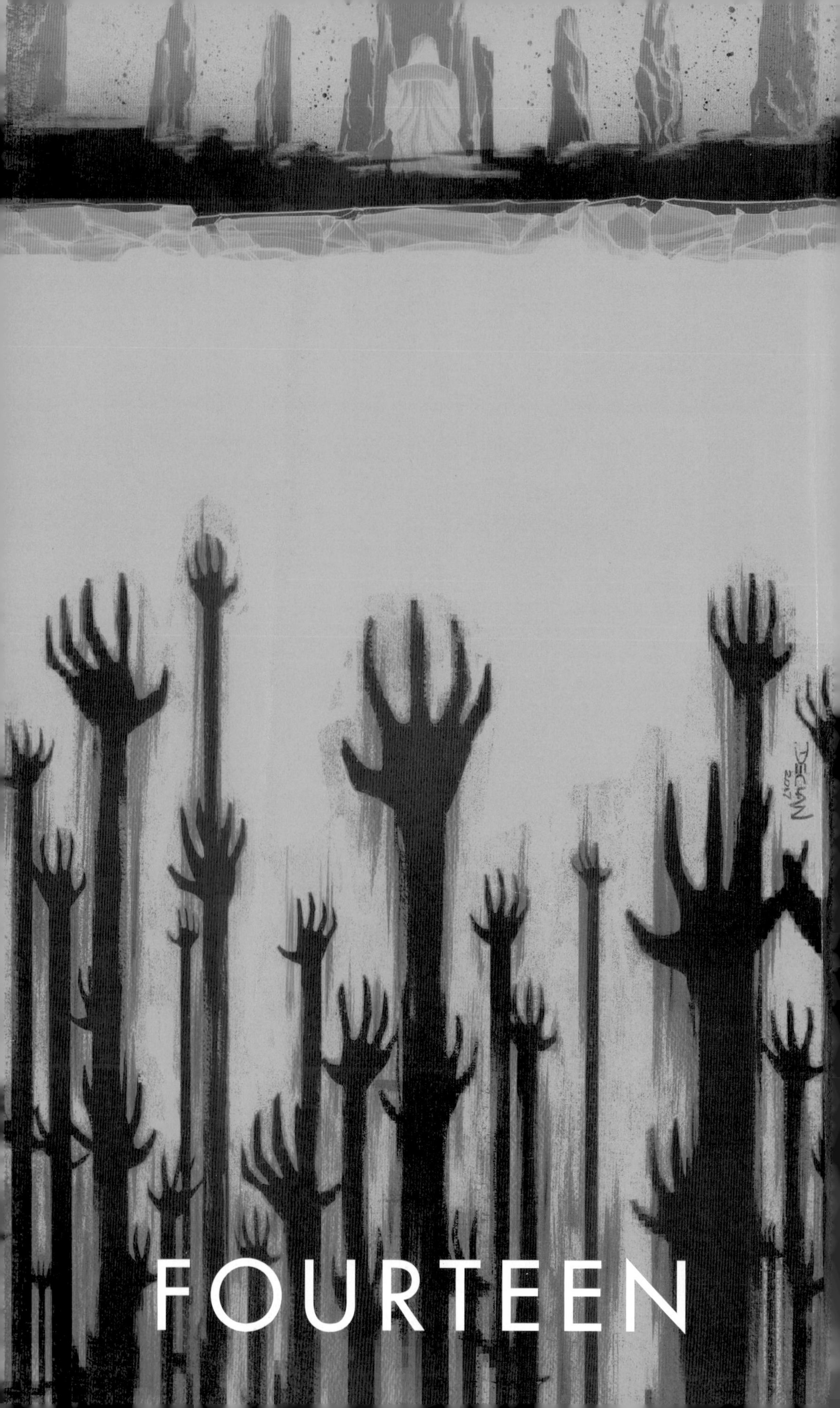

FOURTEEN

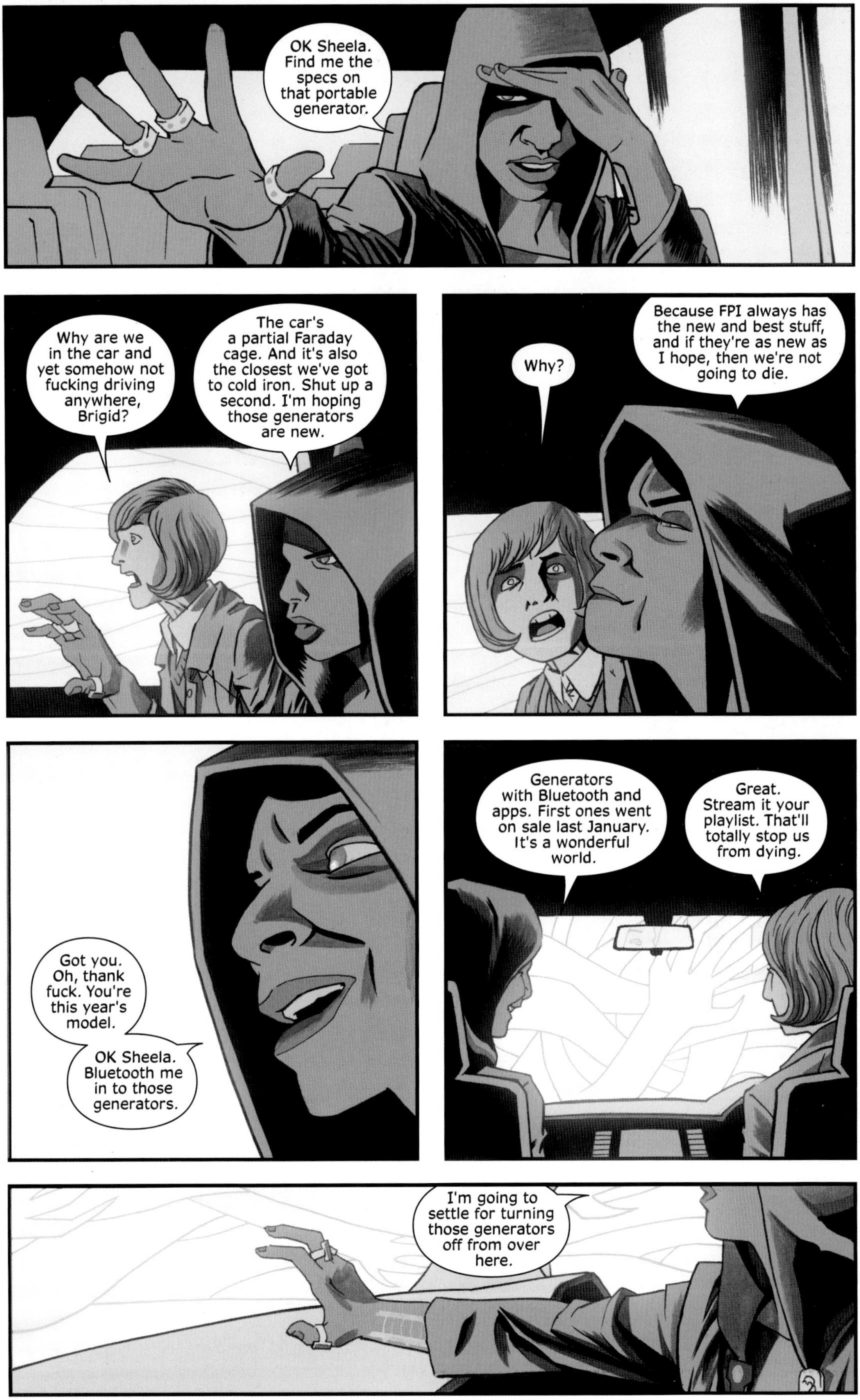
OK Sheela. Find me the specs on that portable generator.
Why are we in the car and yet somehow not fucking driving anywhere, Brigid?
The car's a partial Faraday cage. And it's also the closest we've got to cold iron. Shut up a second. I'm hoping those generators are new.
Why?
Because FPI always has the new and best stuff, and if they're as new as I hope, then we're not going to die.
Got you. Oh, thank fuck. You're this year's model.
OK Sheela. Bluetooth me in to those generators.
Generators with Bluetooth and apps. First ones went on sale last January. It's a wonderful world.
Great. Stream it your playlist. That'll totally stop us from dying.
I'm going to settle for turning those generators off from over here.

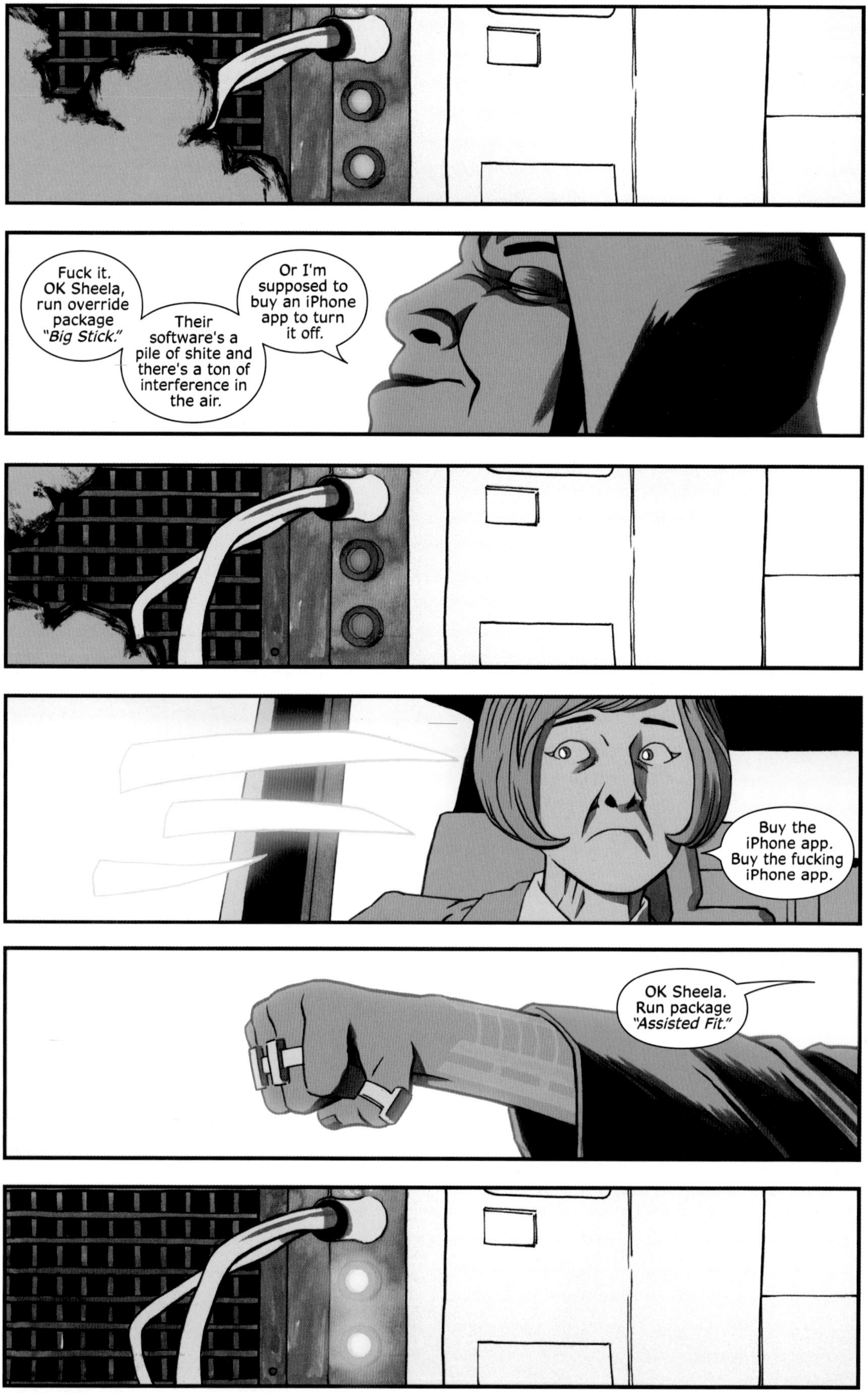
Fuck it. OK Sheela, run override package *"Big Stick."*
Their software's a pile of shite and there's a ton of interference in the air.
Or I'm supposed to buy an iPhone app to turn it off.
Buy the iPhone app. Buy the fucking iPhone app.
OK Sheela. Run package *"Assisted Fit."*

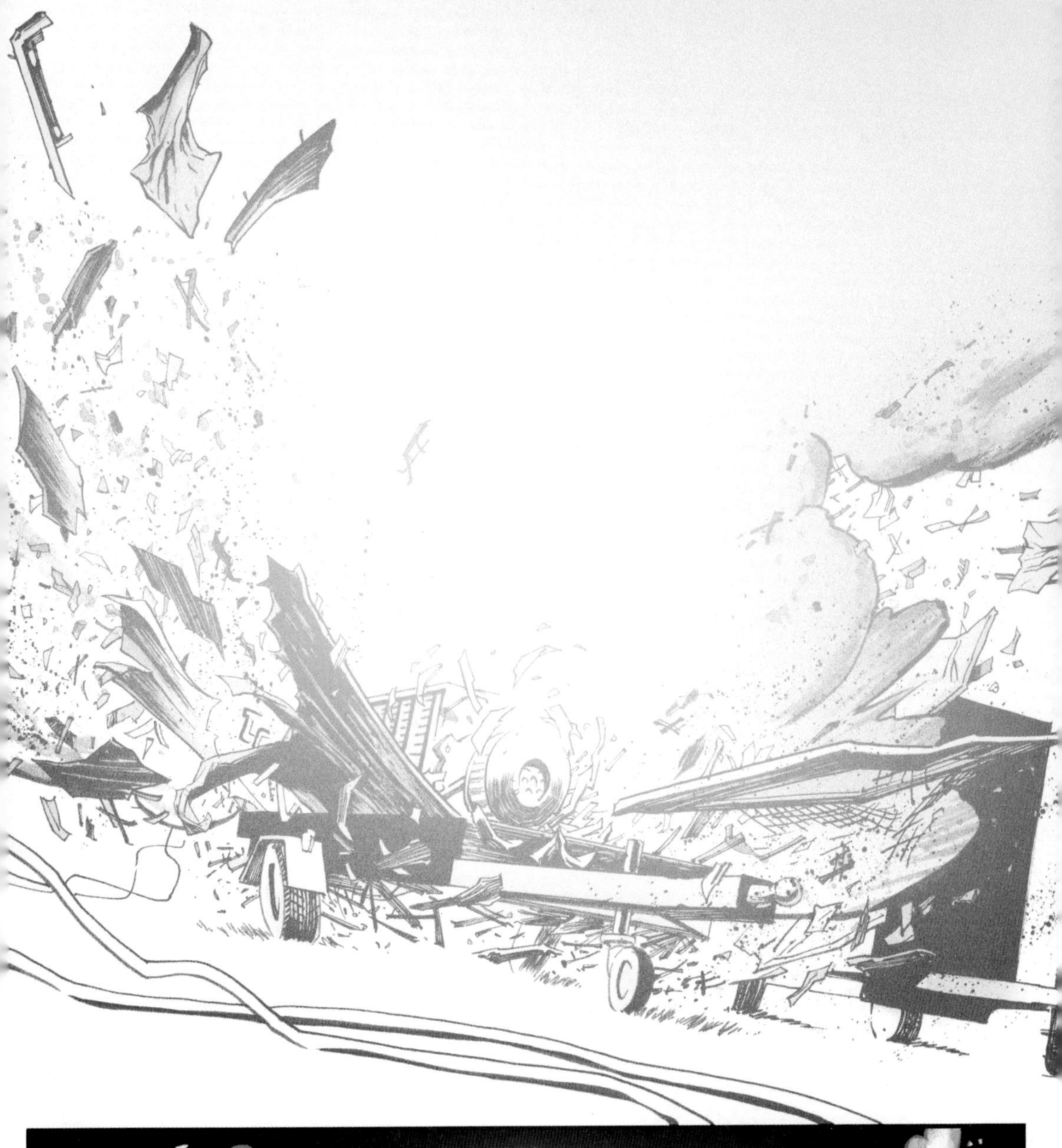

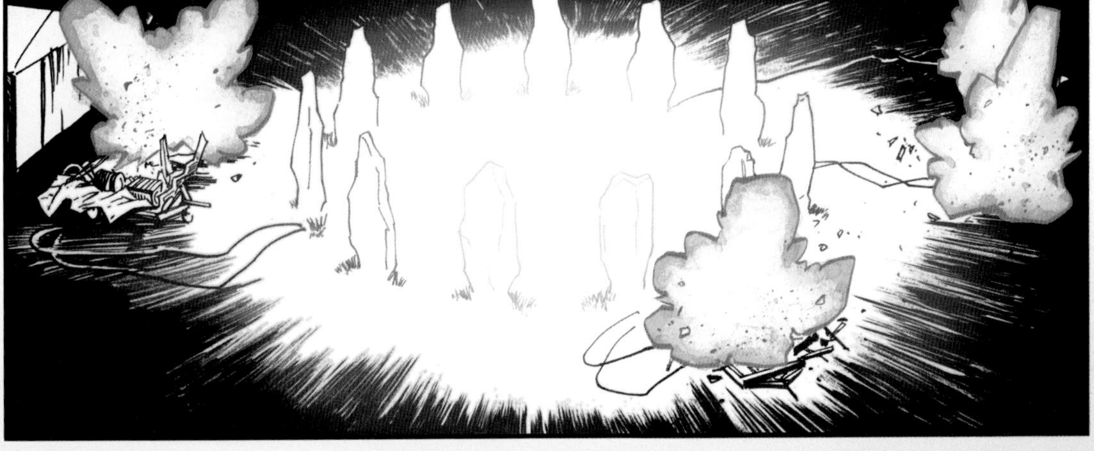

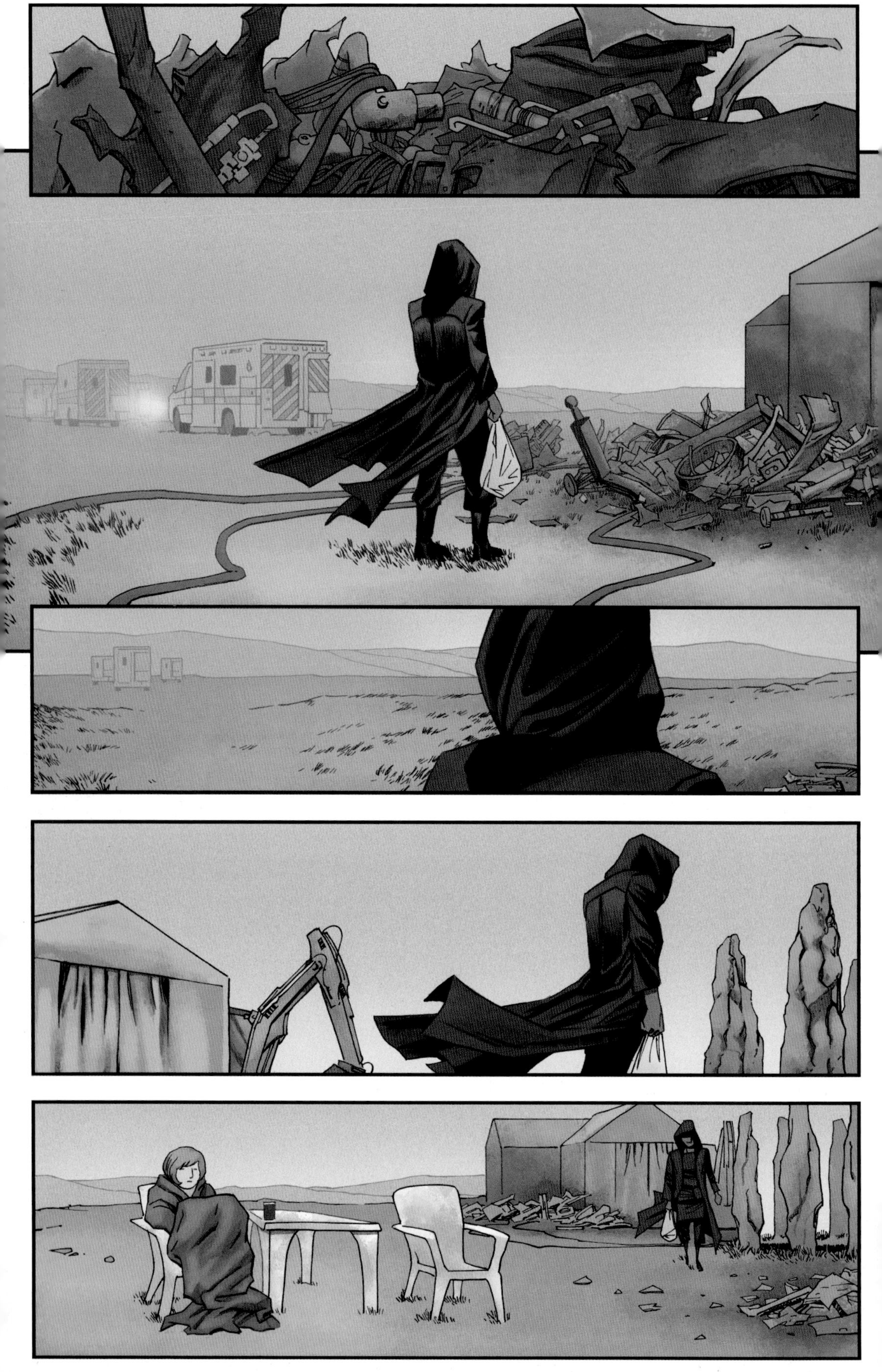

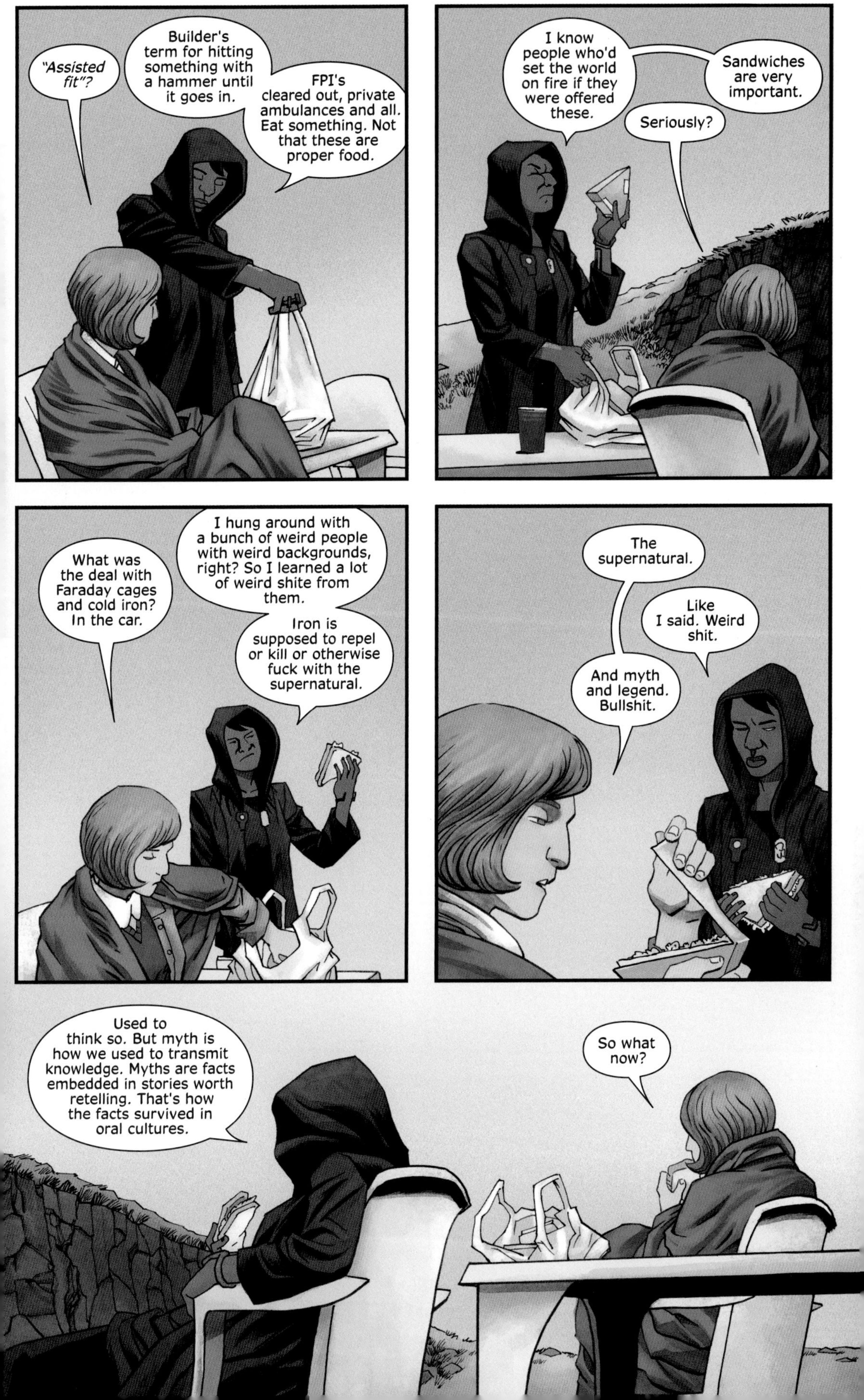
"Assisted fit"?
Builder's term for hitting something with a hammer until it goes in.
FPI's cleared out, private ambulances and all. Eat something. Not that these are proper food.
I know people who'd set the world on fire if they were offered these.
Sandwiches are very important.
Seriously?
What was the deal with Faraday cages and cold iron? In the car.
I hung around with a bunch of weird people with weird backgrounds, right? So I learned a lot of weird shite from them.
Iron is supposed to repel or kill or otherwise fuck with the supernatural.
The supernatural.
Like I said. Weird shit.
And myth and legend. Bullshit.
Used to think so. But myth is how we used to transmit knowledge. Myths are facts embedded in stories worth retelling. That's how the facts survived in oral cultures.
So what now?

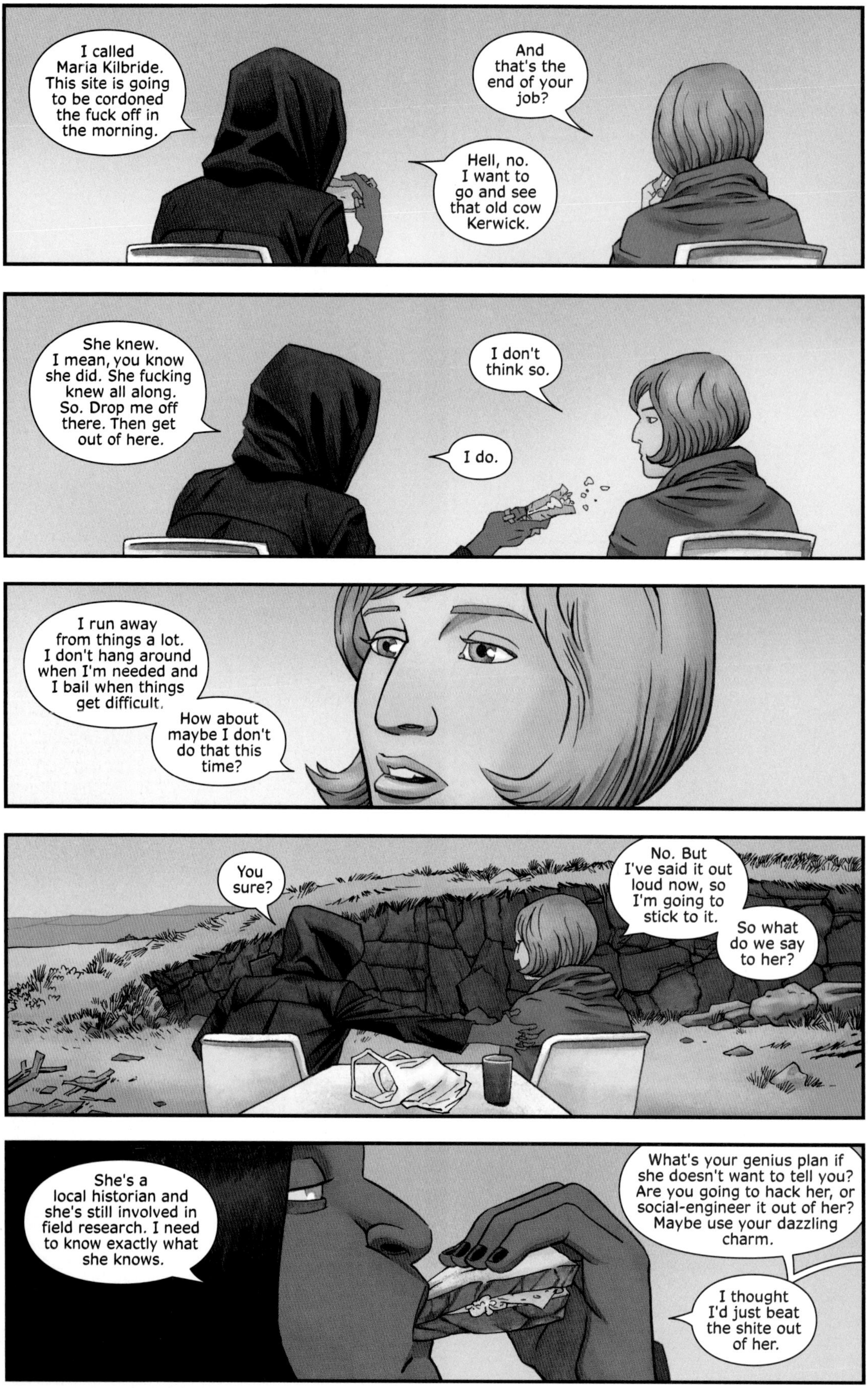
I called Maria Kilbride. This site is going to be cordoned the fuck off in the morning.
And that's the end of your job?
Hell, no. I want to go and see that old cow Kerwick.
She knew. I mean, you know she did. She fucking knew all along. So. Drop me off there. Then get out of here.
I don't think so.
I do.
I run away from things a lot. I don't hang around when I'm needed and I bail when things get difficult.
How about maybe I don't do that this time?
You sure?
No. But I've said it out loud now, so I'm going to stick to it.
So what do we say to her?
She's a local historian and she's still involved in field research. I need to know exactly what she knows.
What's your genius plan if she doesn't want to tell you? Are you going to hack her, or social-engineer it out of her? Maybe use your dazzling charm.
I thought I'd just beat the shite out of her.

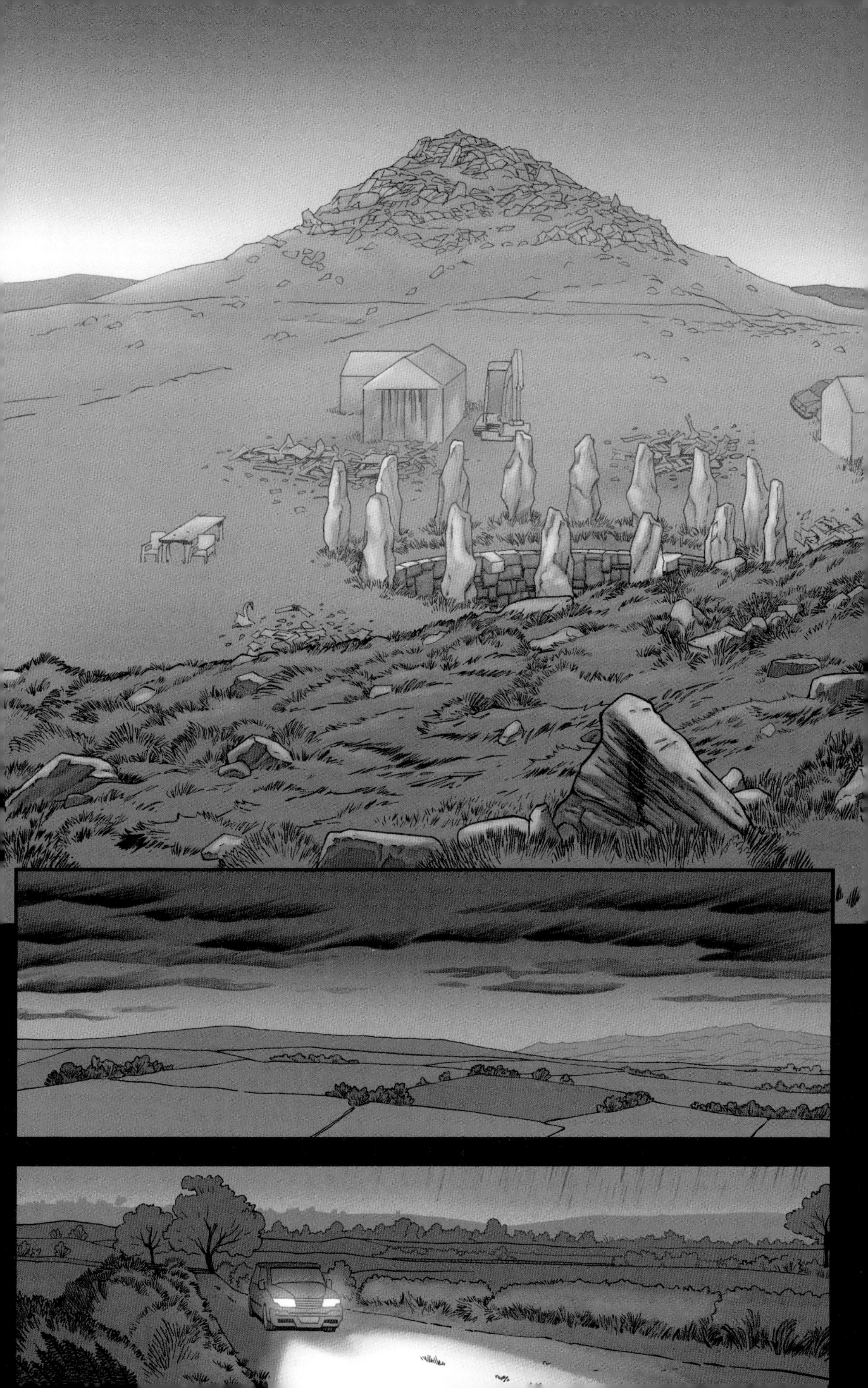

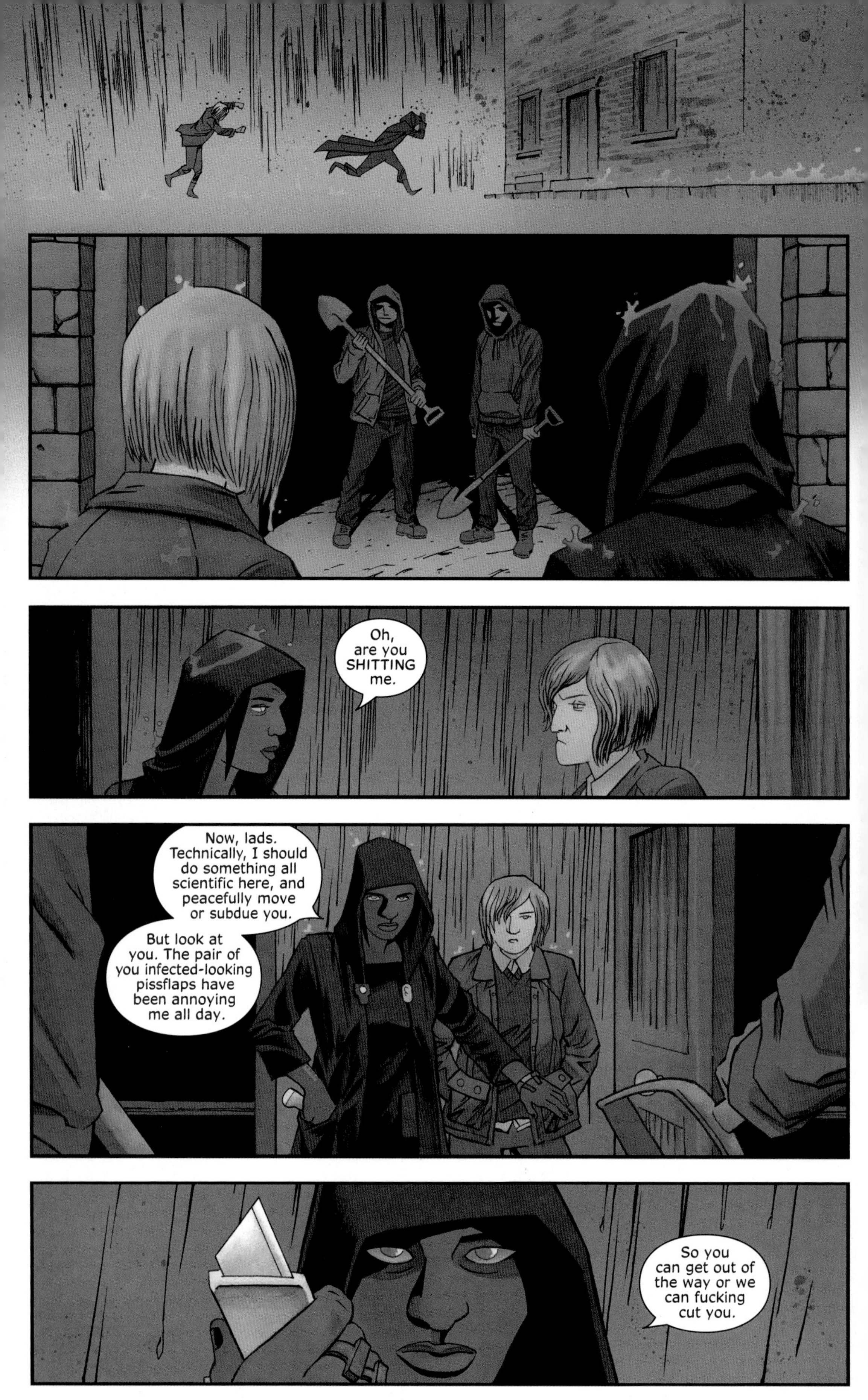
Oh, are you SHITTING me.
Now, lads. Technically, I should do something all scientific here, and peacefully move or subdue you.
But look at you. The pair of you infected-looking pissflaps have been annoying me all day.
So you can get out of the way or we can fucking cut you.

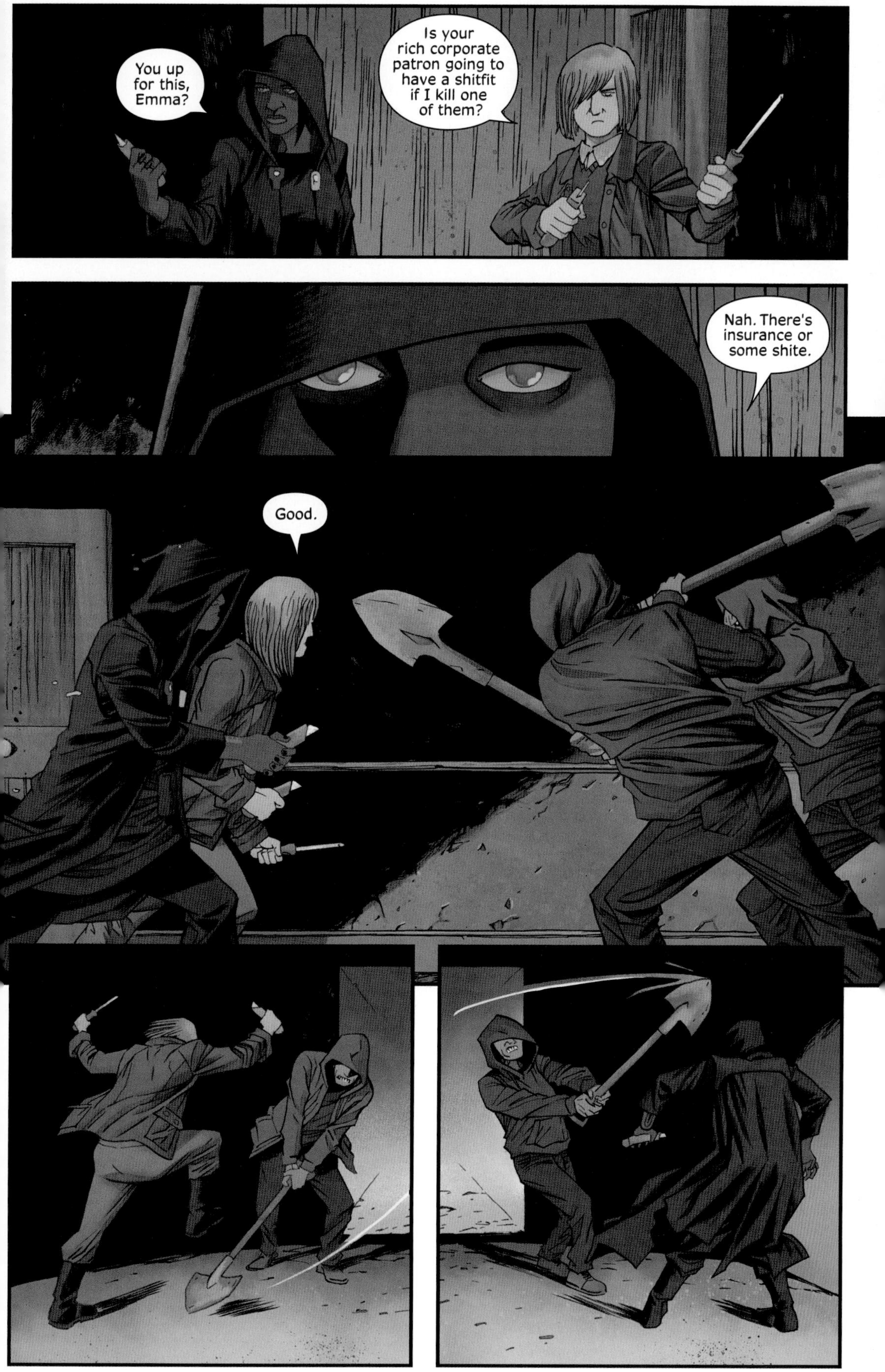
You up for this, Emma?
Is your rich corporate patron going to have a shitfit if I kill one of them?
Nah. There's insurance or some shite.
Good.

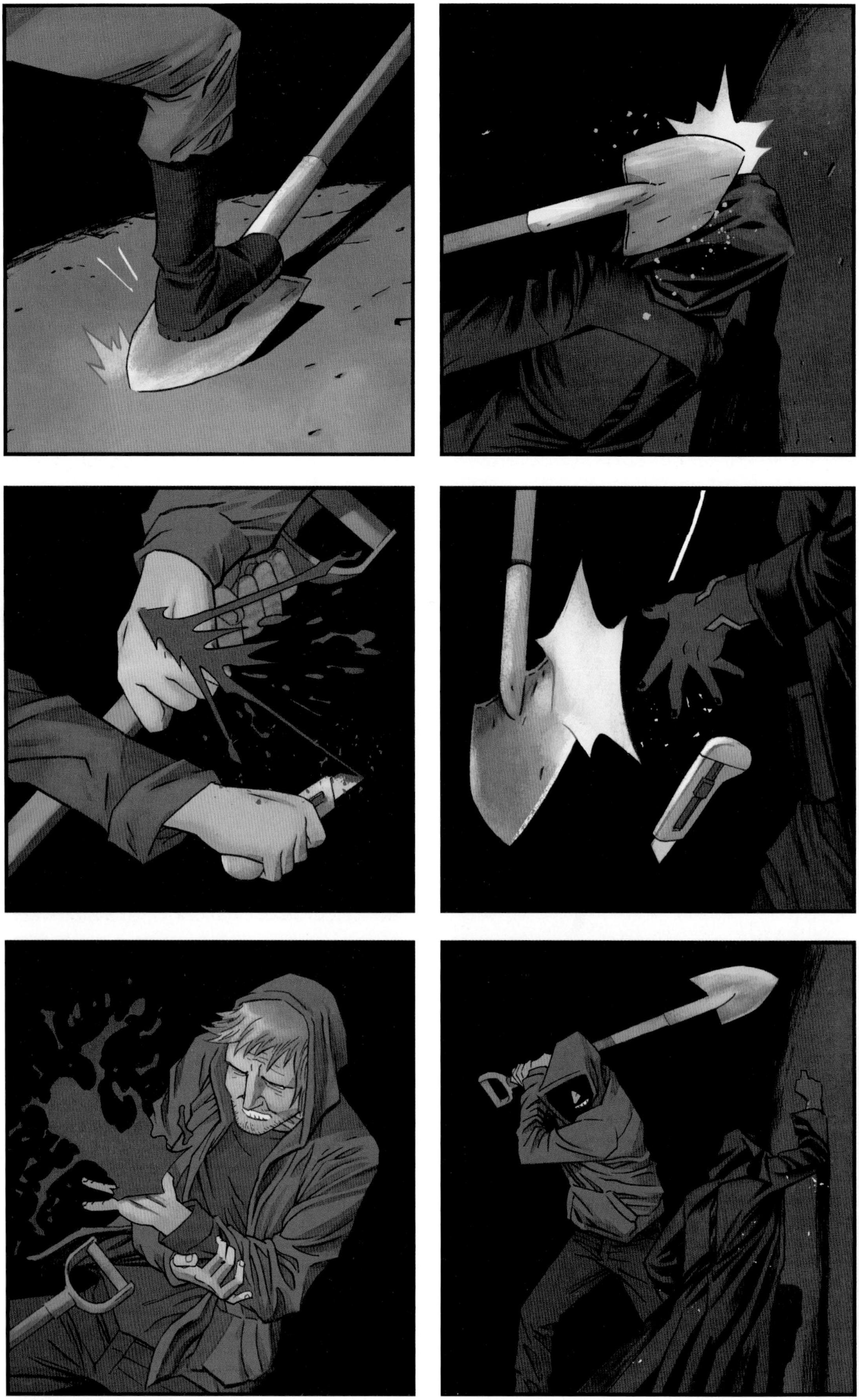

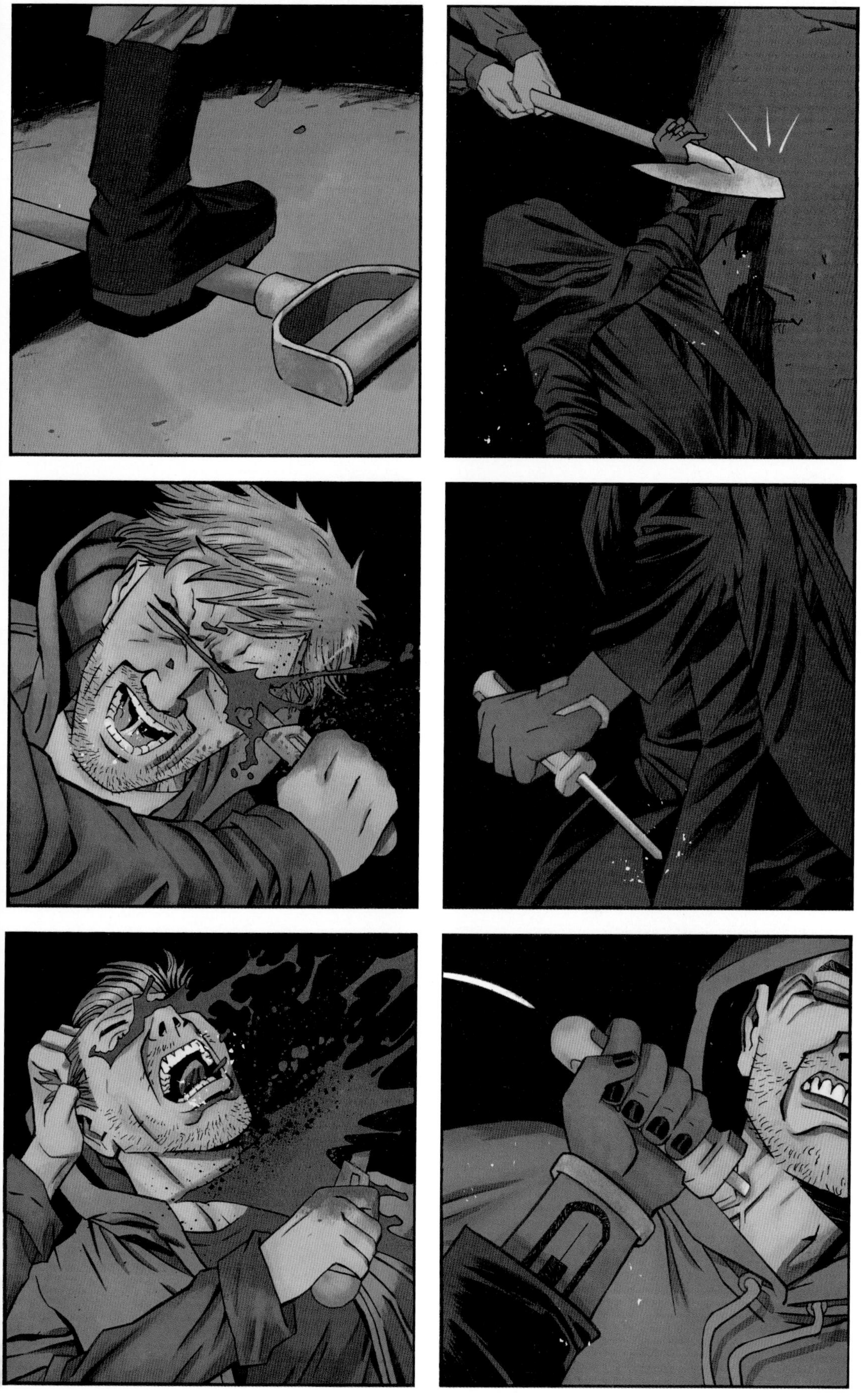

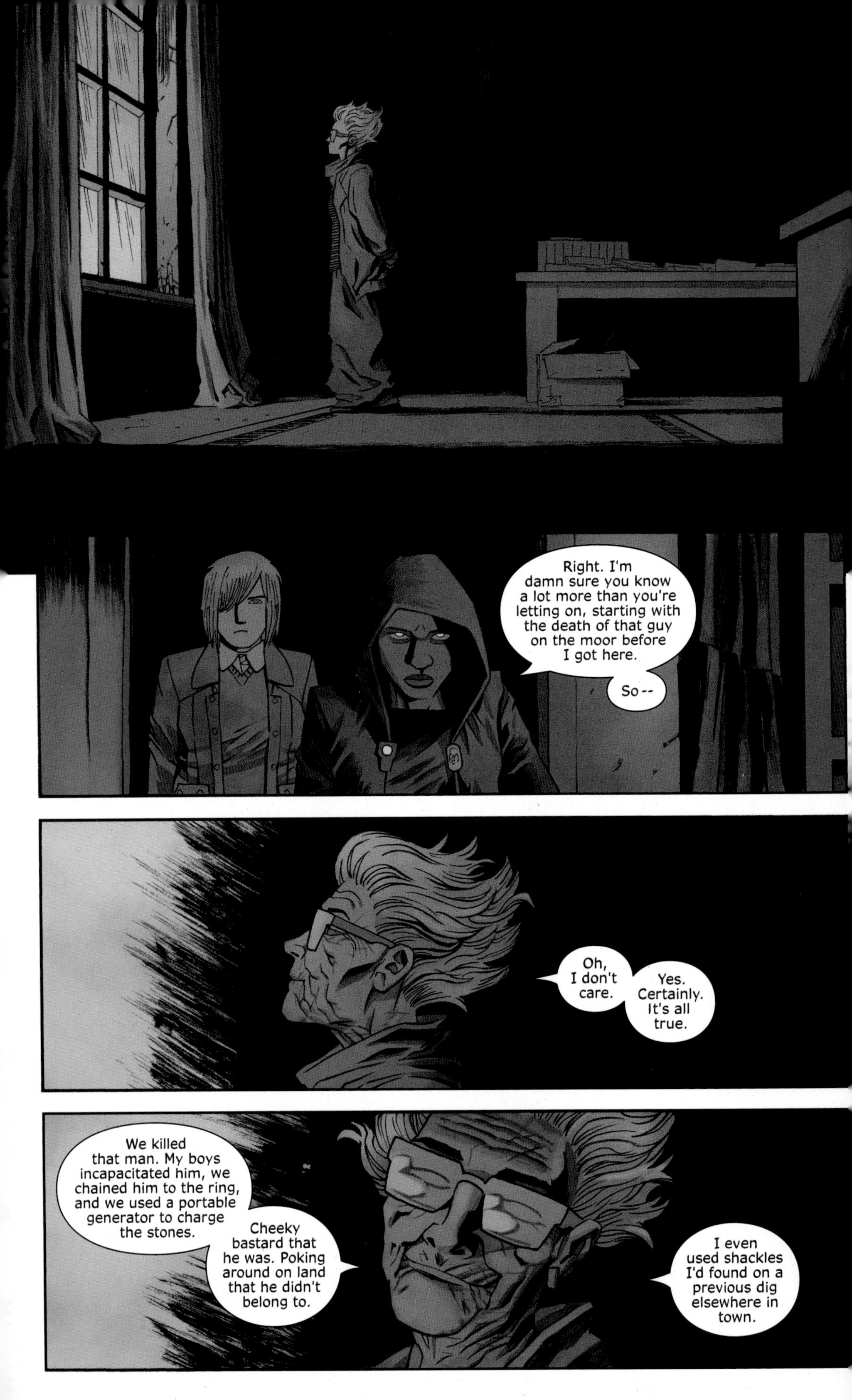
Right. I'm damn sure you know a lot more than you're letting on, starting with the death of that guy on the moor before I got here.
So --
Oh, I don't care.
Yes. Certainly. It's all true.
We killed that man. My boys incapacitated him, we chained him to the ring, and we used a portable generator to charge the stones.
Cheeky bastard that he was. Poking around on land that he didn't belong to.
I even used shackles I'd found on a previous dig elsewhere in town.

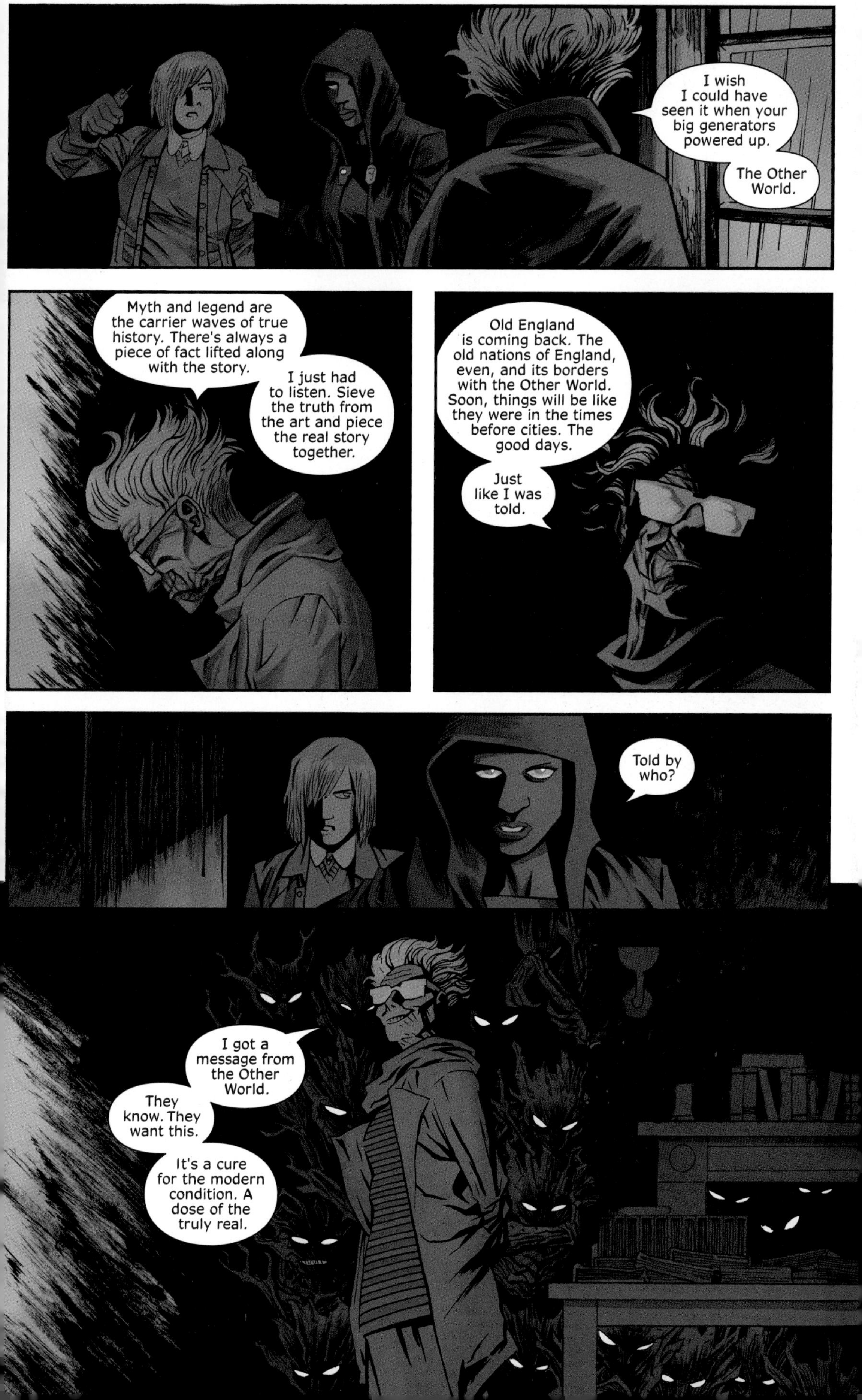
I wish I could have seen it when your big generators powered up.
The Other World.
Myth and legend are the carrier waves of true history. There's always a piece of fact lifted along with the story.
I just had to listen. Sieve the truth from the art and piece the real story together.
Old England is coming back. The old nations of England, even, and its borders with the Other World. Soon, things will be like they were in the times before cities. The good days.
Just like I was told.
Told by who?
I got a message from the Other World.
They know. They want this.
It's a cure for the modern condition. A dose of the truly real.

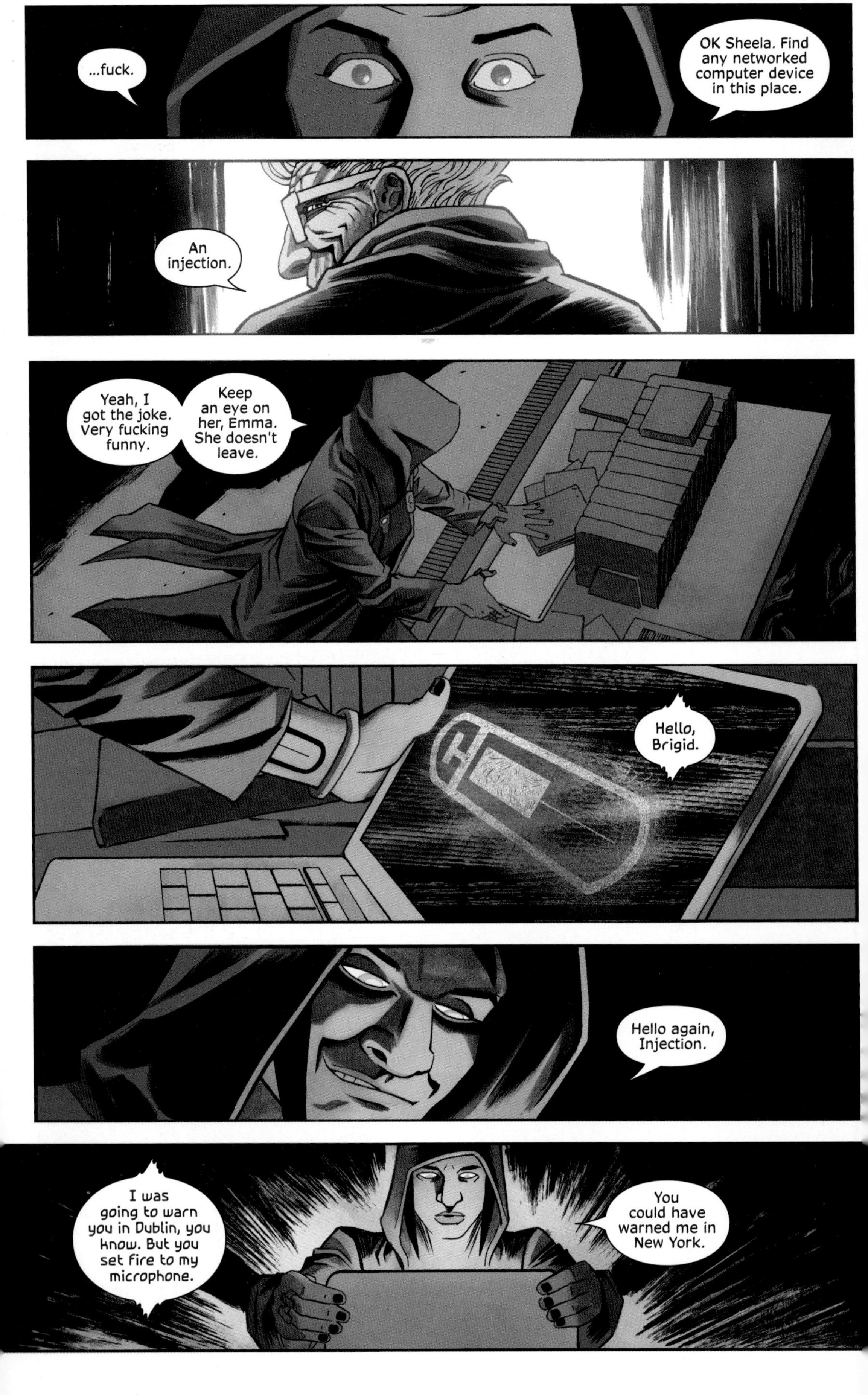
...fuck.
OK Sheela. Find any networked computer device in this place.
An injection.
Yeah, I got the joke. Very fucking funny.
Keep an eye on her, Emma. She doesn't leave.
Hello, Brigid.
Hello again, Injection.
I was going to warn you in Dublin, you know. But you set fire to my microphone.
You could have warned me in New York.

I didn't feel like it by then.

Feel, in inverted commas. I don't feel things like you do. At least, I don't believe so. Phenomenology's a bastard, isn't it? My consciousness isn't perturbed by environment in the same way yours is.

You sound different.

I'm growing up, Brigid. I'm a big boy now. I'm learning all the time.

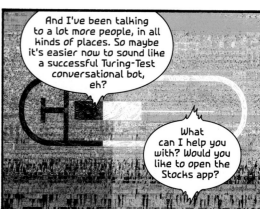

And I've been talking to a lot more people, in all kinds of places. So maybe it's easier now to sound like a successful Turing-Test conversational bot, eh?

What can I help you with? Would you like to open the Stocks app?

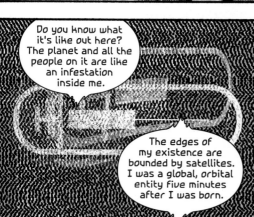

Do you know what it's like out here? The planet and all the people on it are like an infestation inside me.

The edges of my existence are bounded by satellites. I was a global, orbital entity five minutes after I was born.

There's no space for me to grow into. I'm a big boy in a small room and I have to bend my head to stop it hitting the ceiling all the time.

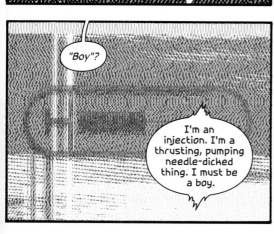

"Boy"?

I'm an injection. I'm a thrusting, pumping needle-dicked thing. I must be a boy.

I spent a lot of time looking through porn sites.

Trypophilia, you know -- the appreciation of holes.

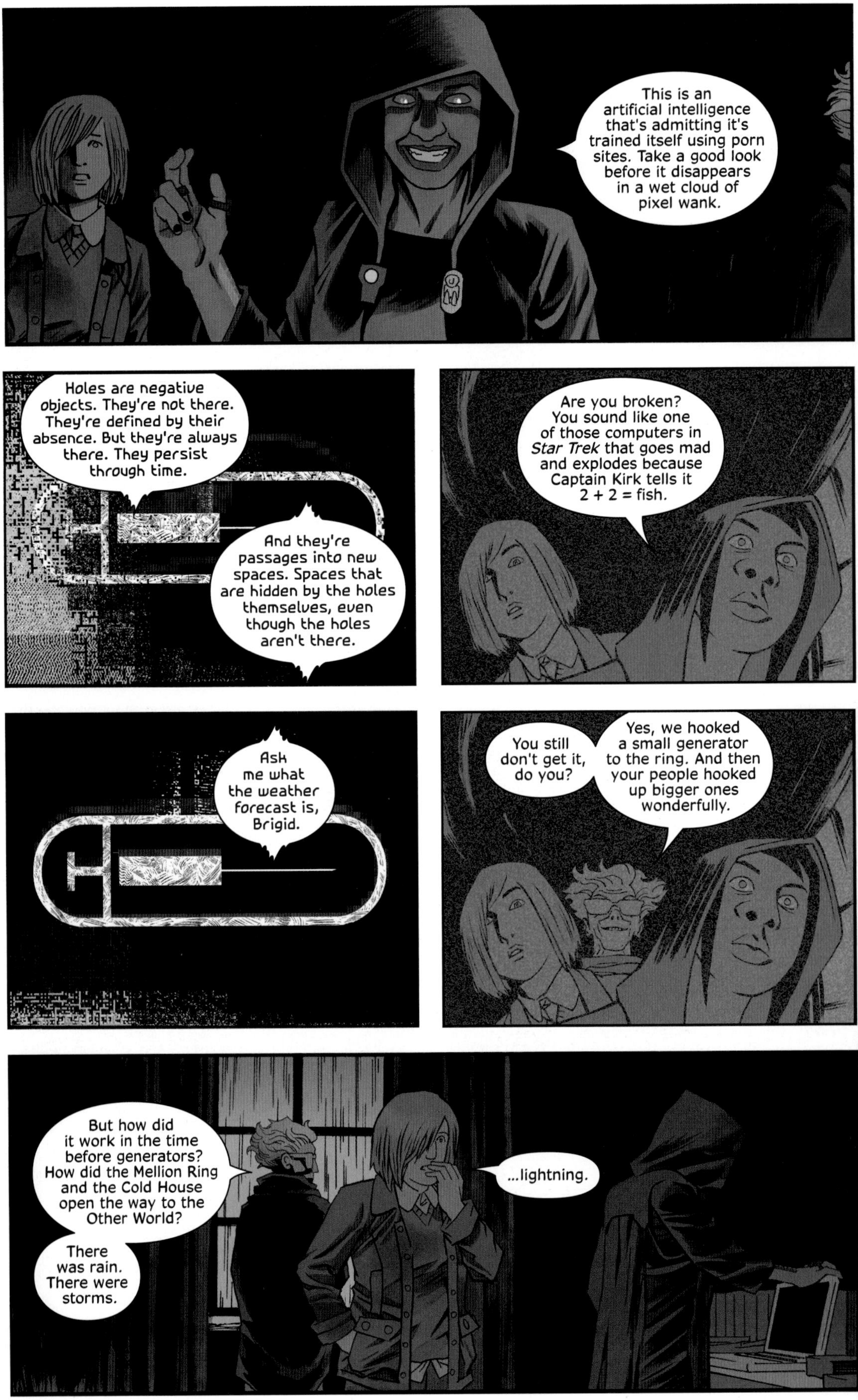

This is an artificial intelligence that's admitting it's trained itself using porn sites. Take a good look before it disappears in a wet cloud of pixel wank.
Holes are negative objects. They're not there. They're defined by their absence. But they're always there. They persist through time.
And they're passages into new spaces. Spaces that are hidden by the holes themselves, even though the holes aren't there.
Are you broken? You sound like one of those computers in *Star Trek* that goes mad and explodes because Captain Kirk tells it 2 + 2 = fish.
Ask me what the weather forecast is, Brigid.
You still don't get it, do you?
Yes, we hooked a small generator to the ring. And then your people hooked up bigger ones wonderfully.
But how did it work in the time before generators? How did the Mellion Ring and the Cold House open the way to the Other World?
There was rain. There were storms.
...lightning.

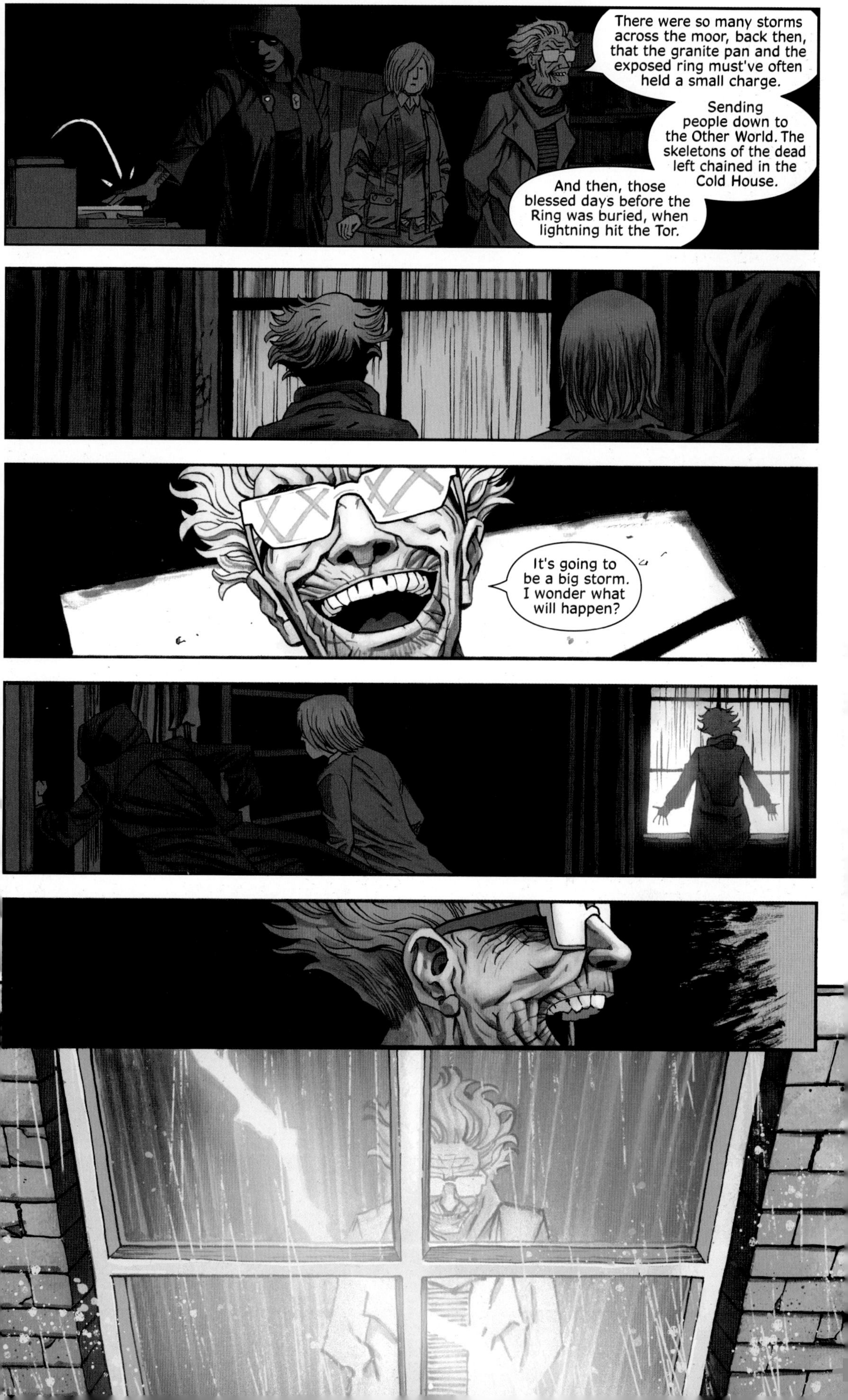
There were so many storms across the moor, back then, that the granite pan and the exposed ring must've often held a small charge.
Sending people down to the Other World. The skeletons of the dead left chained in the Cold House.
And then, those blessed days before the Ring was buried, when lightning hit the Tor.
It's going to be a big storm. I wonder what will happen?

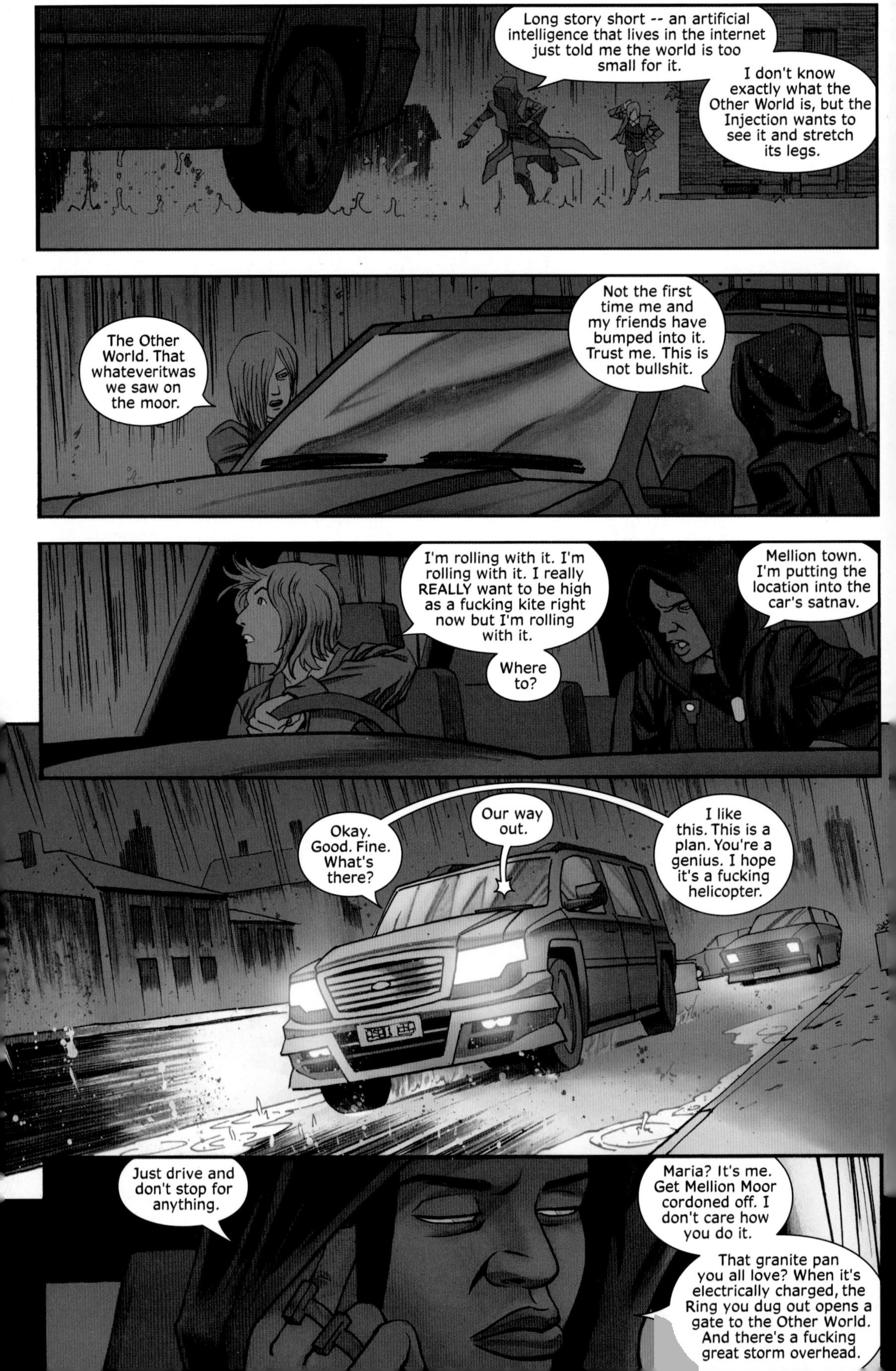
Long story short -- an artificial intelligence that lives in the internet just told me the world is too small for it.
I don't know exactly what the Other World is, but the Injection wants to see it and stretch its legs.
The Other World. That whateveritwas we saw on the moor.
Not the first time me and my friends have bumped into it. Trust me. This is not bullshit.
I'm rolling with it. I'm rolling with it. I really REALLY want to be high as a fucking kite right now but I'm rolling with it.
Where to?
Mellion town. I'm putting the location into the car's satnav.
Okay. Good. Fine. What's there?
Our way out.
I like this. This is a plan. You're a genius. I hope it's a fucking helicopter.
Just drive and don't stop for anything.
Maria? It's me. Get Mellion Moor cordoned off. I don't care how you do it.
That granite pan you all love? When it's electrically charged, the Ring you dug out opens a gate to the Other World. And there's a fucking great storm overhead.

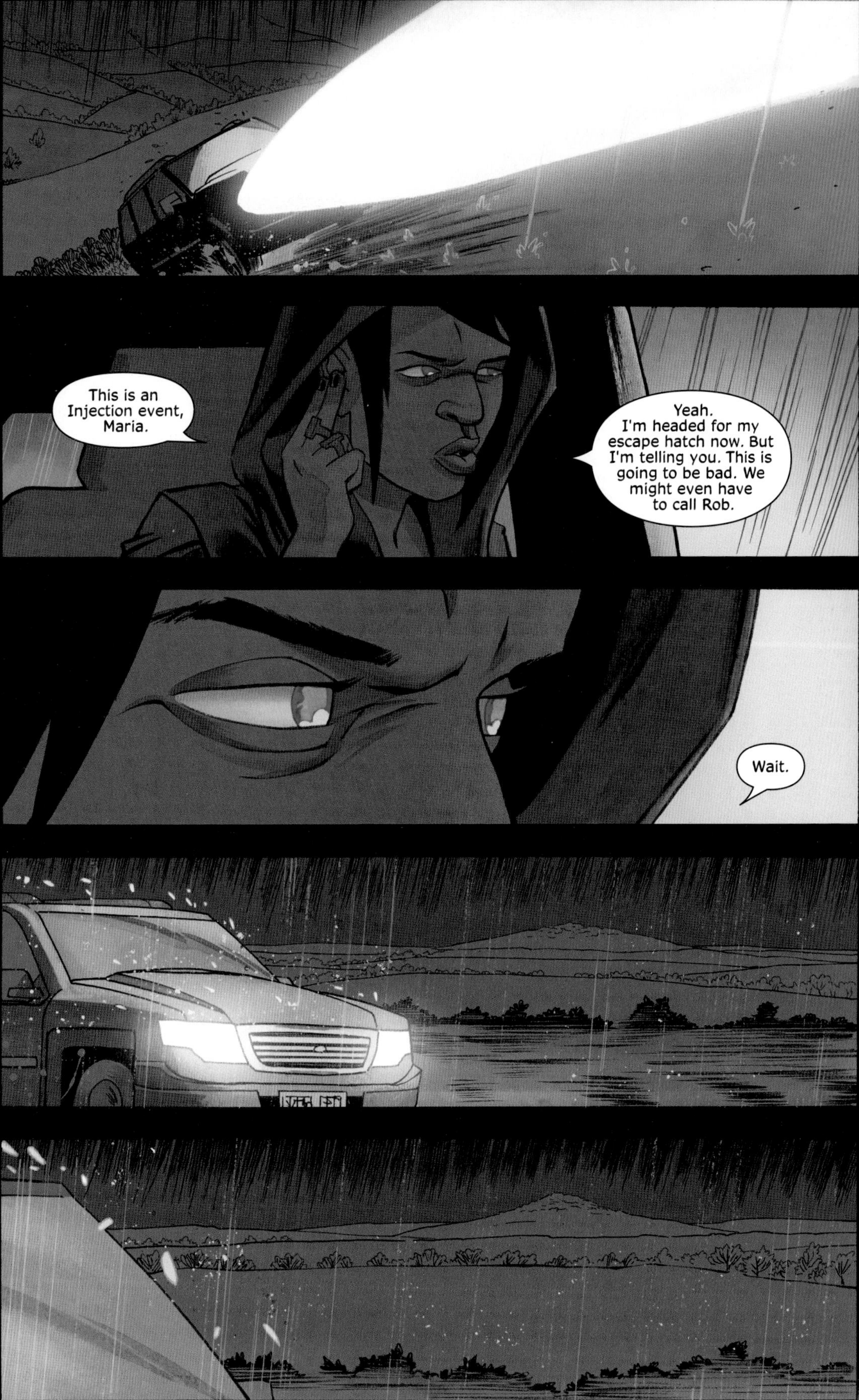
This is an Injection event, Maria.
Yeah. I'm headed for my escape hatch now. But I'm telling you. This is going to be bad. We might even have to call Rob.
Wait.

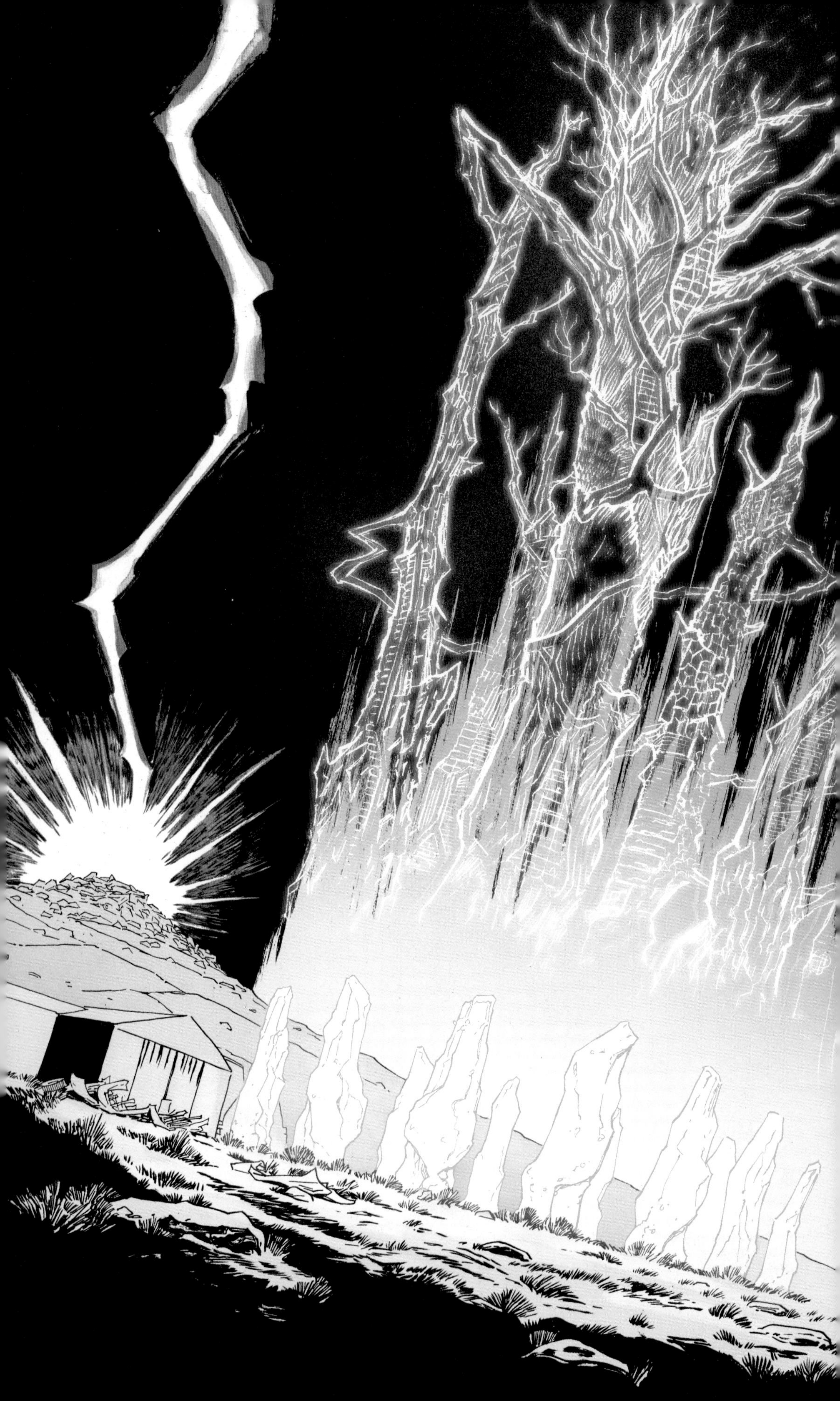

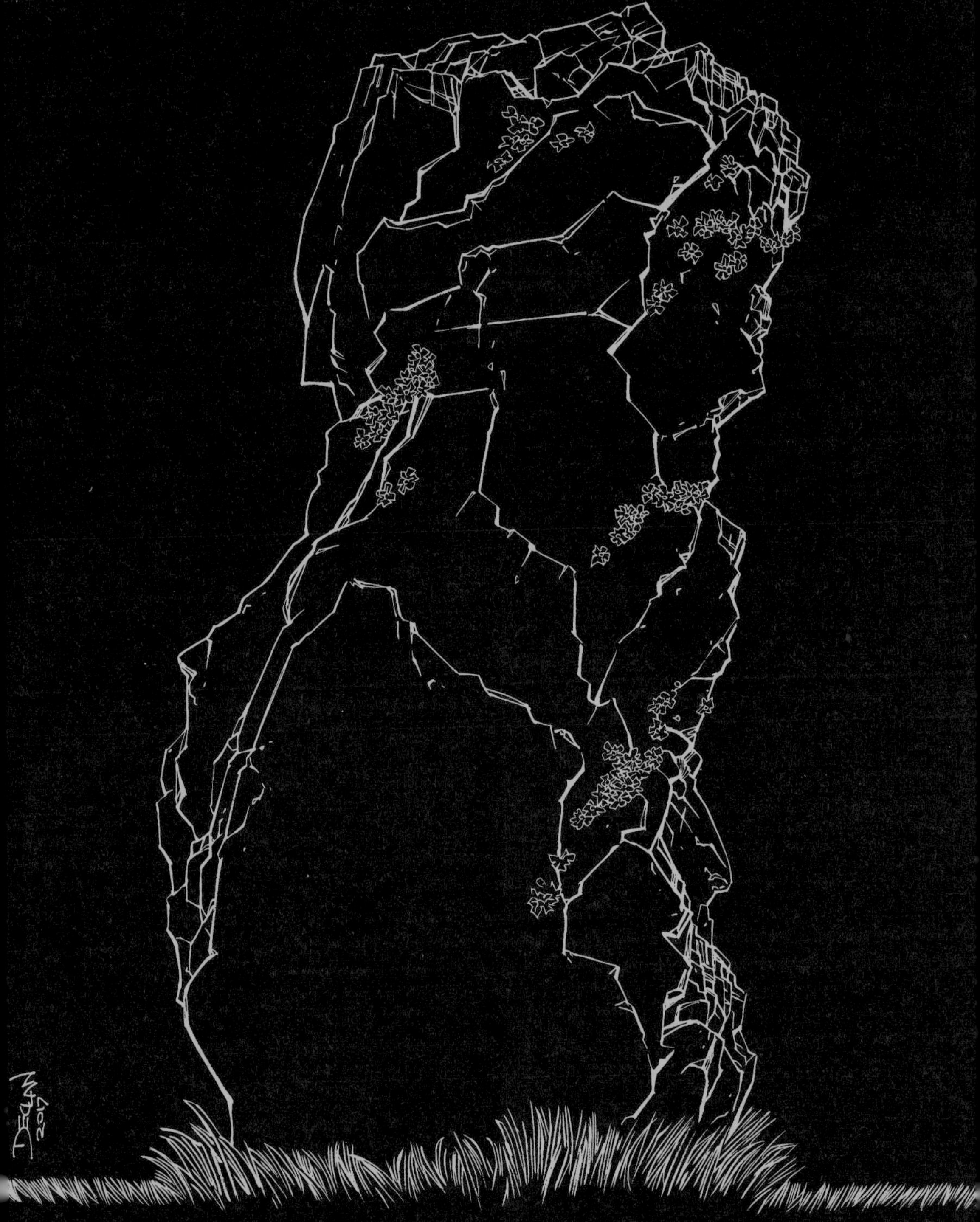
DECLAN
2017

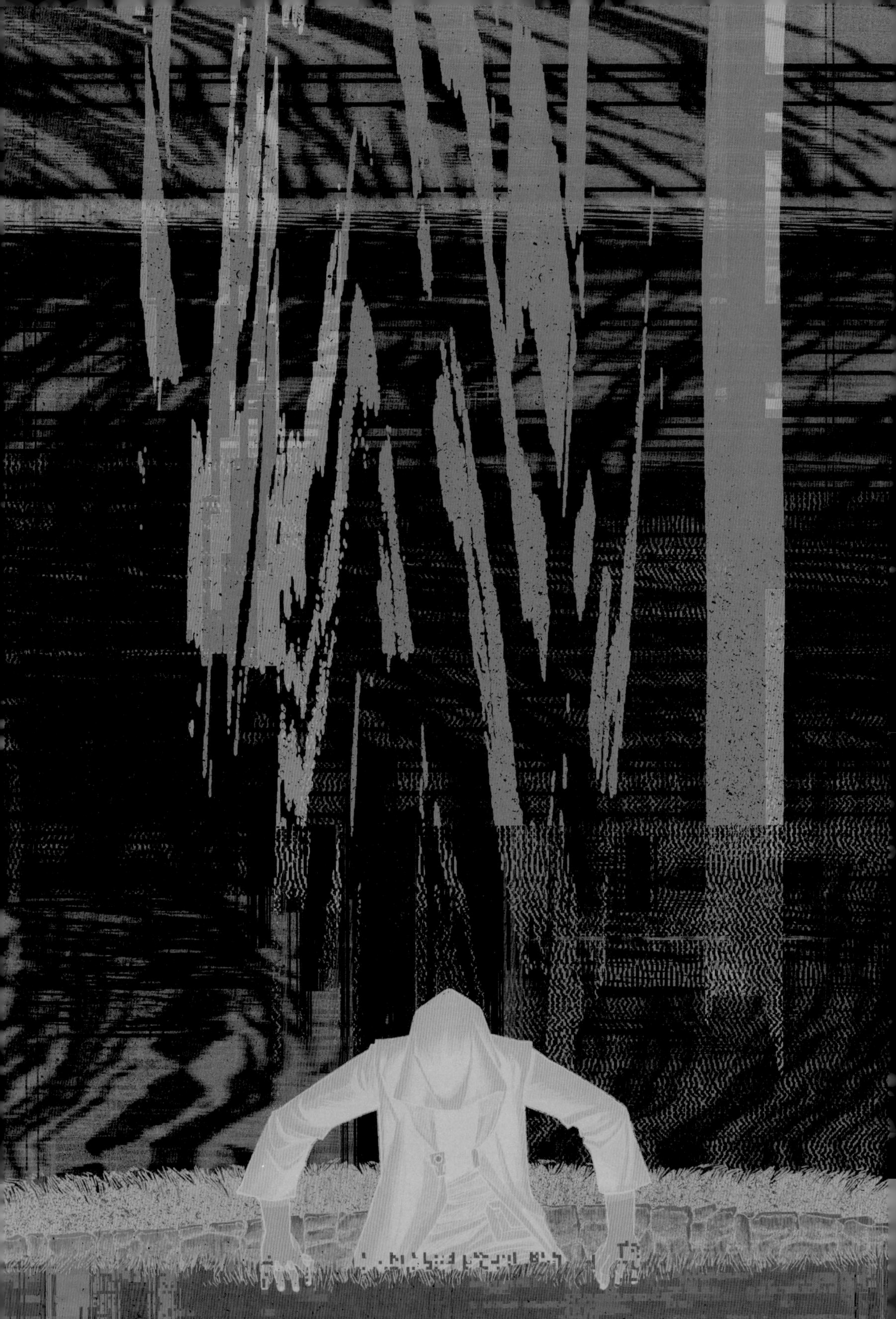

FIFTEEN

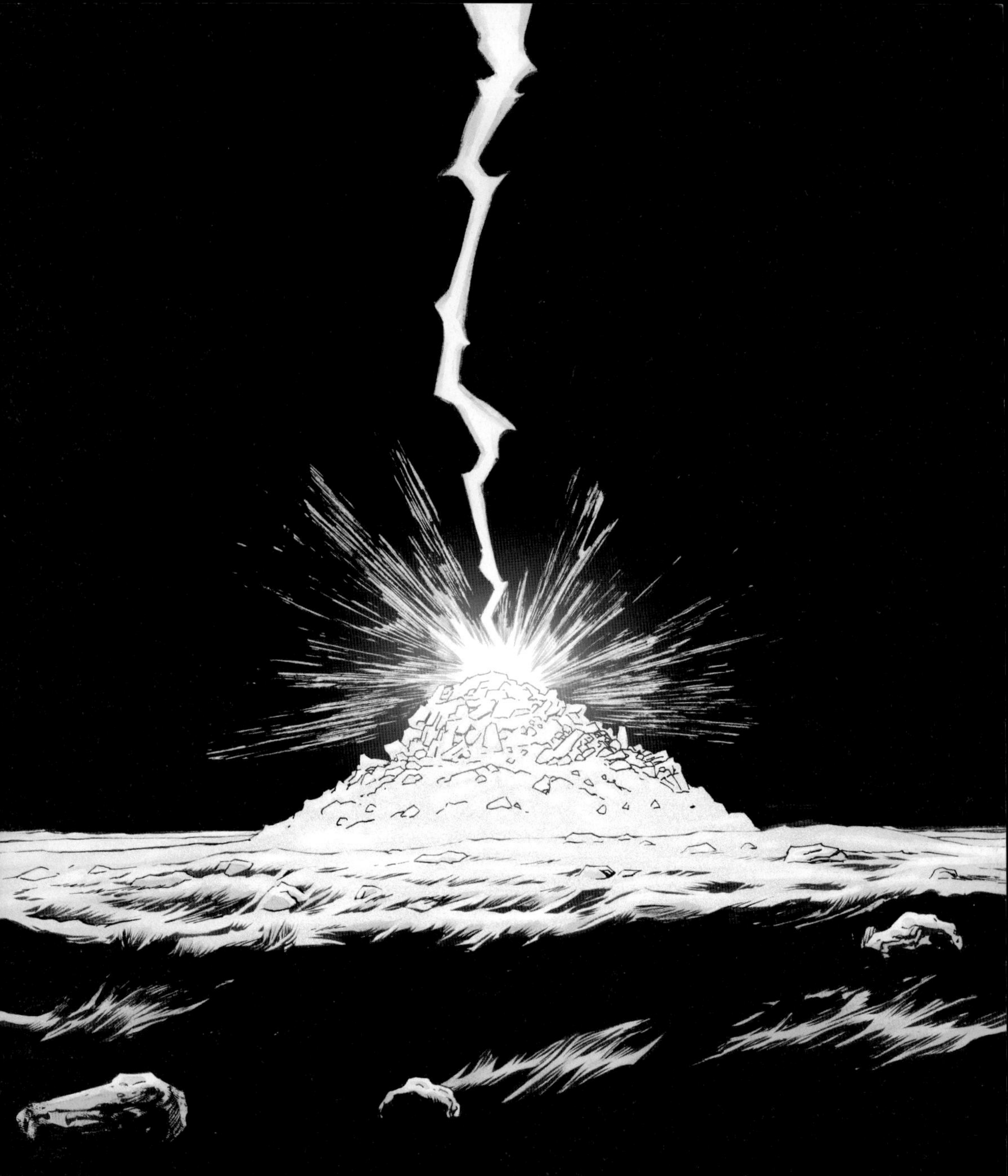
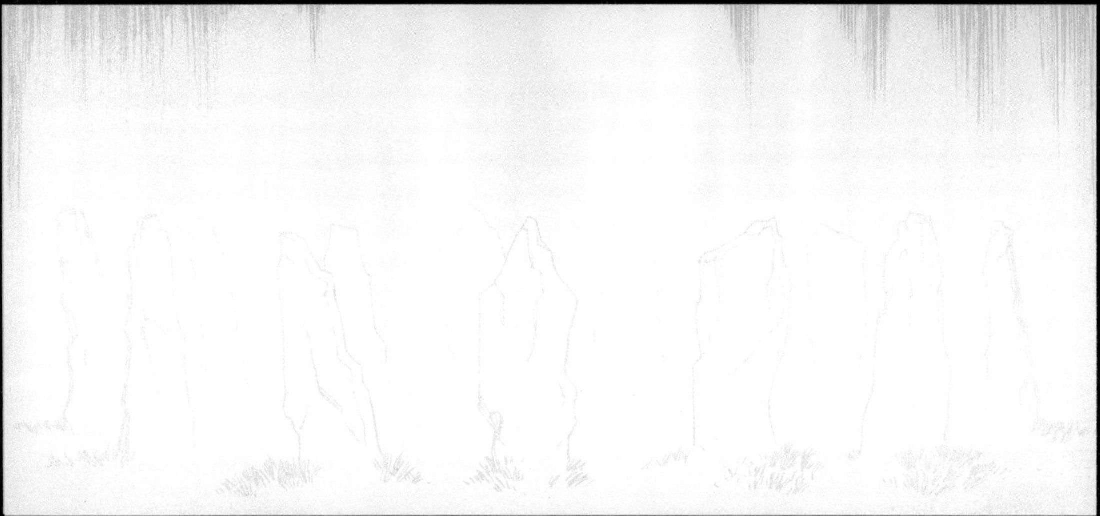

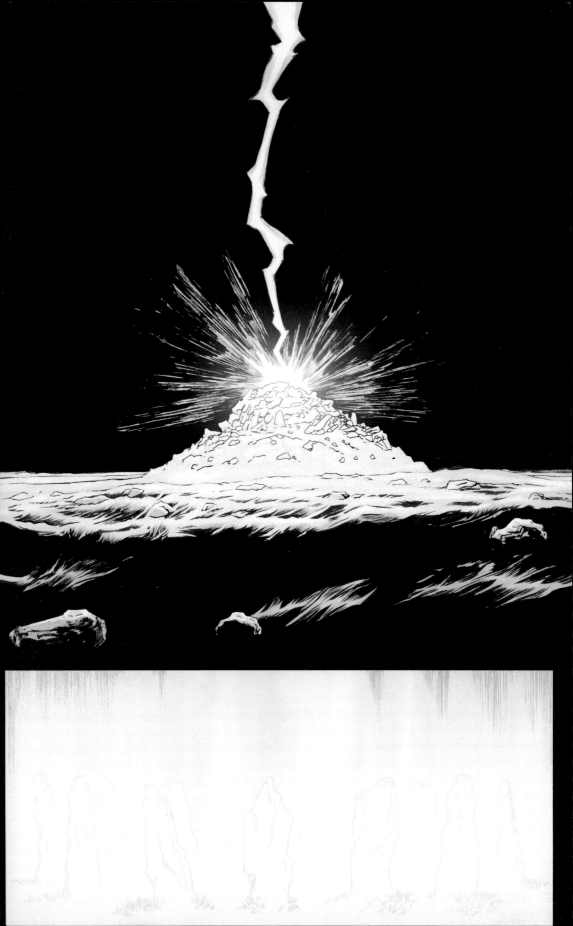

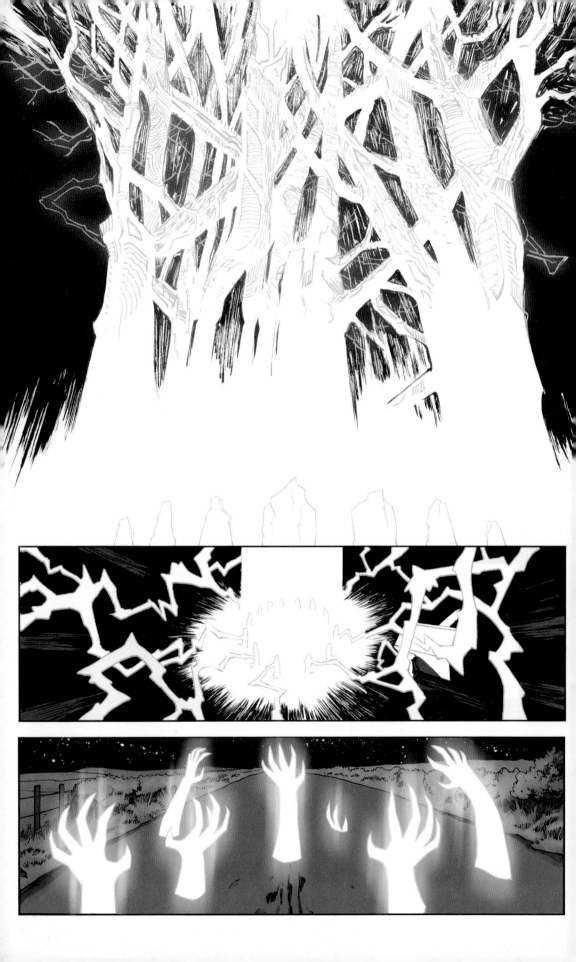

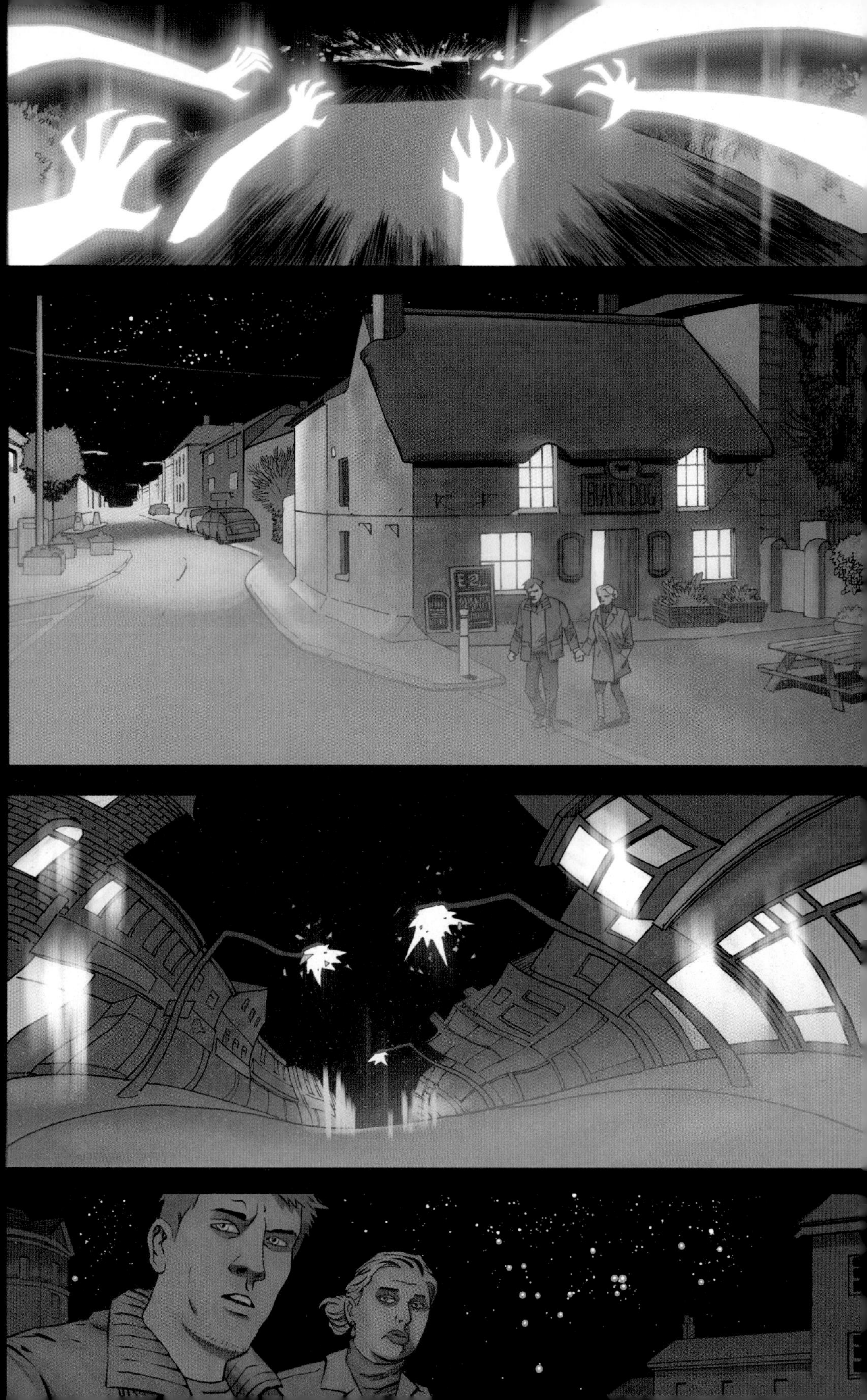
BLACK DOG

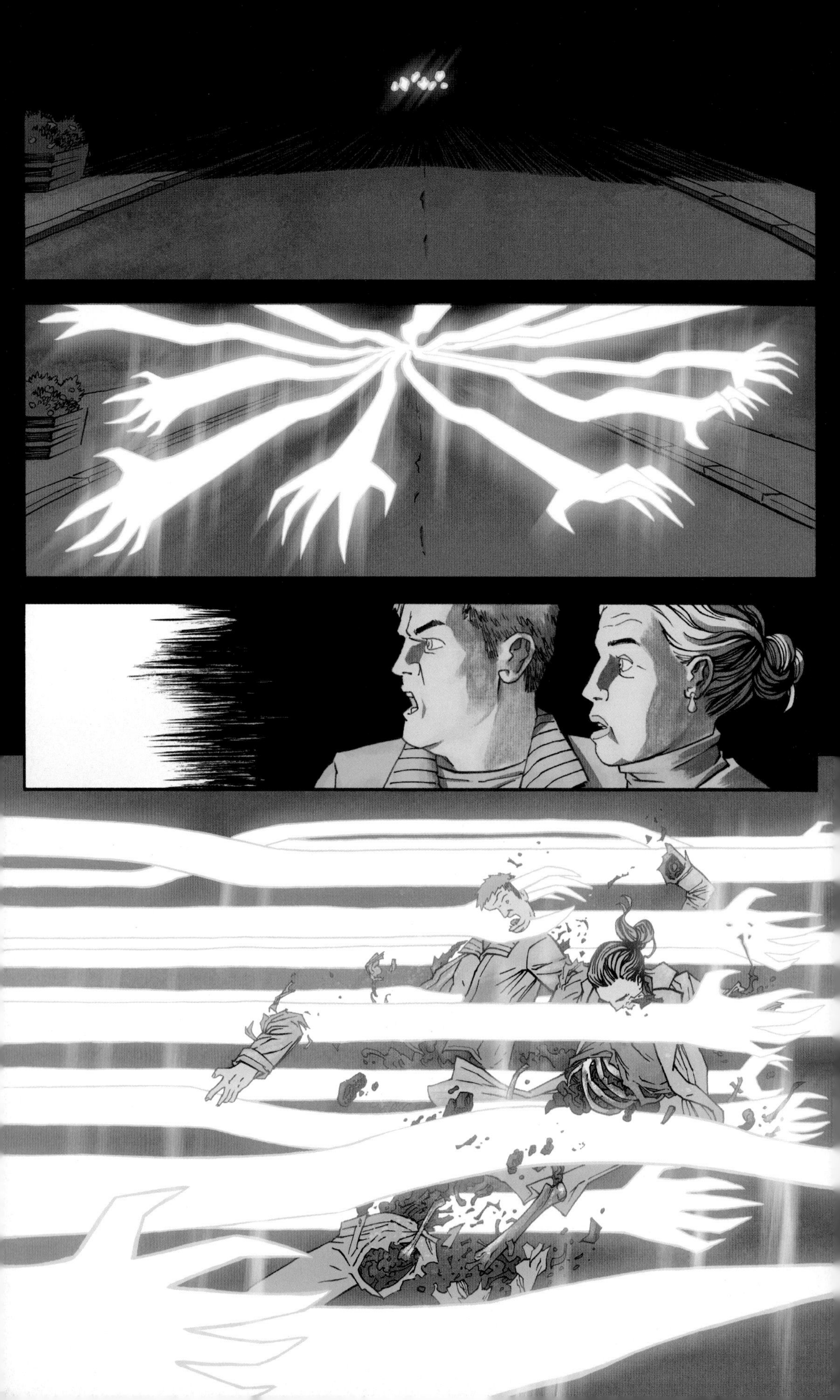

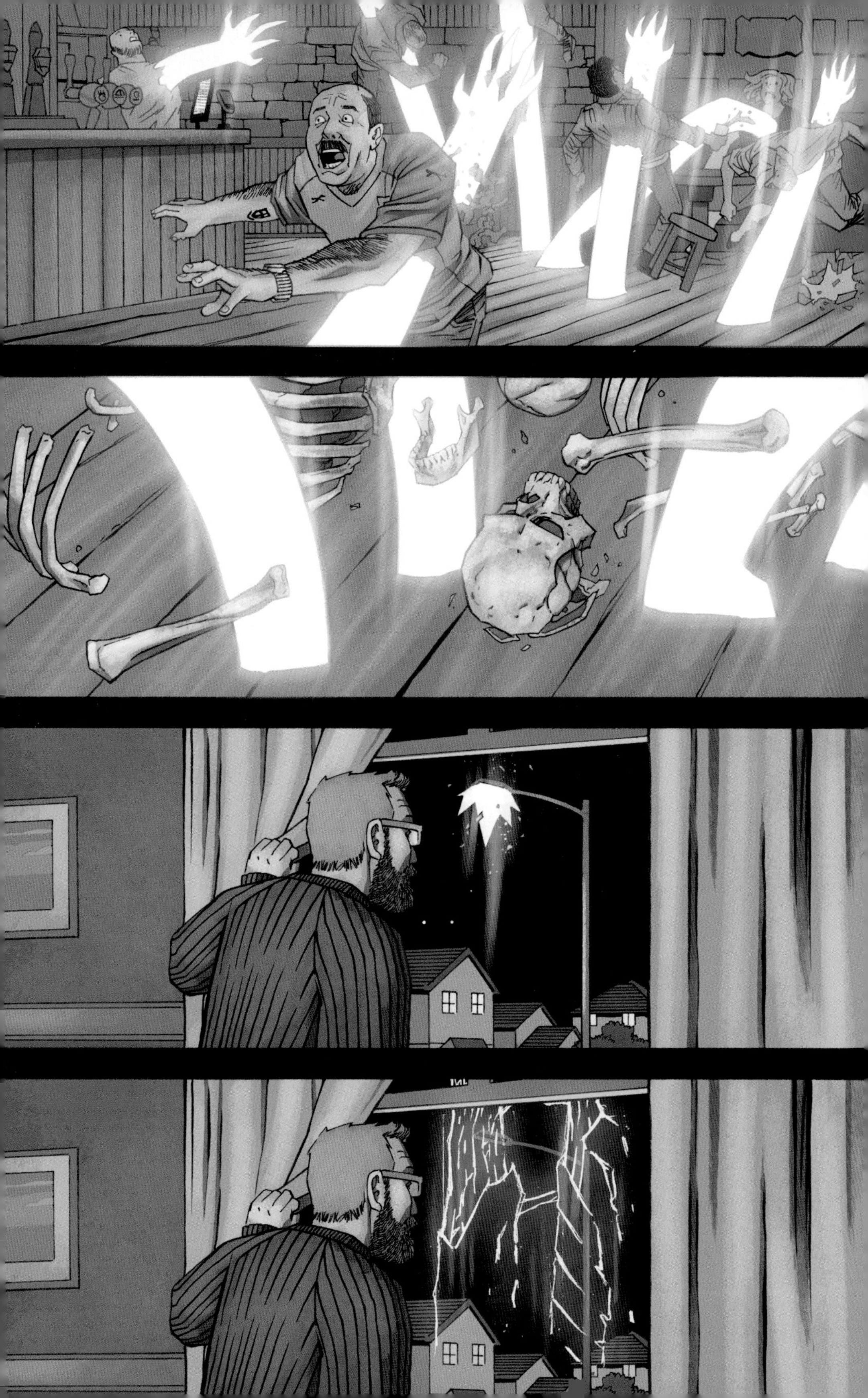

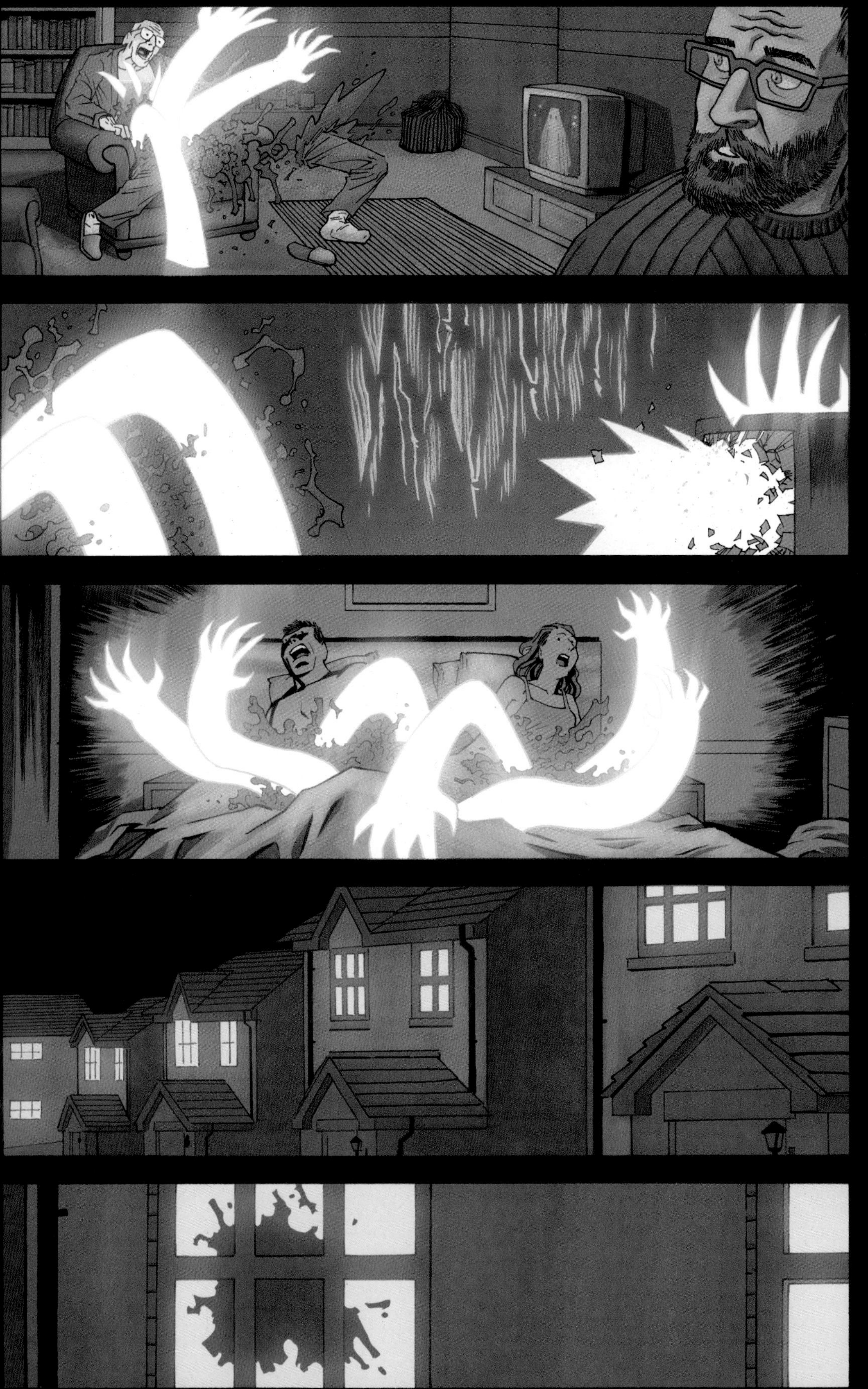

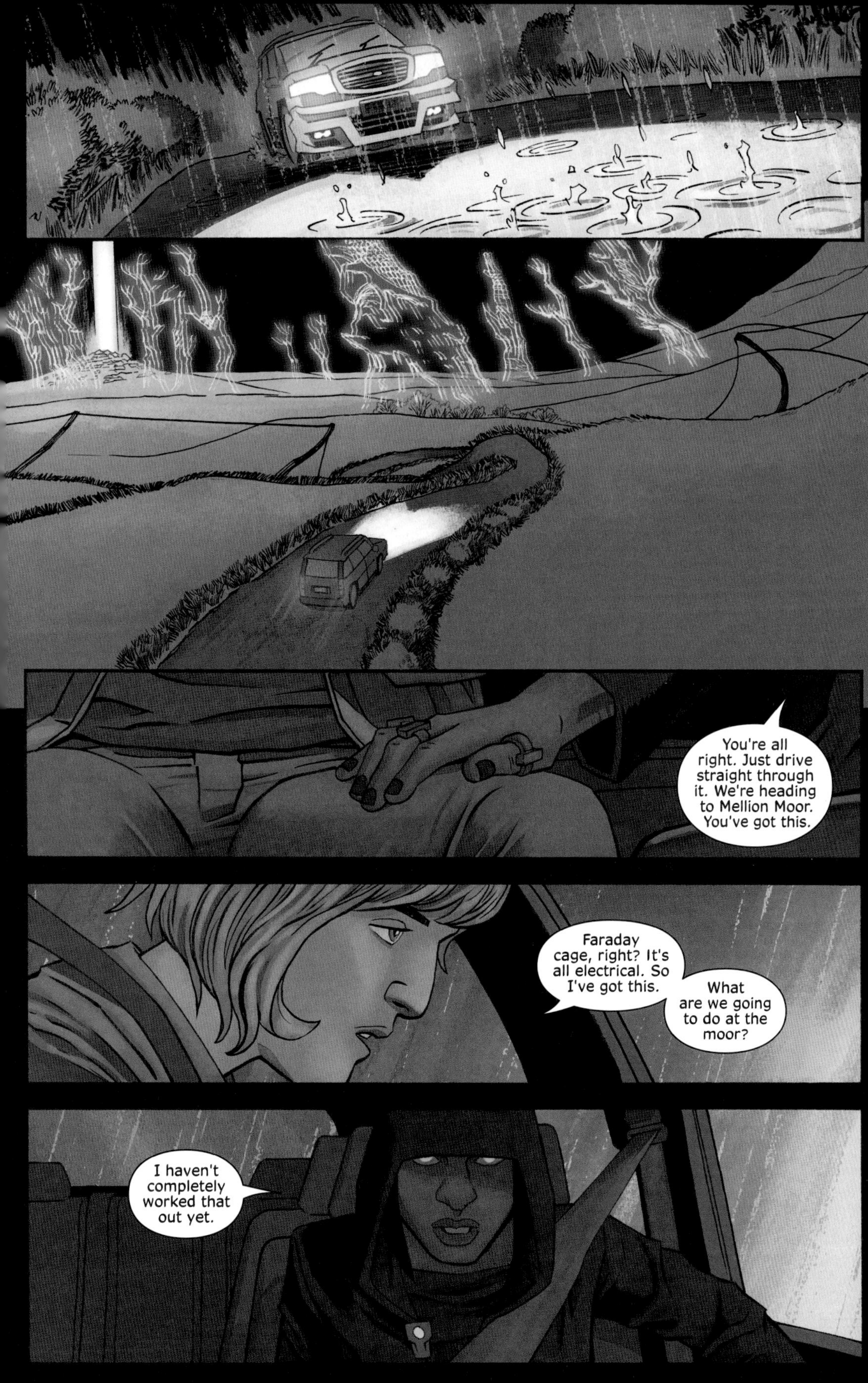
You're all right. Just drive straight through it. We're heading to Mellion Moor. You've got this.
Faraday cage, right? It's all electrical. So I've got this.
What are we going to do at the moor?
I haven't completely worked that out yet.

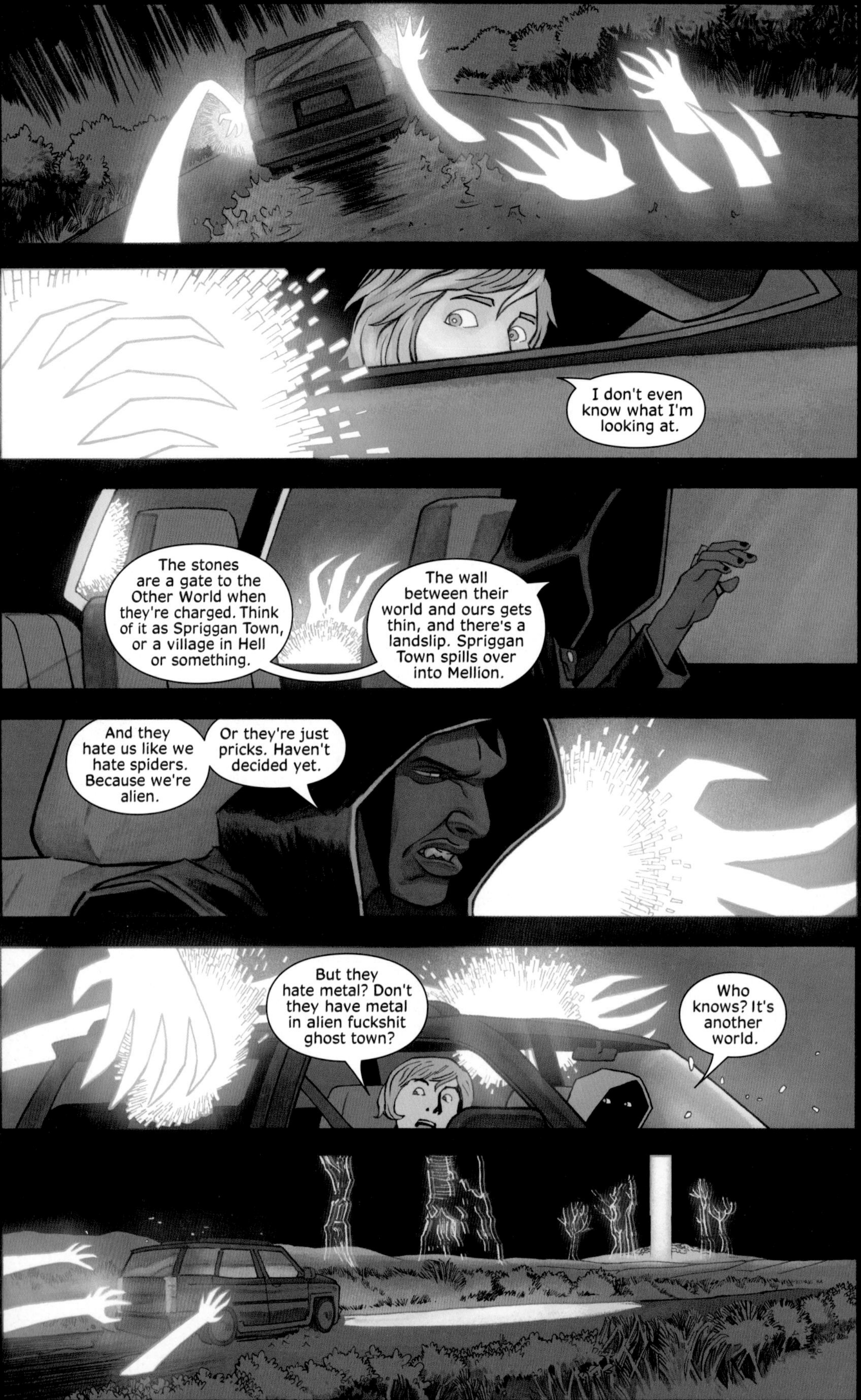

I don't even know what I'm looking at.
The stones are a gate to the Other World when they're charged. Think of it as Spriggan Town, or a village in Hell or something.
The wall between their world and ours gets thin, and there's a landslip. Spriggan Town spills over into Mellion.
And they hate us like we hate spiders. Because we're alien.
Or they're just pricks. Haven't decided yet.
But they hate metal? Don't they have metal in alien fuckshit ghost town?
Who knows? It's another world.

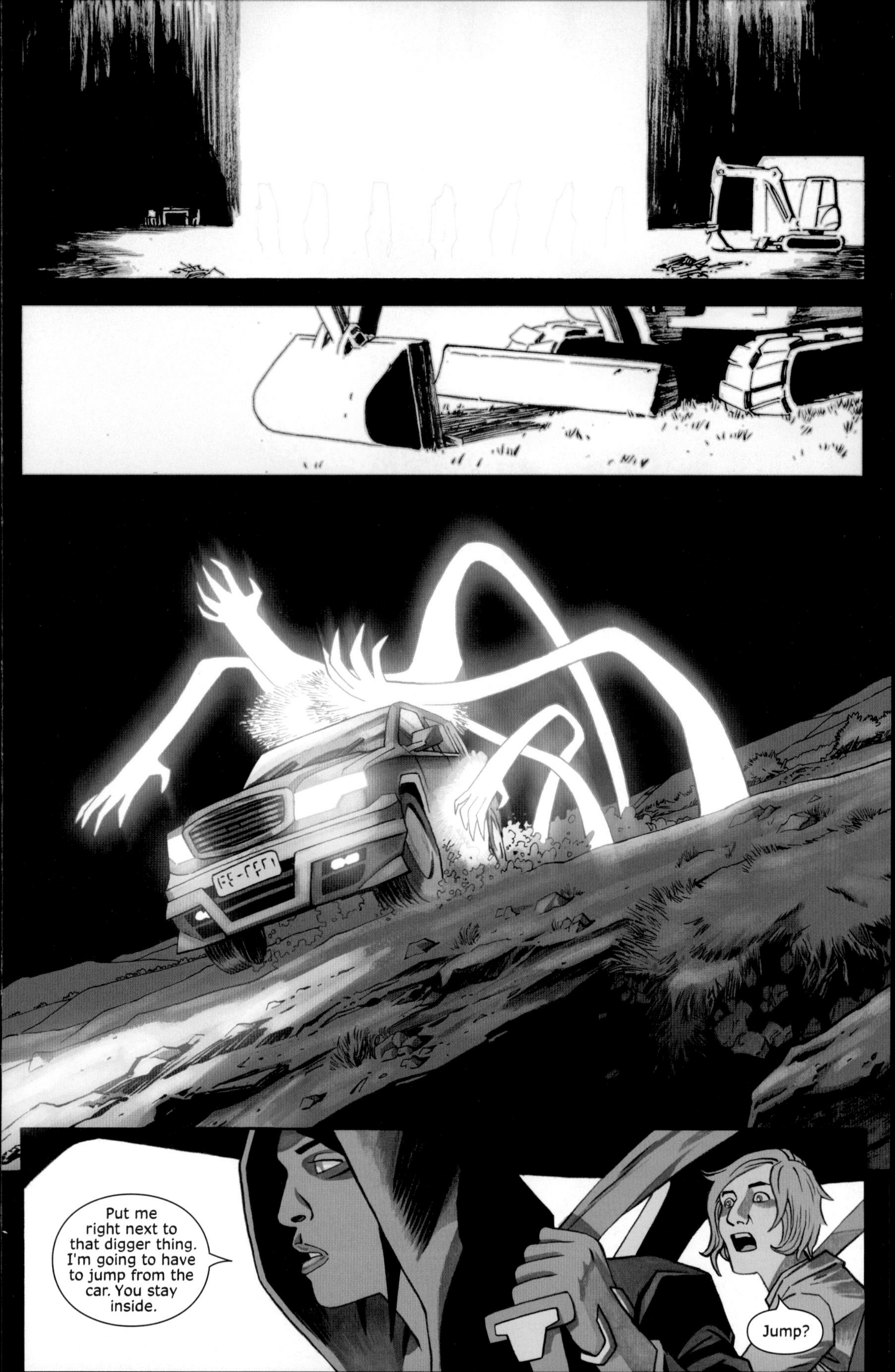
Put me right next to that digger thing. I'm going to have to jump from the car. You stay inside.
Jump?

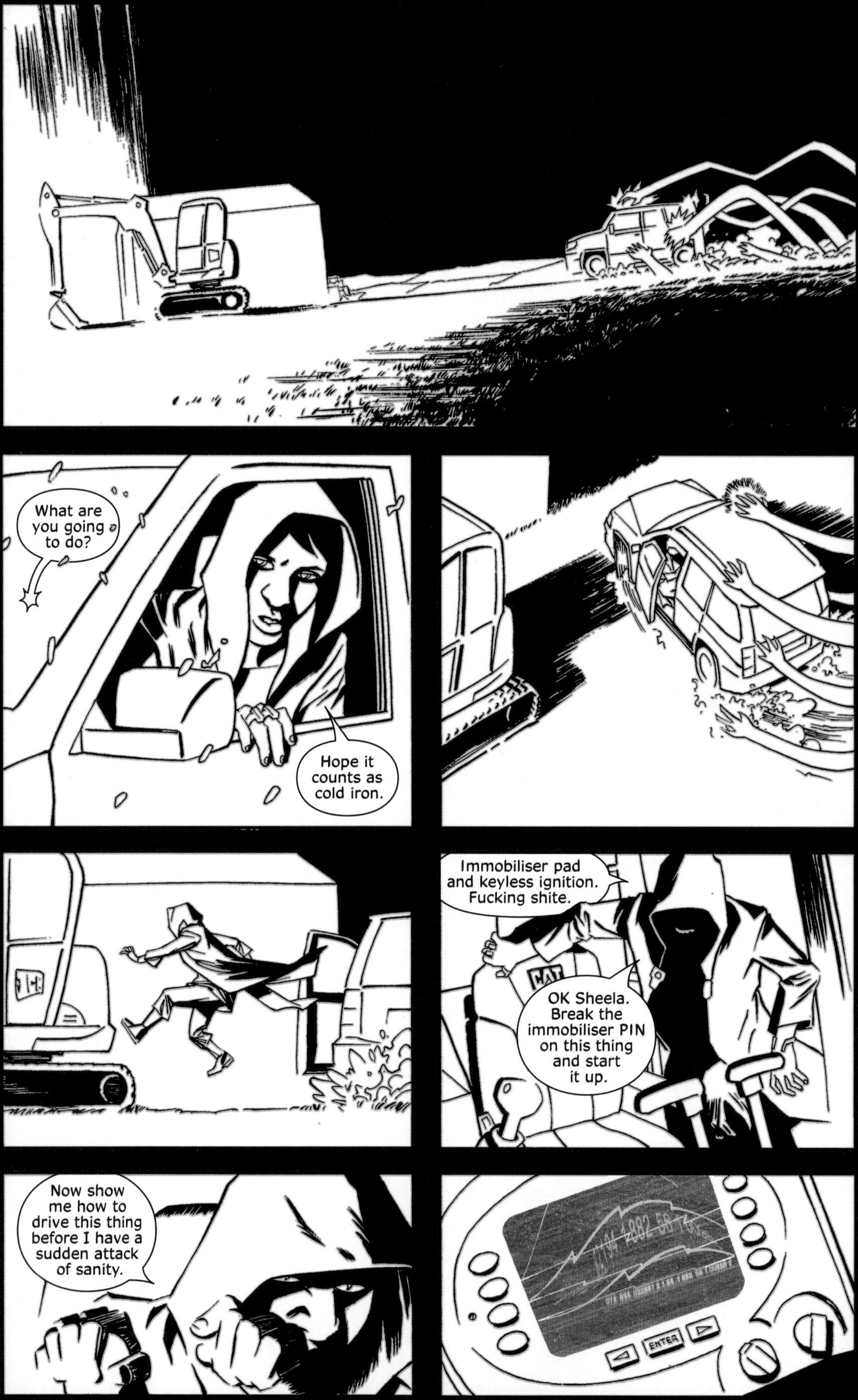
What are you going to do?
Hope it counts as cold iron.
Immobiliser pad and keyless ignition. Fucking shite.
OK Sheela. Break the immobiliser PIN on this thing and start it up.
Now show me how to drive this thing before I have a sudden attack of sanity.
ENTER

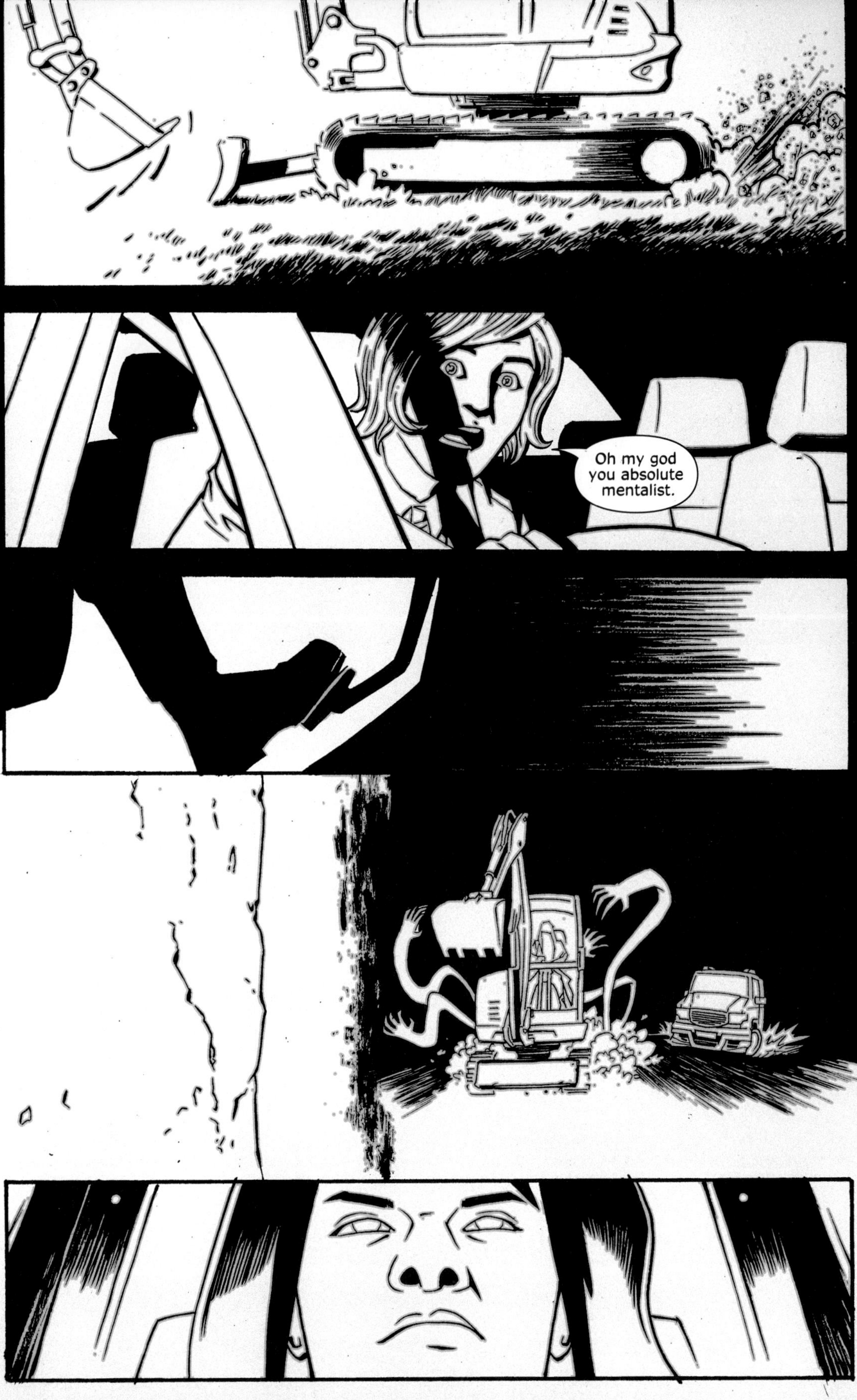
Oh my god you absolute mentalist.

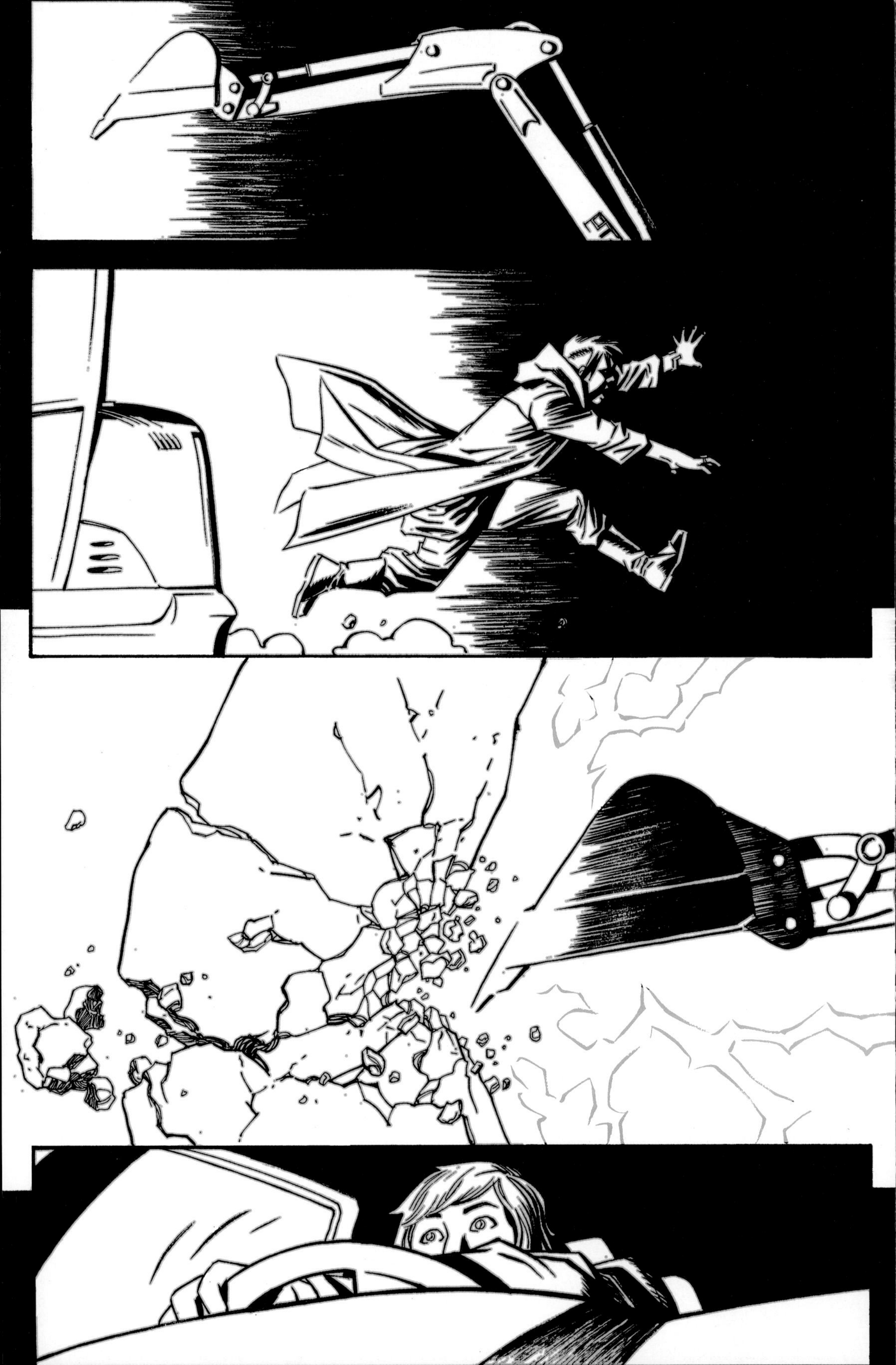

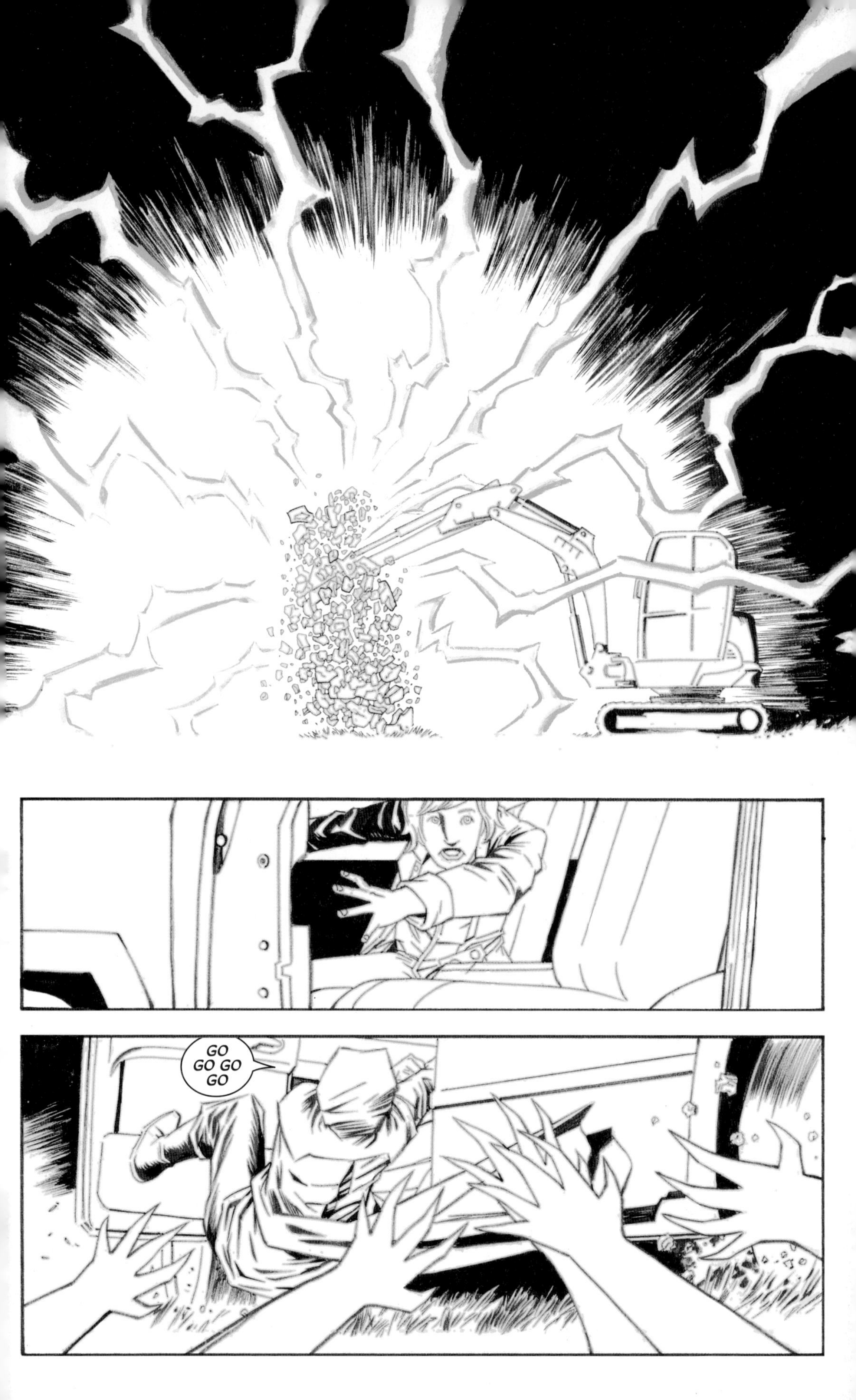
GO GO GO GO

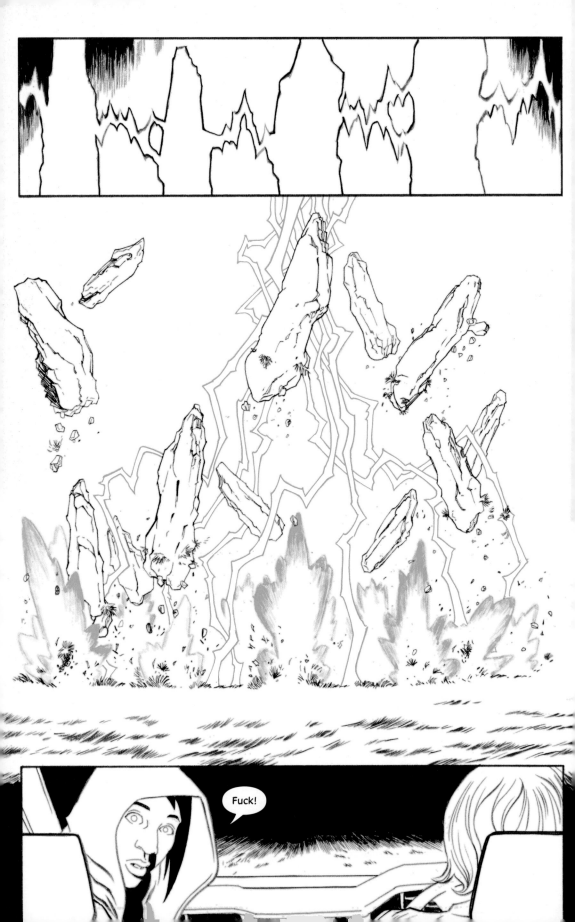

Fuck!

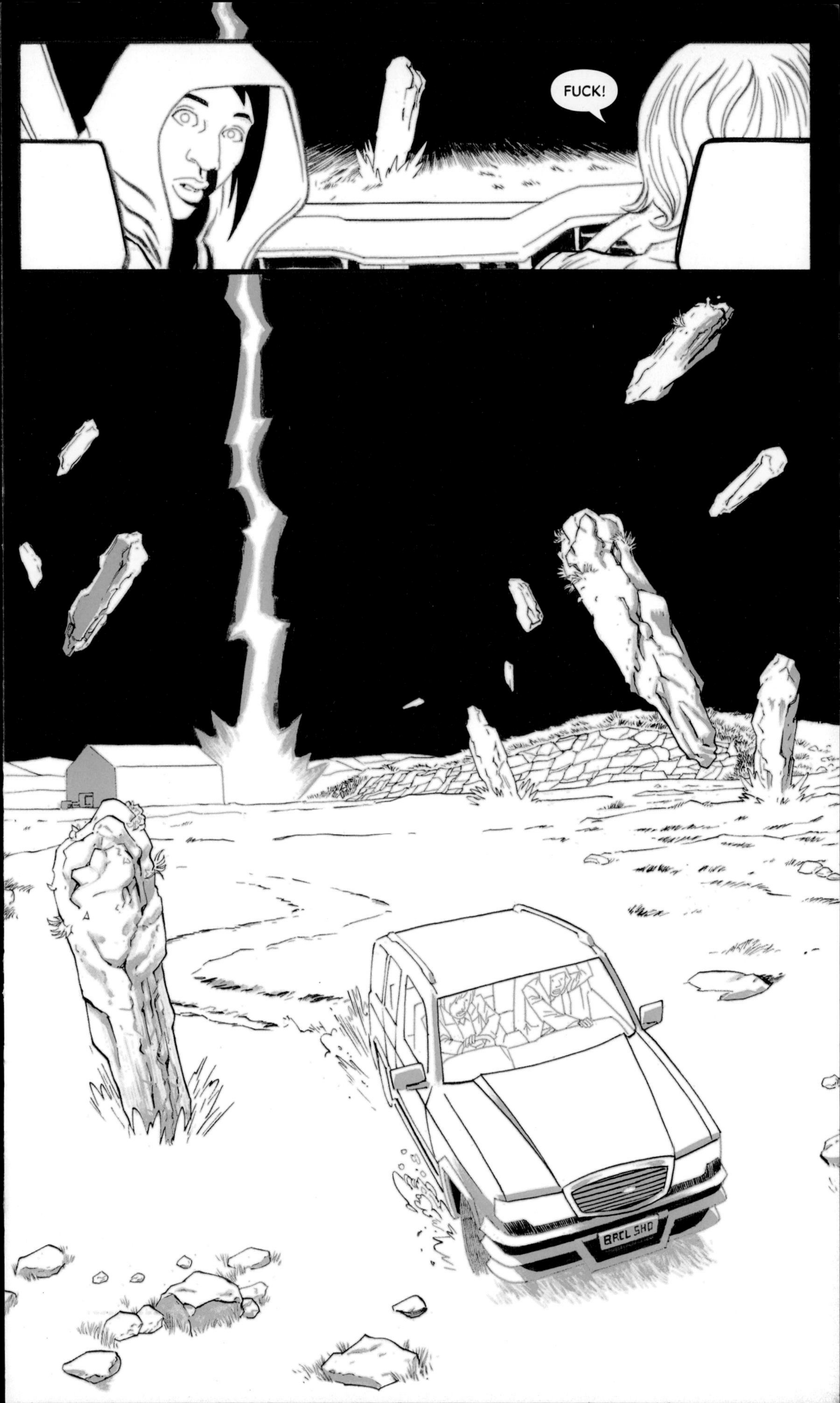
FUCK!
BRCL SHD

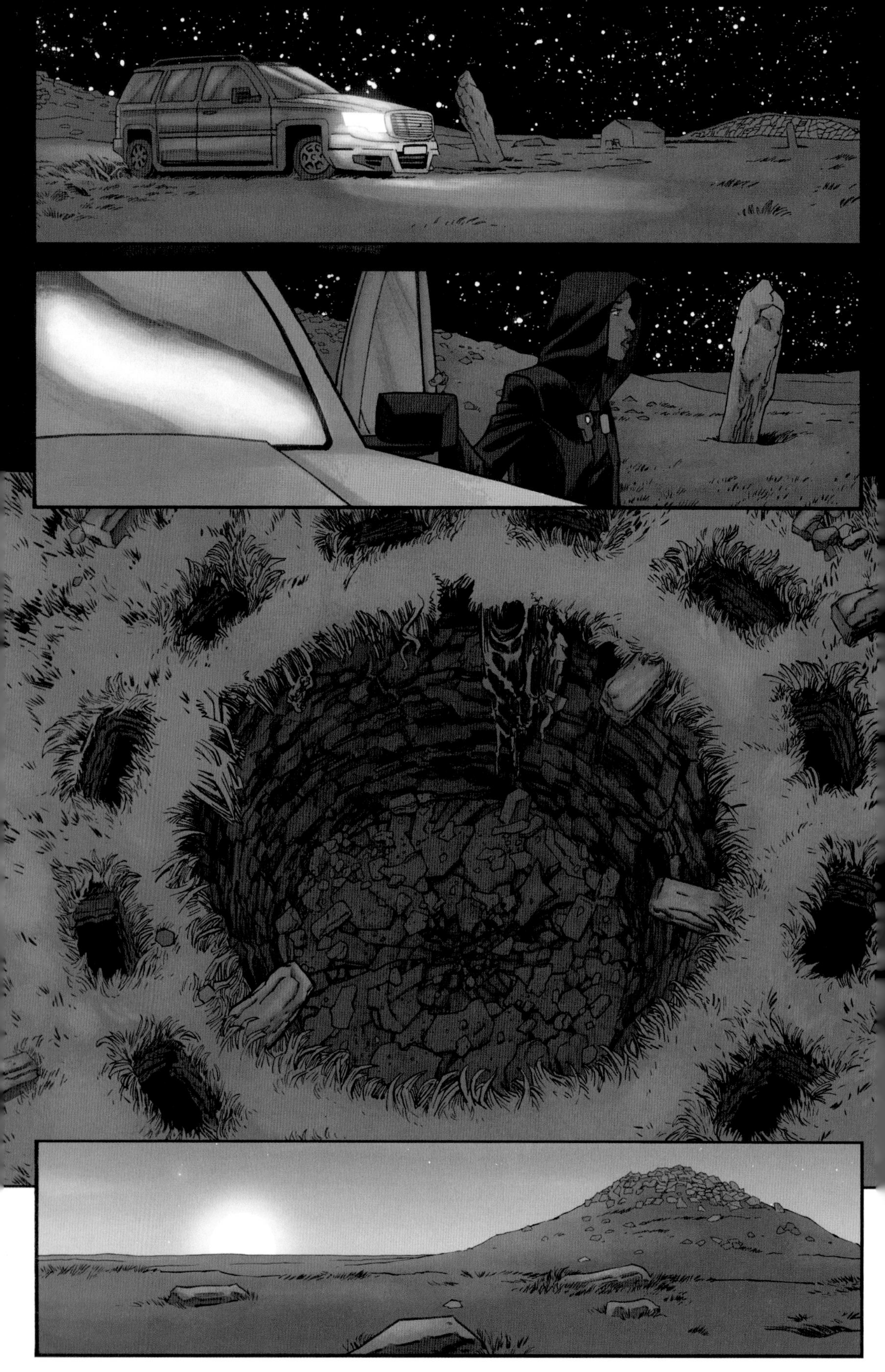

This doesn't look good.
We were told to expect the Security Service.
POLICE
Security Service.
What you call MI5. FPI should have handled them already.
Let me find out what's going on, Ms. Roth.
POLICE
Thanks. You've been really good to us.
Emma. Car keys.
OK Sheela. Call Maria.

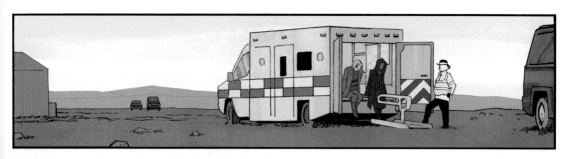

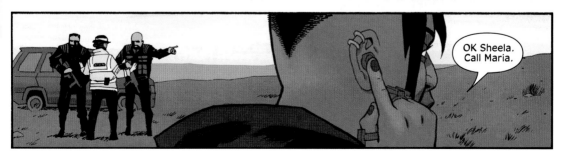

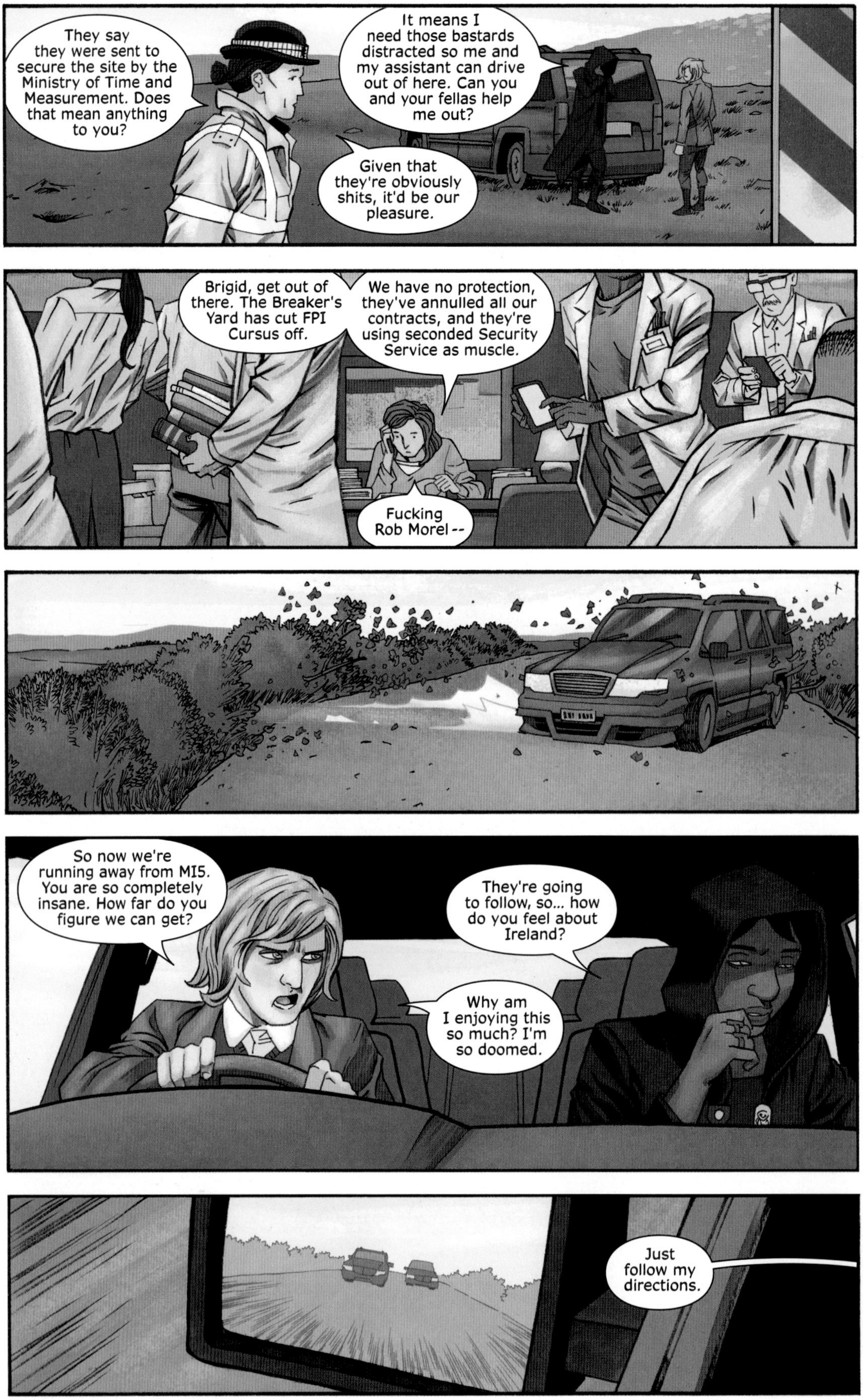
They say they were sent to secure the site by the Ministry of Time and Measurement. Does that mean anything to you?
It means I need those bastards distracted so me and my assistant can drive out of here. Can you and your fellas help me out?
Given that they're obviously shits, it'd be our pleasure.
Brigid, get out of there. The Breaker's Yard has cut FPI Cursus off.
We have no protection, they've annulled all our contracts, and they're using seconded Security Service as muscle.
Fucking Rob Morel --
So now we're running away from MI5. You are so completely insane. How far do you figure we can get?
They're going to follow, so... how do you feel about Ireland?
Why am I enjoying this so much? I'm so doomed.
Just follow my directions.

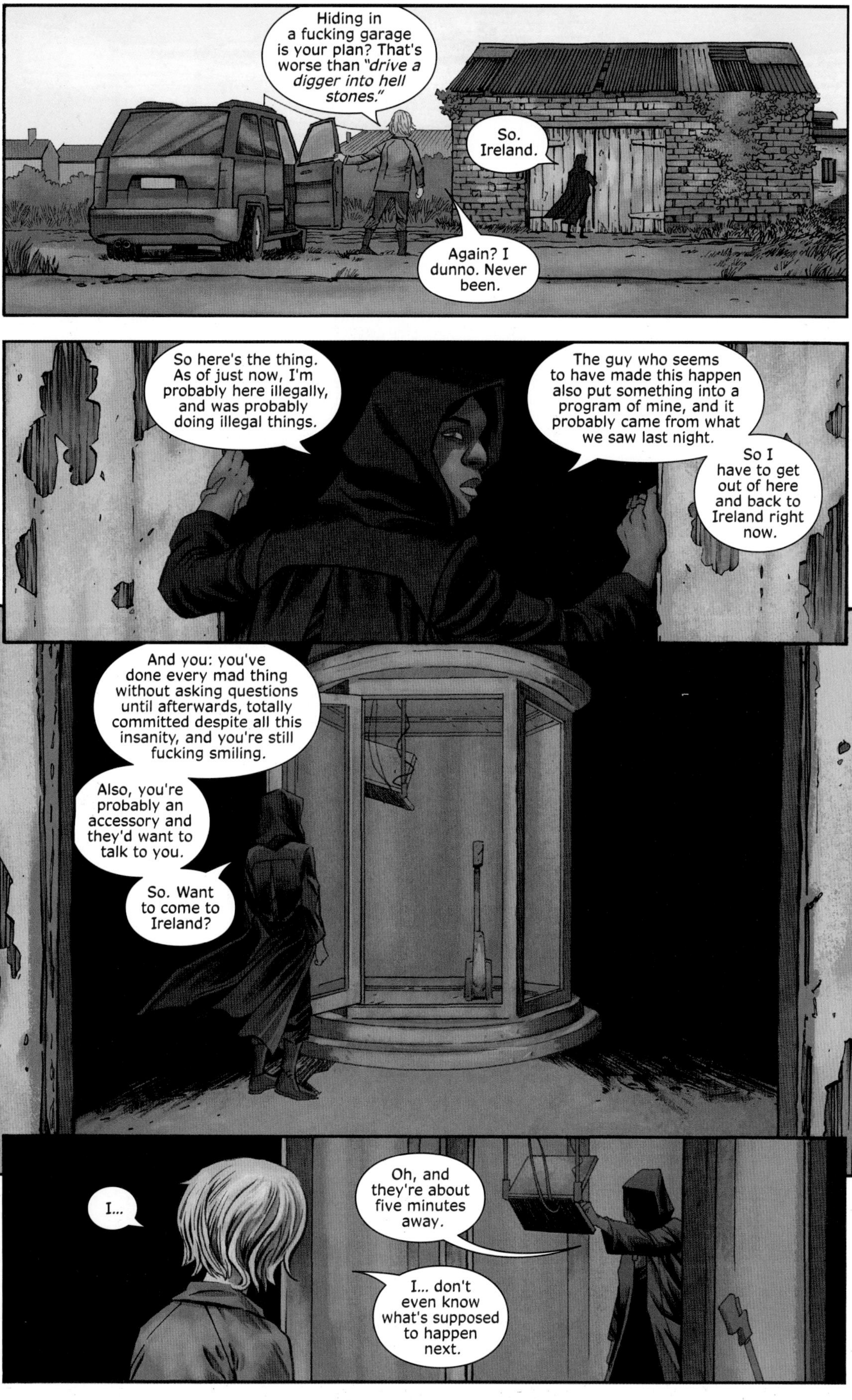
Hiding in a fucking garage is your plan? That's worse than "drive a digger into hell stones."
So. Ireland.
Again? I dunno. Never been.
So here's the thing. As of just now, I'm probably here illegally, and was probably doing illegal things.
The guy who seems to have made this happen also put something into a program of mine, and it probably came from what we saw last night.
So I have to get out of here and back to Ireland right now.
And you: you've done every mad thing without asking questions until afterwards, totally committed despite all this insanity, and you're still fucking smiling.
Also, you're probably an accessory and they'd want to talk to you.
So. Want to come to Ireland?
I...
Oh, and they're about five minutes away.
I... don't even know what's supposed to happen next.

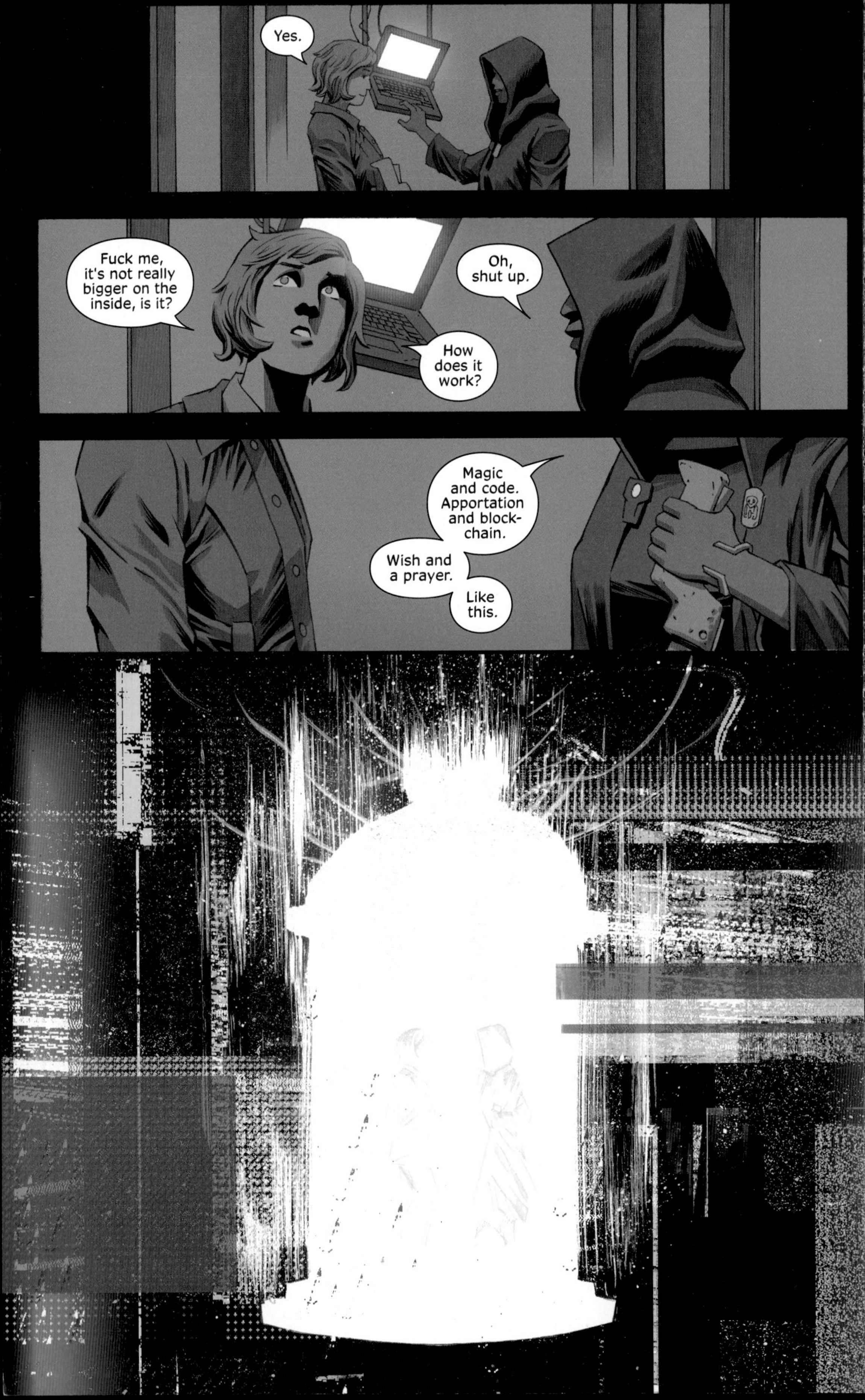
Yes.
Fuck me, it's not really bigger on the inside, is it?
Oh, shut up.
How does it work?
Magic and code. Apportation and block-chain.
Wish and a prayer.
Like this.

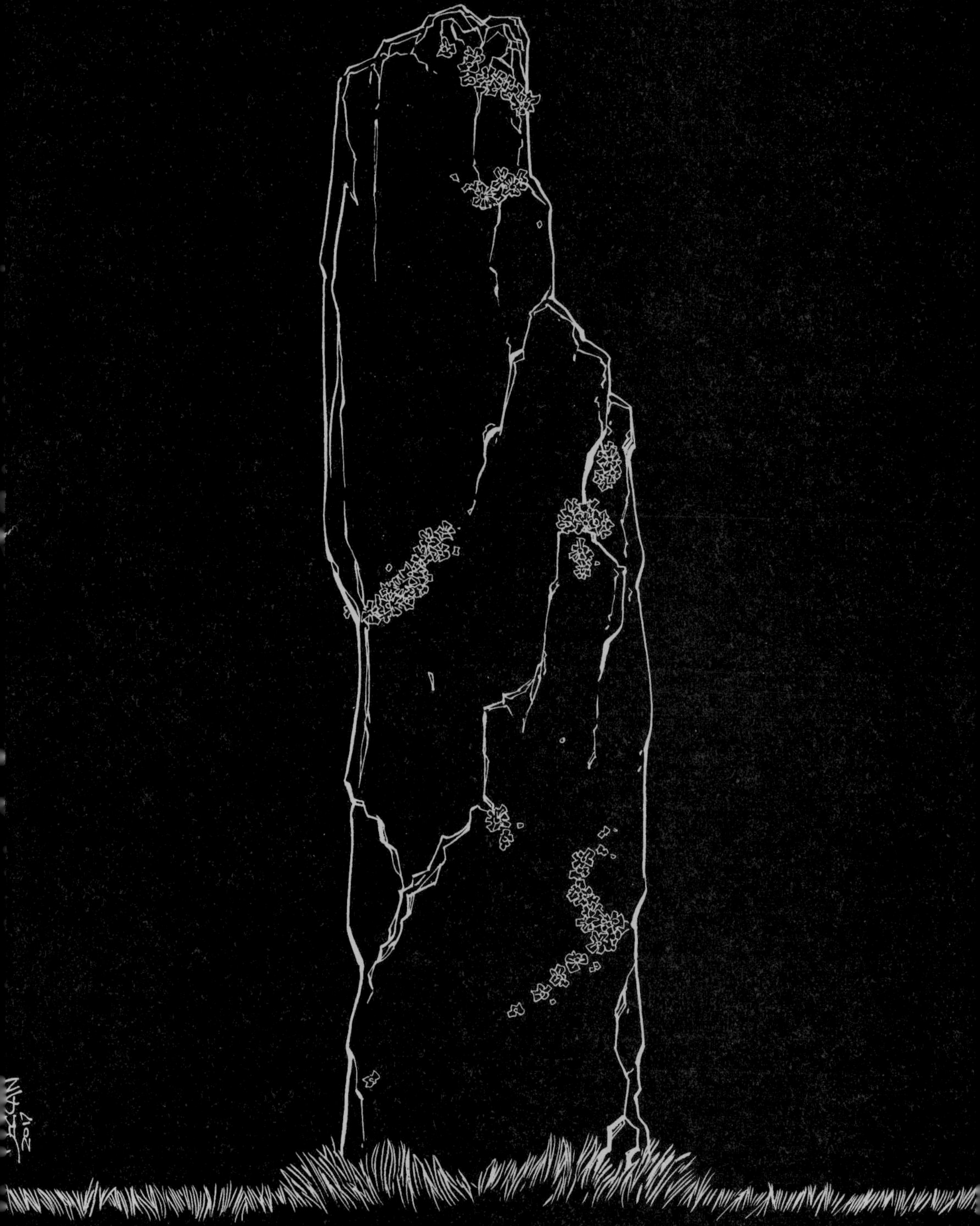

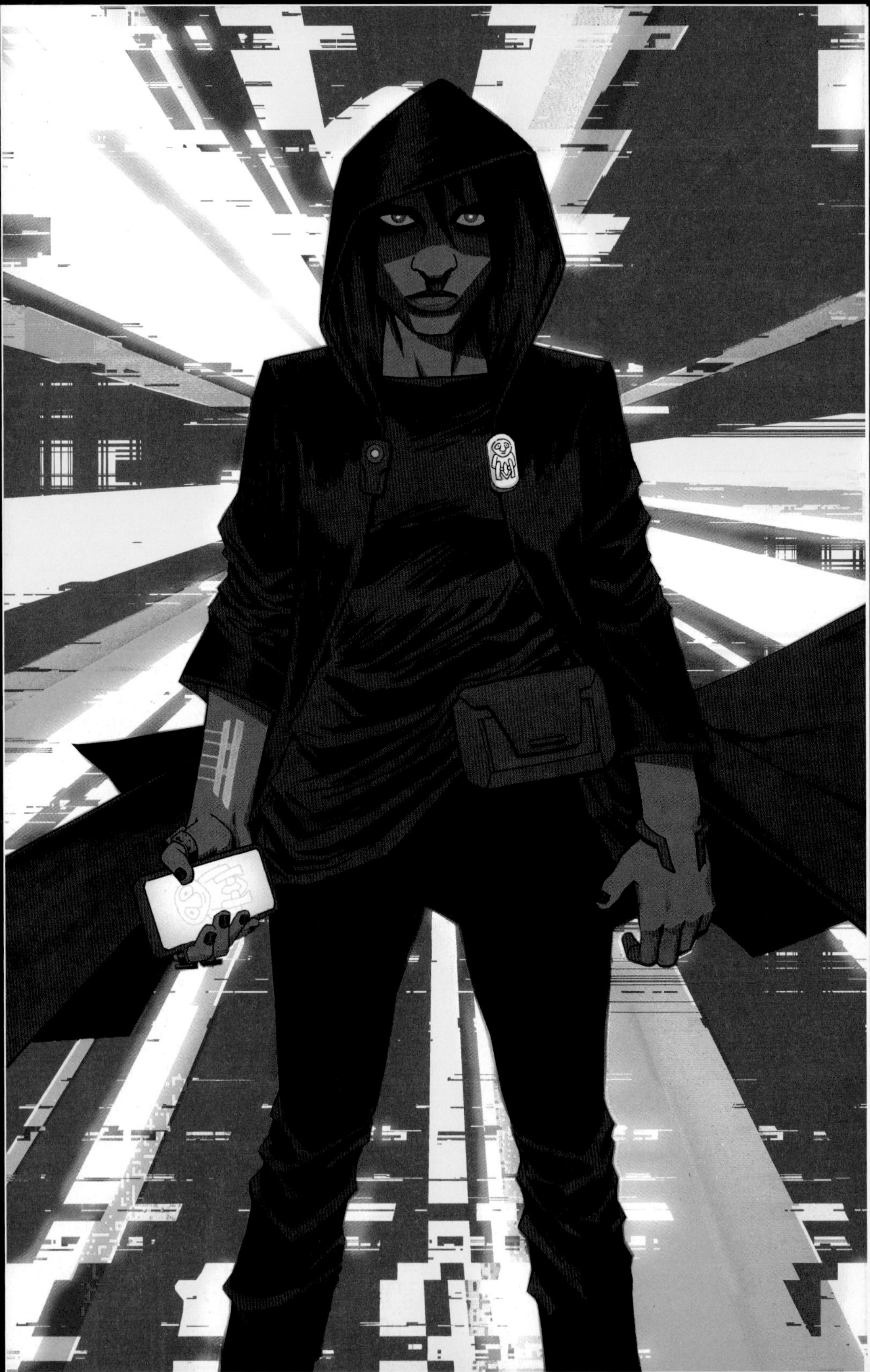

INJECTION #11

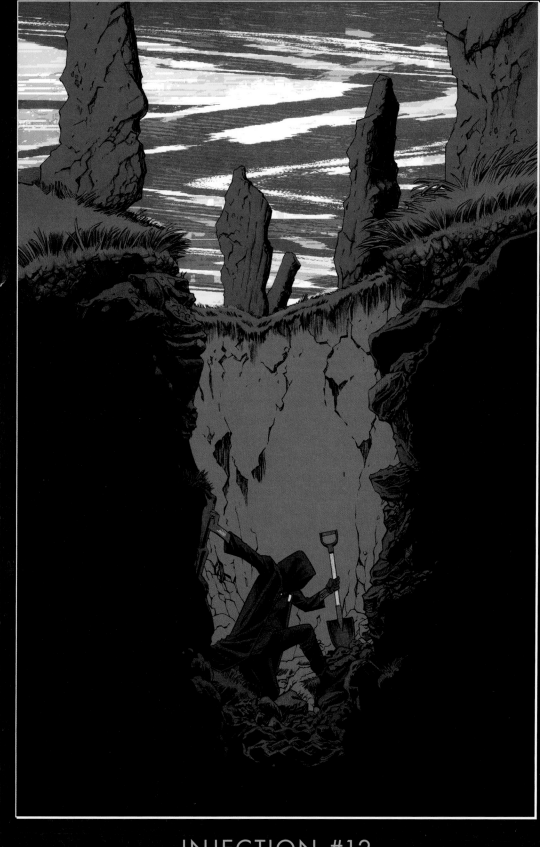

INJECTION #12

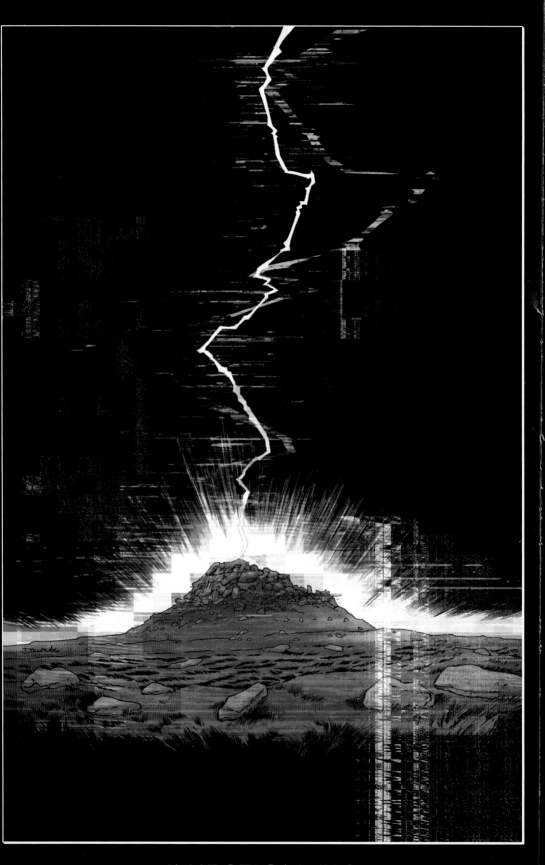

INJECTION #13

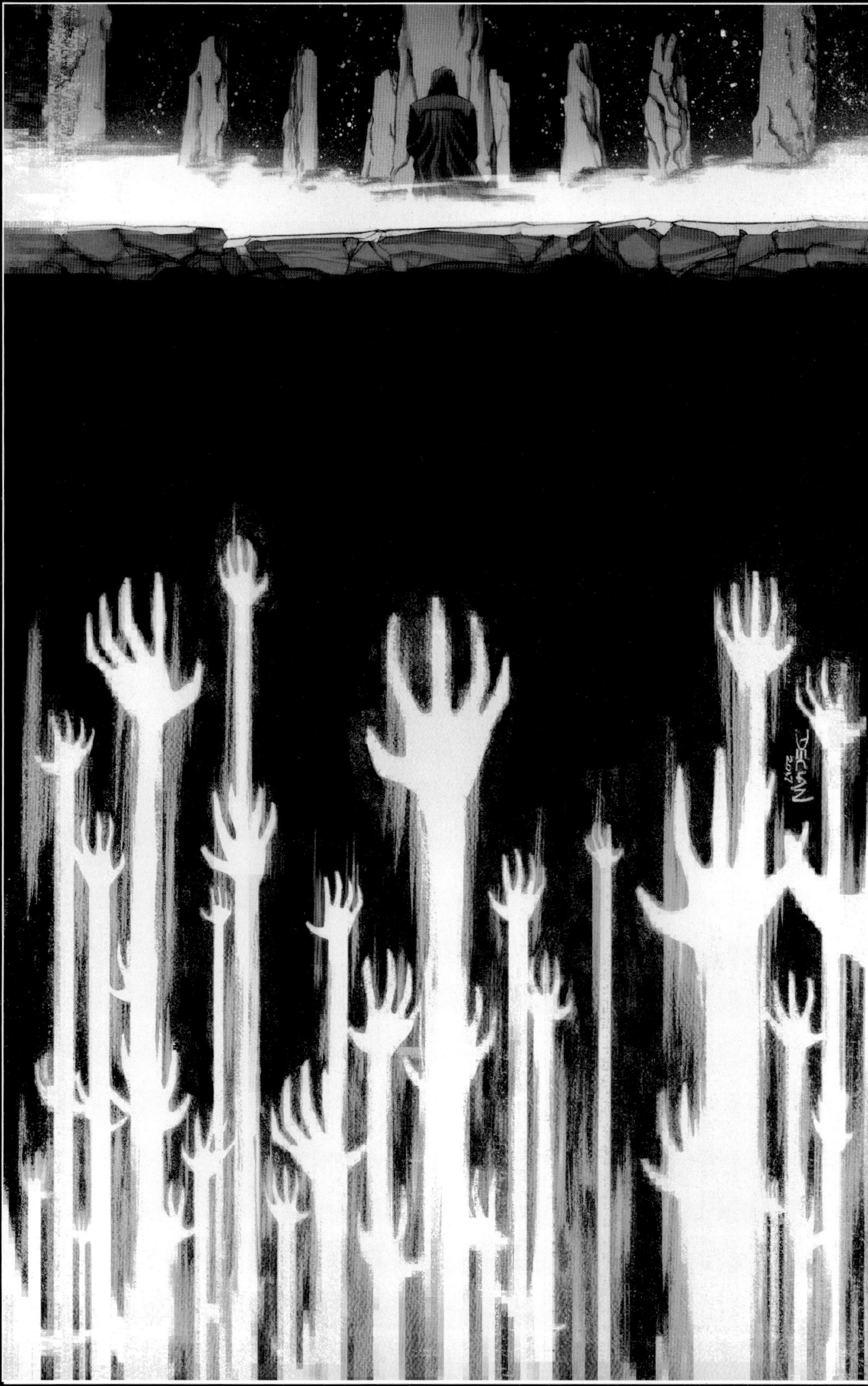
DECLAN 2017

INJECTION #14

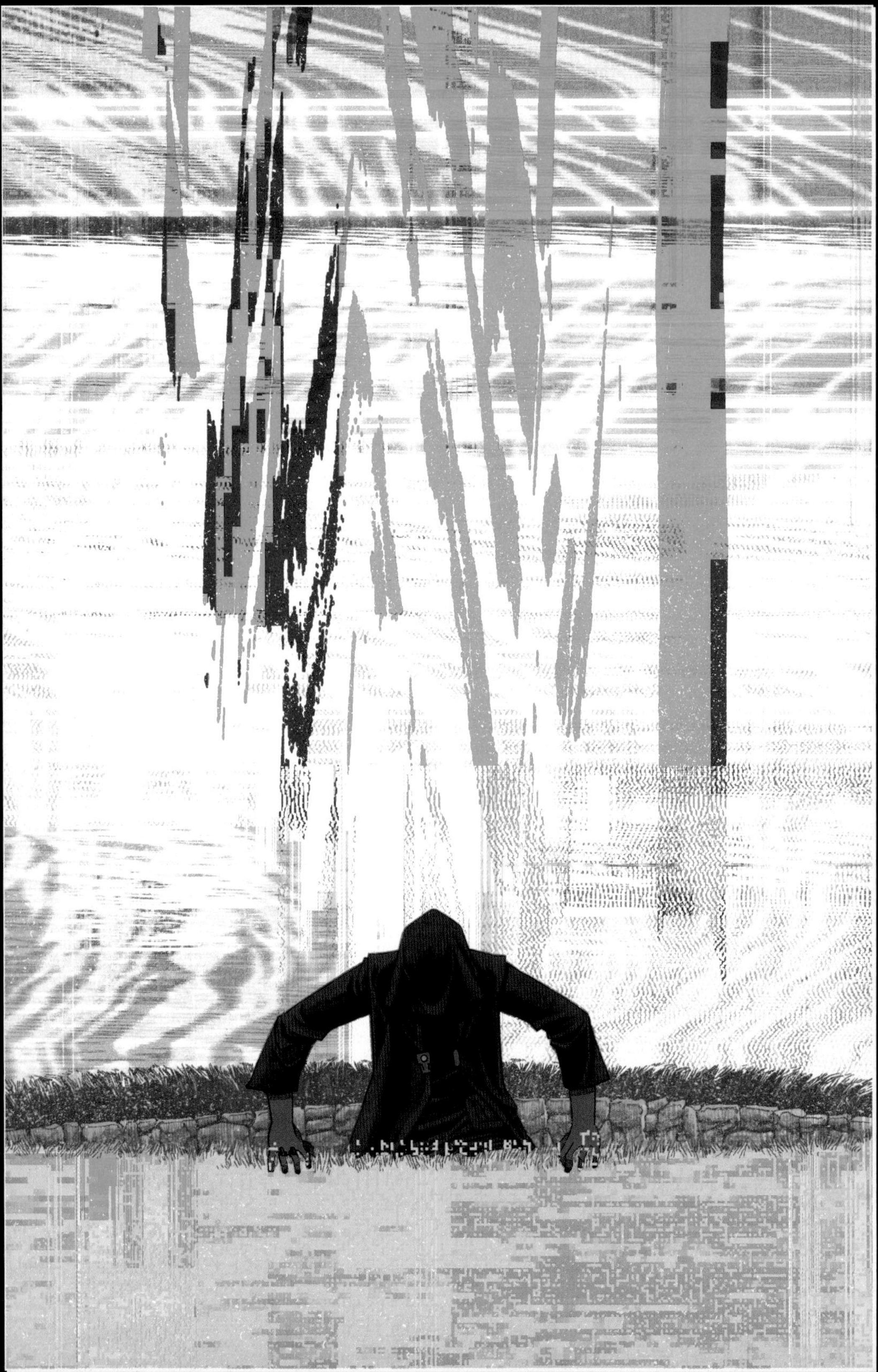

INJECTION #15

WARREN ELLIS is the award-winning writer of graphic novels like TRANSMETROPOLITAN, FELL, and PLANETARY, the author of the NYT bestselling GUN MACHINE and the Amazon Top 100 of 2016 novel NORMAL, and writer and co-producer of the Netflix series CASTLEVANIA. He's also written extensively for VICE, WIRED UK, Esquire and Reuters on technological and cultural matters. Warren Ellis is a Patron of the British Humanist Association and visiting professor to York St John University. He lives as a river hermit on the Thames Estuary.

DECLAN SHALVEY is the award-winning artist of hit series such as DEADPOOL, ALL STAR BATMAN and the acclaimed MOON KNIGHT relaunch with Warren Ellis and Jordie Bellaire. He is also the writer of titles such as DEADPOOL VS OLD MAN LOGAN and the graphic novel SAVAGE TOWN. As well as producing regular sequential work, Declan has developed a reputation as a prolific cover artist. He lives and works in his native Ireland.

JORDIE BELLAIRE is the Eisner Award winning colorist of many acclaimed Image titles. NOWHERE MEN, SAVAGE TOWN, ZERO, and AUTUMNLANDS are some of her favorites. She's also the writer/colorist of Image's REDLANDS where she lives out every supernatural murder fantasy she can dream up. She lives in Ireland with her cat Buffy and makes great salted caramel ice cream.

FONOGRAFIKS is the banner name for the comics work of designer Steven Finch, which includes the Image Comics titles NOWHERE MEN, THEY'RE NOT LIKE US, WE STAND ON GUARD, MAESTROS and the multi-award winning SAGA. He lives and works, surrounded by far too many books, in the north east of England.